Electronic Evidence and Discovery: What Every Lawyer Should Know

Michele C.S. Lange
Kristin M. Nimsger

Section of Science & Technology Law

Defending Liberty
Pursuing Justice

Cover design by ABA Publishing.

The materials contained herein represent the opinions and views of the authors and editors, and should not be construed to be the action of either the American Bar Association or the Section of Science & Technology Law unless adopted pursuant to the bylaws of the Association.

Nothing contained in this book is to be considered as the rendering of legal advice for specific cases, and readers are responsible for obtaining such advice from their own legal counsel. This book and any forms and agreements herein are intended for educational and informational purposes only.

08 07 06 05 04   5 4 3 2 1

Library of Congress Cataloging-in-Publication Data

Lange, Michele C. S., 1977–
    Electronic evidence and discovery : what every lawyer should know / by Michele C.S. Lange, Kristin M. Nimsger.
        p. cm.
    ISBN 1-59031-334-8
    1. Evidence, Documentary—United States. 2. Discovery (Law)—United States. 3. Electronic records—Law and legislation—United States. 4. Computer files—Law and legislation—United States. I. Nimsger, Kristin M., 1973– II. Title.

    KF8947.L36 2004
    347.73′64—dc22

                                                            2004010319

Discounts are available for books ordered in bulk. Special consideration is given to state bars, CLE programs, and other bar-related organizations. Inquire at Book Publishing, ABA Publishing, American Bar Association, 321 N. Clark, Chicago, IL 60610-4714.

www.ababooks.org

FOREWORD

The protodigital age is now ending for the legal profession. For a quarter century or more, we utilized computer technology to perform complicated calculations, print our documents, and send messages to our colleagues. We viewed computers as tools to help us go about our daily professional lives. Some of us even recognized that computers might be the repositories of discoverable information, the place to find "data compilations from which information can be obtained, translated, if necessary, by the respondent through detection devices into reasonably useable form," to use the quaint language of the 1970 amendments to the Federal Rules of Civil Procedure. But we were thinking in protodigital terms. We thought of computers as tools to make conventional business tasks faster and easier, the same way we once thought of radio as wireless telegraph technology or the automobile as a horseless carriage.

In the protodigital age, it was useful to think about computers and computer operations using metaphors or analogies. We spoke of "spreadsheets," "word processing documents," "electronic mail," "web pages," and other allusions to fixed, tangible objects of the paper media world. The 1970 amendments to Fed. R. Civ. P. 34 placed "data compilations" under the rubric "documents" and the Advisory Committee Notes dwelt on the need for the respondent to "supply a printout of the computer data." That made sense in the protodigital age, when computers were viewed as powerful business tools to create paper records. As late as 1977, Kenneth Olsen, the founder and CEO of Digital Equipment Corporation, declared "there is no reason for any individual to have a computer in their home." *See* Greatest-Quotations.com, http://www.greatest-quotations.com/search.asp?quote=Home&page=14 (visited October 31, 2003).

Twenty-five years later, we cannot imagine *not* having a computer in our home. We have no choice. We are surrounded by computers, sensors, recorders, players, and digital storage devices of every description. What marks the end of protodigital thinking is the realization that computers have done more than perform complicated calculations; they have changed the nature of calculation. They have done more than print our documents; they have changed the way we compose and present our thoughts. And they have done much more than send messages to our colleagues; they have changed the way we communicate. The role played by computer technology in our lives now has little to do with generating business papers. Analogies to the paper media world are no longer useful.

The law always follows social development. When the Rules of Civil Procedure were amended in 1970 and the Rules of Evidence shortly thereafter, email as we know it didn't exist. Today is it a primary target of discovery in both civil and criminal cases. One in every seven U.S. companies has been ordered by a court or regulatory agency to produce email. Gregg Keizer, "Lack of E-Mail Policies Could Put Companies in Hot Water," InformationWeek, June 17, 2003. http://www.informationweek.com/story/showArticle.jhtml?article ID=10700336. Computer data is routinely presented as evidence in both civil and criminal courts. Electronic case filing is being implemented across the country. Government agencies are required to do business electronically and make public information available in digital form. High-profile business executives have been arrested and tried for the destruction of electronic evidence—evidence that they, or their lawyers, may not yet think of as "real" because the evidence was never reduced to paper form, nor is it even susceptible to being printed out.

The common law development was slow at first but is quickly picking up speed. In the 1980's and 1990's, only a handful of reported cases dealt squarely with the discovery or use of electronic evidence. Since 2000, the case law has exploded, and the cases deal with a number of complicated questions, including cost allocation, the duty to preserve electronic evidence, and the effect of inadvertent production of privileged electronic communications. Judges are becoming experts in computer technology and electronic records management issues, as evidenced by Judge Facciola's discussion of backup tapes in *McPeek v. Ashcroft*, 202 F.R.D. 31 (D. D.C., 2001); Judge Nevas' exploration of computer forensics in *United States v. Triumph Capital Group*, 211 F.R.D. 31 (D.Conn. 2002); and Judge Scheindlin's mini-treatise on electronic storage technology in *Zubulake v. UBS Warburg*, 217 F.R.D. 309 (S.D.N.Y. 2003).

But some things have not changed. Discovery and the presentation of evidence in court are truth-seeking processes central to the administration of justice. These processes are conducted under rules that we often overlook. Rule One of the Federal Rules of Civil Procedure establishes that the rules that follow are to be "construed and administered to secure the just, speedy, and inexpensive determination of every action." Similarly, Rule Two of the Federal Rules of Criminal Procedure states that "[t]hese rules are to be interpreted to provide for the just determination of every criminal proceeding, to secure simplicity in procedure and fairness in administration, and to eliminate unjustifiable expense and delay." Finally, Rule 102 of the Federal Rules of Evidence states that "[t]hese rules shall be construed to secure fairness in administration, elimination of unjustifiable expense and delay, and promotion of growth and development in the law of evidence to the end that the truth may be ascertained and proceedings justly determined."

In the protodigital age, it was very easy to ignore the unique aspects of electronic evidence and concentrate those tangible manifestations that looked and felt like objects from the analog world—paper printouts, photographs and drawings, or images on screens. By concentrating on these manifestations, or deliberately ignoring the more complete electronic files and computer operations that produced them, the truth-seeking purpose of discovery and evidence law was not being served. But an opposite and equal danger existed. Litigants could become obsessed with computer and information technology and lose sight of the truth-seeking goal, impeding the "speedy and inexpensive" determination of the action.

The key to striking a balance between these two extremes, at least in civil cases, is Fed. R. Civ. P. 26. Rule 26 lays out a clear division of burdens between the requesting and responding parties. This division creates opposing forces which assist the court in steering a course down the middle.

The requesting party has the burden of showing that the information being sought is relevant to the issues at hand—relevant first to the claims or defenses of the parties, and if good cause is shown, relevance to the subject matter of the dispute. In the computer world, there will likely be metadata, embedded edits and commentary, deleted files, and system data waiting to be discovered. There may be special procedures for discovering computer evidence, such as on-site inspection of computers or special procedures for preserving the evidence, such as creating bit-stream images of computer hard drives. But the burden is on the requesting party to demonstrate that any of these data sources are relevant to the claims and defenses of the parties (or the subject matter of the dispute) or that the procedures are necessary to obtain or preserve relevant and discoverable evidence. This case law is full of examples of overbroad discovery requests being denied and unjustified procedures being prohibited.

The responding party has the burden to either produce the information sought by the requesting party or demonstrate that there are privileges, undue burdens, alternative sources of information, or other reasons to object to the discovery. Simply stating that the information is in the computer and not in a preexisting tangible form that can be handed to the requesting party is not enough. It is worse for the responding party to state that it does not know whether it has the requested information or cannot assure the court that relevant data will be preserved because it either does not understand or does not control its own information technology. The case law is full of examples of broad discovery being ordered when the responding party is uncooperative and sanctions being imposed for failures and misrepresentations to the court.

The allocation of burdens between the requesting and responding parties and the consequence of failure to meet those burdens existed in the pre-digital age when discovery consisted almost entirely of interrogatories, depositions, and requests for paper documents. The issues become much sharper and the burdens on the requesting and responding parties much clearer as we enter the digital world. When businesses operate though vast, complex databases and data management systems, "documents" in the conventional sense no longer exist. Although perhaps framed as a document request in the conventional sense of Fed. R.Civ. P. 34, a request for "electronic documents" is really a request to the responding party to query its database and generate reports based on certain criteria, more akin to the request under Fed. R. Civ. P. 33(c).

Where the requesting party in the past has the luxury of requesting documents relevant to a specific claim or defense, the requesting party must now be more specific in identifying not just the topic, but the elements of data that the party needs and the form that they require. If chronology or authorship of particular files is an issue, then a request for metadata may be appropriate. If evolution of a contract or memorandum is relevant, then a request for embedded edits may be appropriate. If fraud is alleged, a request for system data or to image a hard drive may be appropriate. Each of these requests must be backed up by a showing of relevance.

On the responding side, it is also no longer business as usual. Conventional searches of paper files are clearly inappropriate in most business litigation, as are conventional litigation "hold" orders to employees to save their paper. Production of "documents" in the form of printouts or static computer images may also be inappropriate if the claims and defenses of the parties suggest more. But most importantly, blanket objections based on burden or overbreadth are out. Every response must be shown to be reasonable and every objection of undue burden must be backed up by a realistic showing of the cost, business disruption, and other burdens involved.

And that's why this book, and continuing education on electronic discovery and evidence for both lawyers and judges, is so important. Requesting parties need to know what is out there and must be able to relate their claims or defenses to the information they seek. Responding parties need to know how to respond and what the real costs are likely to be. Judges need to know what is reasonable to expect from both parties.

Michele Lange and Kristin Nimsger have distilled their practical trailblazing experience into the first edition of a guidebook through this territory. Using this guide, readers will be able to identify the major rivers and mountains and safely conduct themselves through what appears to be a jungle. But this is just the first edition guidebook. More trekkers will follow, the paths will get smoother, and the settled areas more commodious as case law develops, new rules are adopted, and technology evolves.

Kenneth J. Withers
Federal Judicial Center

ABOUT THE AUTHORS

MICHELE C.S. LANGE

Michele C.S. Lange is a staff attorney in the Electronic Evidence Services group at Kroll Ontrack Inc. Ms. Lange tracks the evolving common and statutory law in the areas of electronic discovery and computer forensics. She also helps practicing attorneys integrate electronic discovery into their case strategy. Ms. Lange has published numerous articles on the topics of electronic discovery, computer forensics, and technology's role in the law. Most notably, her articles have appeared in the *National Law Journal, New York Law Journal, Law Technology News,* and *Corporate Counsel* magazine, as well as on Law.com.

Prior to joining Kroll Ontrack, Ms. Lange worked for an international alternative dispute provider, specializing in the area of domain name disputes, researching and writing on many aspects of Internet law and commerce. Ms. Lange graduated from the University of Wisconsin—La Crosse with highest honors (B.S. Political Science and Public Administration) and the University of Minnesota Law School (J.D. *cum laude*).

KRISTIN M. NIMSGER

Kristin M. Nimsger is the Director of the Electronic Evidence Product Line at Kroll Ontrack Inc. Ms. Nimsger is responsible for the evolution of the products and service offerings of the E-Evidence business group, which primarily serves law firms, corporate counsel, and government agencies. Ms. Nimsger speaks regularly on the topics of electronic discovery, computer forensics and technology's role in the law. Recently, she has appeared in media outlets such as *CourtTV, Fox News, The New York Times, Chicago Tribune,* CNet Radio, and Bloomberg Radio on topics relating to Electronic Evidence, and has authored articles appearing in publications such as *TRIAL magazine, Legal Times, Federal Lawyer, Computer World,* and *Canada's The Lawyers Weekly.*

Prior to joining Kroll Ontrack, Ms. Nimsger practiced law in the areas of complex product liability litigation, and property and casualty insurance defense. Much of her practice involved the investigation and litigation of fire cases (subrogation and defense work) in multi-million dollar matters involving nationally recognized clients and cases. Ms. Nimsger is a graduate of the University of Minnesota, Duluth (B.A. English) and William Mitchell College of Law (J.D. *cum laude*).

KROLL ONTRACK INC.

Kroll Ontrack Inc., a wholly-owned subsidiary of Kroll Inc., provides electronic evidence and data recovery services to help corporations, law firms, federal agencies, and individuals quickly and cost-effectively recover electronic information. Specifically, the Electronic Evidence team focuses on assisting attorneys practicing in many areas (including mergers and acquisitions, intellectual property, class actions and complex litigation) with discovery and investigations surrounding electronically stored data. Kroll Ontrack, headquartered in Eden Prairie, Minnesota, operates as the "Technology Services Group" of Kroll, which is one of four business groups dedicated to serving the complex business of providing practical and integrated solutions to organizations worldwide to help safeguard them against risk. Kroll Ontrack can be reached online at http://www.krollontrack.com or by calling 1-800-347-6105.

FROM THE AUTHORS

Today, attorneys do not need to be told that electronic evidence is revolutionizing the practice of law. They see it in their cases every day. Some law schools are beginning to cover the subject of electronic evidence in classes. However, this was not such the case only a few years ago when we both started on this journey of exploration into the area of e-evidence. As lawyers, this is a non-traditional path, but one on which we have learned a tremendous amount, and of which we have grown quite fond.

We are thrilled to be central to the evolution of thought as it relates to e-evidence. Our jobs allow us to draw on our legal training and experience on a daily basis, while at the same time placing us at the brink of cutting-edge electronic discovery and computer forensics technology. This career has been the perfect marriage of the law and technology. It has taken us a long time to become experts in the law and technology associated with e-evidence, and we continue to devote significant time and energy to the ongoing pursuit of knowledge and thought leadership in this area.

It is with this background that we write this book. Our desire is to effectively transfer knowledge that has taken us years to build and acquire. We would like all practicing attorneys to have a grasp of the leading issues associated with e-evidence in order to de-mystify this technology and afford them the chance to take advantage of this new opportunity within the practice of law.

From our vantage point, we see cases come through Kroll Ontrack's doors that could have never been solved ten, five, or in some instances, even two years ago. It is very gratifying to work for the market leader in the electronic evidence industry. It was only with the complete support of Kroll Ontrack that we could have completed this book.

We would also like to express sincere gratitude to several of our colleagues and friends who assisted in editing this work—Greg Olson,

Jim Reinert, David H. Schultz, J. Robert Keena, Linda Kish, Michael Rands, Jason Paroff and Charity Delich. Thank you for correcting our errors and suggesting areas for further development. Our thanks also goes out to the ultimate thought leader in this industry, Ken Withers of the Federal Judicial Center, for writing the foreword to this work, as well as providing edits. In addition, thanks to the American Bar Association for their efforts and support in editing and publishing this book. All of you have made our end-product a much better resource.

Last, we would like to profoundly thank our spouses and families: Ben, Jon, and Sophia, you give us great inspiration and continuously rise to the challenge of living with a lawyer and keeping your sanity.

Michele Lange and Kristin Nimsger

DISCLAIMER

This document is neither designed nor intended to provide legal or other professional advice but is intended merely to be a starting point for research and information on the subject of electronic evidence. While every attempt has been made to ensure accuracy of this information, no responsibility can be accepted for errors or omissions. Recipients of information maintain full, professional, and direct responsibility to their clients for any information rendered by the authors or Kroll Ontrack.

TABLE OF CONTENTS

FIGURES AND TABLES

CHAPTER ❖ 1

Introduction

1.1 Explosion of E-Evidence: Statistics and Case Examples—The Importance of E-Evidence

In recent years technology has had a profound impact on the way human beings communicate, the way business is transacted, and ultimately, the way lawyers practice law. From the convenience of corresponding with clients via e-mail and filing pleadings electronically, to the ease of using a handheld computer to manage a case calendar or access legal research in court, technology's contributions cannot be understated. As positive and powerful as technology has been to the legal industry, however, it has also created new challenges and opportunities.

The advancement of technology has created an entirely new source of evidence—electronic evidence. The rise of the importance of this new brand of evidence has vastly outpaced the rate at which lawyers have adapted to this new reality. Gone are the days of lawyers asking clients to search their office file cabinets to locate the paper documents responsive to a discovery request. The changes to the practice, however, are much more far reaching. The entire landscape of advocacy is shifting dramatically. With increasing momentum, case law is embracing the realities of the digital age. Courts are moving toward requiring a level of technological sophistication in order for lawyers to adequately advocate previously open-and-shut discovery disputes. Today, lawyers must work with clients to capture responsive electronic documents from a multitude of locations and formats in order to comply with a garden variety discovery request.

In addition to the "old-fashioned" method of discovery, electronic evidence is affecting virtually every investigation, whether criminal or civil. Today, there is not usually a "paper-trail" to establish who did what and when. Instead, electronic footprints and fingerprints often provide the clues to solving a multitude of questions of conduct or action. Today's investigators must understand computer forensic best practices as they mine metadata and electronic files for digital clues and evidence to support a case.

Consider these statistics:

- In 2002, the International Data Corporation estimated that 31 billion emails were sent daily. This number is expected to grow to 60 billion a day by 2006.[1]
- Most companies store up to 70 percent of their records in electronic form.[2]
- Within ten years, the total number of electronic records produced on the planet could be doubling every sixty minutes.[3]
- A company operating in all fifty states could face as many as 2,500 potentially relevant laws affecting electronic records within their organization.[4]

One reason the electronic evidence explosion is affecting virtually every lawyer, regardless of practice area, is that as a culture, we are experiencing a revolution on a massive scale. Just as we look back on the industrial revolution as a turning point in the development of society, so will future historians look at our time as one that forever changed the way the world worked—an electronic communication revolution. This boom has left no person untouched.

In corporate America, now more than ever, employees are creating and storing documents solely in an electronic format. In addition, de-

---

[1]Gretel Johnston, IDG News Service, http://www.idg.net/go.cgi?id=749070
[2]Lori Enos, *Digital Data Changing Legal Landscape*, E-Commerce Times (May 16, 2000) http://www.ecommercetimes.com/perl/story/3339.htmlv
[3]http://www.censa.org/html/news.html
[4]Kevin Craine, "Here Come the Lawyers. Is Your IT Department Ready?" http://www.educomts.com/downloads/Herecomethelawyers.pdf

spite warnings about commemorating candid remarks or confidential information in e-mail or instant messaging systems, employees are finding it easier and faster to send e-mails to communicate rather than pick up the telephone. Ease and speed, however, breed candor at a level that can alter the course of a lawsuit with just a few keystrokes. Consider these examples:

- A 1996 e-mail from an administrator within the Wyeth-Ayerst pharmaceutical company regarding side-effects of the Phen-Fen diet drug: ". . . . can I look forward to my waning years signing checks for fat people who are a little afraid of a silly lung problem?" *See* Alicia Mundy, *Dispensing with the Truth*, St. Martin's Press, Inc. (April 2001).

- A 2001 e-mail from Jack Grubman, New York stock analyst: "You know everyone thinks I upgraded [AT&T stock]. . . . Nope. I used Sandy to get my kids in 92nd St. Y preschool (which is harder than Harvard) and Sandy needed Armstrong's vote on our board to nuke Reed in showdown. Once coast was clear for both of us (ie Sandy clear victor and my kids confirmed) I went back to my normal negative self [on AT&T] . . . Armstrong never knew that we both (Sandy and I) played him like a fiddle." *See* "Grubman Informed Weill of Meetings With AT&T" *Wall Street Journal*, Nov. 15, 2002.

- An August 21, 2001 e-mail to a human resources specialist at UBS Warburg suggested that Laura Zubulake, a senior salesperson, be fired "ASAP" after her EEOC charge was filed, in part so that she would not be eligible for year-end bonuses. *See Zubulake v. UBS Warburg*, 2003 WL 21087884 (S.D.N.Y. May 13, 2003).

- In a January 22, 2002 e-mail, former WorldCom controller David Myers instructed Steven Brabbs, WorldCom director of international finance in the U.K. headquarters, to "not have any more meetings with AA [Arthur Andersen] for any reason. I do not want to hear an excuse just stop. Don't make me tell you again," *See* "E-Mail Blackmail—WorldCom Memo Threatened Conscience-Stricken Exec." Jessica Sommar, *New York Post*. Aug 27, 2002. pg. 027.

All of this activity creates a mountain of information that has to be identified, collected, searched, reviewed, and produced in the event of civil litigation or a governmental investigation.

In addition to its impact on civil litigation and government investigations, electronic evidence routinely plays a key role in criminal law—either as the instrumentality of the crime or the primary source of evidence relating to a more traditional charge. For example, drug dealers have jumped on the information superhighway and are arranging and carrying out transactions via their handheld personal digital assistants. Pedophiles are finding it easier to reach their targets by logging onto the Internet and visiting "chat rooms." With the click of a button, hackers can send viruses and computer bombs to sizeable audiences wreaking enormous financial and physical damage. These are only a few instances where technology has been used for foul play. Even in the investigation of more traditional criminal matters, such as murder, theft or other age-old crimes, perpetrators often leave electronic traces of their malfeasance.

The *State v. Guthrie*, 627 N.W.2d 401 (S.D. 2001), case is one example of computer forensic protocols filtering into the criminal case law. In this case, the defendant, a Presbyterian minister, was prosecuted for murdering his wife of thirty-four years. The defendant's wife was found face down in the bathtub of her home, with her husband on his hands and knees sobbing for help. Autopsy results revealed that she had consumed large amounts of prescription drugs shortly before her death. The medical examiner could not resolve whether the death was suicide or homicide. During the search of the defendant's home and church, the police seized a computer from the defendant's office. A computer specialist conducted several forensic searches on the computer, finding that it had been used to conduct Internet searches on "household accidents," "bathtub accidents," and prescription drugs. In addition, the forensic analysis was able to reveal that a computer printed suicide note, offered to exculpate the defendant, was created several months after the victim's death. This computer forensic analysis was part of the evidence relied upon in finding the defendant guilty of first-degree murder.

These examples reveal that the computer is becoming a critical point of investigation in any case. Almost every interaction with a computer or other piece of electronic media creates an electronic trail of evidence. Computer media is often the best place to begin looking for potential evidence, whether on one hard drive, a network of servers and desktops, or a pile of backup tapes. In order to discharge their duties to clients, lawyers practicing in the 21st century must now be prepared to handle this modern form of evidence, along with all the new and unique technical and legal issues that come along with it.

This book is designed to arm lawyers with the information, tools, and knowledge gained from the combined wisdom of our organization's collective experience in the e-evidence industry and our experience of living the evolution of the practice of law. This book is a practical guide to all things e-evidence. A mastery of the topics discussed herein will adequately prepare any lawyer for zealous advocacy in the 21st century.

1.2 The Difference between Electronic and Paper Evidence

In physical form, a computer file is observably different from a piece of paper contained in a filing cabinet. Understanding the similarities and differences between these two evidentiary sources is essential to understanding the comparisons and contrasts between traditional paper discovery practices and electronic evidence practices.

A preliminary topic which must be understood in order to lay the foundation for understanding electronic evidence is the process of how data is stored on a computer or other digital media. When documents, files, and programs are saved on a computer, they are "written to" the hard disk drive in a number of places. Data stored on a hard drive is written to a "platter" or series of "platters," very similar to a CD-Rom, in a number of "sectors." The data is written randomly to the drive, rather than sequentially or chronologically, or in any other logical order. The computer system determines how and where files are placed on a hard drive with the goal of trying to optimize the data retrieval process, which is generally instructed by the computer's central processing unit (CPU).

The computer then creates a "table of contents" or "index" for the locations of data stored on the drive. This is known as the File Allocation Table (FAT) for the most common type of operating systems. When a user tries to retrieve a file, the file system uses the File Allocation Table to determine where on the hard drive the file has been placed, if it is a FAT-based file system.

The file system can be likened to a library card catalogue system that attempts to organize the location of books within the library in the most optimal manner. To find a book, one looks up the name in the card catalogue, which then points to the book's location. This system of writing and retrieving data becomes critically important in the context of computer forensic investigations, with respect to deleted data in particular, discussed later in this chapter.

A principle difference between paper and electronic data relates to its destructibility. While somehow less tangible than paper documents, digital data is much more difficult to destroy. When a paper document custodian places a document into a paper shredder, sets it on fire, or uses other destructive means to dispose of information, that document is gone and is not likely to be resurrected. For all intents and purposes, the bits and pieces of paper cannot be glued together to bring the information back.

In contrast, electronic documents and e-mail are not so easily destroyed. Despite a user's intention, e-evidence tends to remain accessible on a computer hard drive even after it has been "deleted." Every electronic document or transaction leaves an electronic fingerprint on the computer's hard drive, as described above. When the data is deleted, the space occupied by that file is simply marked as available for overwriting by the file allocation table (FAT). Using computer forensic protocols, portions of the "deleted" data are recoverable by experts, unless and until new data is written to each and every sector that was previously occupied by that file. (See Chapter 3.1 "Computer Forensics" for further discussion). The phrase "delete does not mean delete" concisely describes the deletion misnomer and has come to be a commonly used phrase among those who live and work with electronic evidence on a daily basis.

Another central distinction between electronic evidence and paper is the sheer volume of information that is created and maintained on an ongoing basis. The creation of digital data not only outpaces its paper counterpart by leaps and bounds, but once created, it is rarely destroyed. The main reason that electronic data tends to live in perpetuity relates to the ease with which it is stored.

Everyone knows that storing volumes of paper requires significant physical storage space. Organizations sign long and expensive contracts with offsite storage facilities to perform just this task—keeping all paper documents for a specified period, keeping them "retrievable" as need be, and ultimately destroying them. In contrast, computer storage takes very little physical space and is relatively inexpensive. The ease with which volumes of electronic files are created and stored results in exponentially more information and documents which must be considered in the context of discovery. The key difference between electronic and paper based information is felt most acutely at this sorting and production phase. Unlike paper documents, electronic documents are not necessarily stored in any organized rationale, significantly complicating its review and production. This is where electronic evidence technology steps in, as will be discussed in this text.

Another factor highlighting the dissimilarities between computer-based documents and paper documents that creates both opportunity and obligation for practicing lawyers is the information available about the document itself. Metadata (perhaps better described as "data about the data") is information regarding document creation and modification, which can tell the tale about the life of a particular electronic document. This information is automatically saved with the computer document by the applications that created it. Available metadata varies with the type of electronic document. Some common examples are the date, time, and perhaps the identity of the person who created, sent and/or received the e-mail, or the name of the person who last accessed the document. This type of information is not included with hard copy documents unless typewritten on their face, or manually "coded" as part of a labor-intensive document review process. The beauty of metadata, from a lawyer's perspective, is that this information can save time and money by taking the place of a long and expensive, objective coding process. Instead, it can all be done automatically through the electronic document handling process. Obviously, the sword is double-edged. This type of information is often important evidence in litigation, and parties are increasingly demanding access to this information from one another. Thus, the term metadata is another word with its origins in technology that has not only wound its way into the vocabulary of the modern lawyer but has also developed its own meaning to lawyers—one that goes beyond what the average "techie" might believe about the term. This topic will be discussed in detail in the technology section of this text.

The final distinction between paper and electronic data may also be the most important; or at the very least, one that has garnered the most attention to the topic of e-evidence. The pure reality is that for some reason, human beings continue to believe there is something transient, impermanent, and casual about electronic communication. We are not psychologists and will not delve into the alluring question of "why" humans behave this way, but this we know to be true: electronic communication may contain more unguarded and spontaneous remarks than any other previous form of human communication. As illustrated previously, the examples are endless.

The bare fact is that things that individuals would *never* have memorialized on paper in the past are now carelessly written in e-mail messages, instant messages, and comments appended to electronic documents. These "stray remarks" may secure a cause of action that would otherwise be questionable if only paper-based documents existed. These pieces of electronic communication capture, like nothing else available, the present sense and contemporaneous reactions, opinions, and feelings of individuals as they live in the moment. What else could any litigator want than an unadulterated statement made by an opposing party at the specific time and in the precise circumstances that gave rise to litigation? Thus is the power of electronic evidence. This is one of the foremost reasons parties seek electronic evidence despite some of the challenges associated with collecting, retrieving, and producing this information.

Figure 1.1 Computer Forensics and Electronic Discovery:
What's the Difference?

Electronic Evidence	
Computer Forensics	**Electronic Discovery**
■ Investigative & detailed analysis ■ Typically a single hard drive or PC ■ Searching for deleted information ■ Determine who, what, when ■ Recreation of time critical events ■ Breaking of passwords/encryption ■ Reporting & expert testimony	■ Gathering, searching, filtering & producing large volumes of relevant information for legal review ■ E-mail systems, network shares, desktops and backups ■ Data is accessed but not analyzed ■ Includes active and archival data ■ Typically does NOT include discarded, hidden or deleted data

Despite these and other differences between traditional and electronic sources of evidence, counsel should not face digital data with trepidation. The discovery of electronic evidence evokes the same game that litigators have faced for years, only today we witness the evolution of a new rulebook. While courts expect attorneys to understand technology and the burden, expense, and process associated with producing that information, litigators who learn what electronic evidence is, how to find it, how to use it, and how to avoid problems when dealing with it increase their chances of prevailing in a case and avoiding judicial sanctions.

1.3 Computer Forensics v. Electronic Discovery: How the Two Disciplines Impact the Practice of Law

The broad term electronic evidence describes all computer and technology based evidence, no matter how it is retrieved or for what purpose it is used in litigation—e-mail, instant messages, documents, databases, spreadsheets, and virtually all other electronic data. This digital data can be stored on various types of media—hard drives, personal digital assistants (PDAs), cell phones, floppy disks, CDs, DVDs, USB drives, backup tapes, servers, and more.

Electronic evidence can best be broken down into two separate disciplines: computer forensics and electronic discovery. These terms are mistakenly used interchangeably in both legal and technical circles. Understanding the difference between computer forensics and electronic discovery can be crucial to developing the most effective electronic evidence case strategy. Often cases have an element of both computer forensics and electronic discovery.

The following quick reference chart and the accompanying text distinguishes between computer forensics and electronic discovery.

A more thorough discussion of the technology and processes will be discussed in later chapters. The case examples described below are taken from actual cases we have had the opportunity to work on in our organization.

COMPUTER FORENSICS

Overview:

Computer forensics is a discipline. While formal educational programs in computer forensics are only beginning to emerge, experience in the field over the past decade has spawned several qualified and well established experts. Computer forensic technicians train for long periods of time in order to become qualified computer forensic experts. Companies and people offering computer forensic services offer investigative assistance, and they practice the art and science of examining and piecing together computer-related conduct and technology use. Experts trained in computer forensic protocol endeavor to determine the who, what, when, where, and how of computer related conduct. Often, computer forensic services involve the recovery and analysis of deleted information on a single piece of media or a small number of media sources. Computer forensic analysis may include:

- Recreating a specific chain of events or user activity, including Internet activity, e-mail communication, file deletion, etc.;
- Searching for key words and key dates and determining what resulting data is relevant;
- Searching for copies of previous document drafts;
- Searching for privileged information;
- Searching for the existence of certain programs such as file deletion programs;
- Breaking passwords or usurping encrypted files; or
- Authenticating data files and the date and time stamps of those files.

Case examples:

Computer Sabotage

A company sought assistance in its investigation of several former employees who were suspected of stealing and dealing in the company's trade secrets. The night before forensic engineers were to image the hard drives in question, one of the former employees destroyed the computer evidence by apparently deleting the incriminating information and then downloading approximately six gigabytes of MP3 files to the drives. Even though no evidence of the trade secret misappropriation was recoverable, engineers presented findings and analysis of the steps the employee had taken to cover his tracks, which supported the company's data spoliation claims against the former employee. Other examples of computer sabotage that are regularly seen include: bullet holes shot through drive platters, hard drives immersed in water, media recovered from intentionally set fires, disks physically mangled by a hammer, drives that have been reformatted, and the application of software utility programs to "wipe clean" portions of the drive.

Inappropriate E-mail Use

Given the candor and ease with which e-mails are drafted and sent, computer forensic engineers are frequently called upon to investigate e-mail communication. Some of the most common e-mail situations include: online harassment, trade secret misappropriation, divorce scandals, office affairs, and corporate fraud. For example, a corporation sought assistance investigating e-mail evidence in a sexual harassment case. Computer forensic engineers examined an e-mail message allegedly sent from the plaintiff's supervisor to the company chairman (with whom the plaintiff claimed an affair) stating that he had "fired her like you told me to do." Engineers were able to prove that the supervisor had not sent the message, but rather that the plaintiff had generated it. The harassment case was settled, but the judge, having examined the forensic findings, referred the matter to the district attorney. The plaintiff was subsequently tried for a number of charges relating to the forged evidence and was found guilty. A state appellate court upheld the verdict and the prison sentence.

ELECTRONIC DISCOVERY

Overview:

In contrast, to computer forensics electronic discovery services (also known as e-discovery) employ advanced proprietary technology (rather than detailed human and machine analysis) to manage extremely large volumes of electronic information for use in litigation, regulatory compliance, government investigations, or other proceedings. Electronic discovery technology is typically used when a large number of media sources are involved, including e-mail systems, network share systems, the desktops and laptops of many individuals, floppies, backup tapes and other sources of electronic storage media. Active and archival data is accessed and provided to the client for legal review but is not analyzed by the electronic evidence expert. Because not every electronic document found on a custodian's computer or on backup tapes is responsive or relevant to a discovery request, data filtering technology limits the universe of data down to a manageable set.

Case Examples:

Complex Litigation

A law firm representing a client suing a technology company for patent infringement sought assistance in searching over 650 gigabytes of data for responsive e-mail and documents from approximately one hundred custodians. These custodians or "users" consisted of current and former employees of the firm's client. E-discovery engineers collected current employees' data from the client's server and restored backup tapes to obtain the data of former employees. Several engineers were sent onsite to collect the data for processing back at the production lab. Once the processing began, engineers determined that 2.6 million pages of documents were responsive to a keyword list containing 93 terms. Instead of printing these documents to paper, the "hits" were imported into an online repository for attorney review.

Antitrust Compliance

A law firm representing a corporation that had recently struck a deal to acquire one of its major industry competitors sought assistance with producing e-mail and documents pursuant to the Federal Trade Commission's Request for Additional Information, better known as a "Second Request," under the Hart Scott Rodino Act of 1976. Some facts about the situation were as follows:

- The "Second Request" was 18 single-spaced pages in length.
- It sought corporate data that was spread over 11 geographic locations, including several sites in South America and Asia.
- Data responsive to the request came from a total of 265 employees in the acquiring corporation.
- The data had been generated on a wide array of operating systems, e-mail packages, and software applications.

E-discovery engineers were dispatched to retrieve the needed data from various client locations, both domestically and abroad. The data was captured from the eleven locations in less than two weeks from the time of the firm's initial phone call. Throughout the project, potentially relevant data from newly identified individuals came to the processing lab. The production took the form of almost 4.3 million pages.

1.4 Emerging Law: Common Law, Rules, and Statutes Addressing Electronic Evidence

New legal issues are emerging almost daily on the topics of computer forensics and electronic discovery. As electronically created documents continue to play a larger role in litigation, litigators, parties, and courts are taking a keen interest in this new area and are working through the application of existing rules and statutes to meet the technological reality. Very few clear, bright-line legal protocols or rules have developed thus far. One court highlighted the lack of precedential guidance surrounding an electronic discovery issue stating, "There is certainly no controlling authority for the proposition that restoring all backup tapes is necessary in every case. The Federal Rules of Civil Procedure do not require such a search, and the handful of cases are idiosyncratic and provide little guidance." *See McPeek v. Ashcroft*, 202 F.R.D. 31 (D.D.C. 2001).

Unlike the vast majority of legal topics, the case law surrounding e-evidence has expanded on an astounding scale since 2001 when Judge Facciola issued the first *McPeek* decision. But, issues such as those in *McPeek*, including what is discoverable, how should it be produced, and who will bear the costs of production among others, are still being played out in courts across the country. At the same time, the federal and state rule advisory committees and other rule influencing groups are making efforts to determine if any revisions to the statutes and rules are warranted. These groups' main challenge is to decide whether electronic evidence is intrinsically different from paper evidence and whether a procedural system can be designed to deal with ever-changing technological developments. While no clear solution has materialized, both the current case law and rules offer guidance.

COMMON LAW

The most straightforward method for analyzing the body of electronic evidence jurisprudence is to look at cases relating to the electronic discovery and computer forensic disciplines. For detailed case lists in both areas, see the appendix. While this body of law is fast evolving and increasing in importance, some seminal cases have emerged. A quick guide to the most important e-evidence decisions follows:

Figure 1.2 Guide to Seminal E-Evidence Cases

- **Electronic Evidence is Discoverable:** "The law is clear that data in computerized form is discoverable even if paper 'hard copies' of the information have been produced...[T]oday it is black letter law that computerized data is discoverable if relevant." *Anti-Monopoly, Inc. v. Hasbro, Inc.*, 1995 WL 649934 (S.D.N.Y. Nov. 3, 1995). See also *McPeek v. Ashcroft*, 202 F.R.D. 31 (D.D.C. 2001); *Linnen v. A.H. Robins Co.*, 1999 WL 462015 (Mass. Super. June 16, 1999); *Crown Life Ins. Co. v. Craig*, 995 F.2d. 1376 (7th Cir. 1993).
- **Proportionality Applies to E-Discovery Requests:** A party producing electronic evidence must be protected against undue burden and expense associated with the production. *Southern Diagnostic Assoc. v. Bencosme*, 833 So. 2d 801 (Fla. Dist. Ct. App. 2002); *Strasser v. Yalamanchi*, 669 So. 2d 1142 (Fla. Dist. Ct. App. 1996); *In re Brand Name Prescription Drugs Antitrust Litig.*, 1995 WL 360526 (N.D. Ill. June 15, 1995).
- **Deleted Data can be Discoverable:** Deleted electronic evidence is fully discoverable. *Dodge, Warren, & Peters Ins. Servs. v. Riley*, 130 Cal.Rptr.2d 385 (Cal. Ct. App. 2003); *Simon Property Group v. mySimon, Inc.*, 194 F.R.D. 639 (S.D. Ind. 2000).
- **Business and Personal Data can be Discoverable:** It is proper to order discovery of electronic evidence from personal hard drives. *Positive Software Solutions v. New Century Mortgage Corp.*, 259 F. Supp. 2d 561 (N.D.Tex. 2003); *Superior Consultant Co. v. Bailey*, 2000 WL 1279161 (E.D. Mich. Aug. 22, 2000); *Northwest Airlines v. Local 2000*, C.A. No. 00-08DWF/AJB (D. Minn. Feb. 2, 2000) (Order on Defendants' Motion for Protective Order and Plaintiff's Motion to Compel Discovery); *Northwest Airlines v. Local 2000*, C.A. No. 00-08DWF/AJB (D. Minn. Feb. 29, 2000) (Memorandum Opinion and Order).
- **Defining Your Duty to Preserve E-Evidence:** There is a duty to preserve evidence that parties know, or should know, is relevant to the ongoing litigation, including preservation of all data compilations, computerized data and other electronically-recorded information. *Kleiner v. Burns*, 2000 WL 1909470 (D. Kan. Dec. 15, 2000); *Danis v. USN Communications*, 2000 WL 1694325 (N.D. Ill. Oct. 23, 2000).
- **Protocols for Proper Evidence Preservation:** It is proper protocol in a case involving electronic evidence to appoint a neutral expert to create a "mirror image" of the electronic evidence. *Playboy Enters., Inc. v. Welles*, 60 F. Supp. 2d 1050 (S.D. Cal. 1999).
- **Spoliation Sanctions Defined:** Failure to preserve e-mail and electronic documents (whether intentional or inadvertent) is sanctionable as spoliation of evidence. *Metropolitan Opera Assoc., Inc. v. Local 100*, 212 F.R.D. 178 (S.D.N.Y. 2003); *Residential Funding Corp. v. DeGeorge Fin. Corp.*, 306 F.3d 99

(2d. Cir. Sept. 26, 2002); *Gates Rubber Co. v. Bando Chem. Ind.*, 167 F.R.D. 90 (D. Colo. 1996); *William T. Thompson Co. v. General Nutrition Corp.*, 593 F. Supp. 1443 (C.D. Cal. 1984).

■ **Cost Shifting and Sharing:** The producing party must normally obtain, translate, and bear the costs associated with the production of electronic evidence. However, recent cases provide alternatives to this general rule. *In re Brand Name Prescription Drugs Antitrust Litig.*, 1995 WL 360526 (N.D. Ill. June 15, 1995). But see *Rowe Entertainment, Inc. v. The William Morris Agency*, 205 F.R.D. 421 (S.D.N.Y. 2002) (setting forth an eight factor cost shifting protocol); *Murphy Oil USA, Inc. v. Fluor Daniel, Inc.*, 2002 WL 246439 (E.D. La. Feb. 19, 2002) (following *Rowe* protocol); *Zubulake v. UBS Warburg*, 217 F.R.D. 309 (S.D.N.Y. 2003) (revising the *Rowe* eight factor test to a seven-factor test with new factors and deleted factors).

FEDERAL RULES OF CIVIL PROCEDURE

In 1970, Federal Rule of Civil Procedure 34 was amended to include "data compilations from which information can be obtained" in the description of "documents." In addition, Rule 26(a)(1)(B), added in 1993, requires disclosure of "all documents, data compilations, and tangible things in the possession, custody, or control of the party that are relevant to disputed facts . . ." when parties are making initial disclosures. Most lawyers seeking their opponents' electronic documents build their arguments around this broad discovery language.

FEDERAL STATUTES AND AGENCY RULES

In recent years, federal statutes and agency rules have been passed or revised to embrace electronic evidence. For example, in 1984 18 U.S.C. § 1030, commonly referred to as the Computer Fraud and Abuse Act (C.F.A.A.), was created. The C.F.A.A. seeks to regulate fraud and related activity in connection with computers. The United States government has used this statute several times to prosecute computer hackers. One of the first public cases in which the C.F.A.A. was used was *United States v. Lloyd*, 269 F.3d 228 (3rd Cir. 2001). In this case, a unanimous three-judge panel of the 3rd U.S. Circuit Court of Appeals found that a man convicted of planting a computer "time bomb" in his former employer's computer system is not entitled to a new trial on the basis of a juror prejudice. The man was originally convicted in large part due to the testimony of computer forensic experts. The ruling reinstated the trial court's verdict in which the defendant was convicted on one count of computer sabotage.

The prosecution's theory was that the defendant had planted a computer "time bomb" in the central file server of Omega's computer network while he was still employed there and that the program "detonated" after he was fired, causing significant damage and business interruption to Omega's operations.

Kroll Ontrack computer forensic experts testified at the original trial that the "purge" of Omega's files was intentional and that only someone with supervisory-level access to the network could have accomplished such a feat. Uncovering evidence of a string of commands entitled "FUSE.EXE," experts characterized the commands as a "time bomb" because anyone who attempted to log on to the server after the commands were in place detonated the program and caused a massive deletion of data. The program was similar to a Microsoft program called "DELTREE," but reconfigured for Novell. Experts ruled out the possibility of accidental deletion (one of the defense's main contentions) because of the specificity of the commands and also testified that after examining the hard drive recovered from the defendant's home, the exact same strings of commands that comprised "FUSE.EXE" were located. While *United States v. Lloyd* was one of the first cases of its kind, it definitely has not been the last.

In addition to regulating computer fraud and abuse, several new federal statutes and corresponding agency rules, such as the Sarbanes Oxley Act, the Health Insurance Portability and Accountability Act, and the Patriot Act, are imposing requirements on organizations in regards to the retention and destruction of certain electronic records. No longer are companies allowed to blindly destroy e-mails and computer files. Instead, balance must be found between appropriate destruction of stale and non-regulated documents and adequate preservation of potentially significant documents. Such balance is the key to effective electronic document management and the protection of informational assets as required by these laws. For a detailed list of federal rules addressing electronic records management, see the appendix.

STATE STATUTES AND COURT RULES

While most jurisdictions are still considering change, some state legislatures have led the way by passing amendments that incorporate electronic evidence issues. For example, on October 12, 2001 Bill AB 223 (Frommer) was signed into law amending Section 2017 of the California Code of Civil Procedure. This law obliges more judicial supervision over the use of technology in conducting discovery, including requests for and responses to discovery orders, service and presentation of motions, production, storage, and access to electronic information, and choice of a service provider. Further, the e-discovery procedures must meet the following five criteria before the court can make such an order: (A) they promote cost-effective and efficient discovery or motions relating thereto; (B) they do not impose or require undue expenditures of time or money; (C) they do not create an economic burden or hardship on any person; (D) they promote open competition among vendors and providers of services in order to facilitate the highest quality service at the lowest reasonable cost to the litigants; and (E) they do not require parties or counsel to purchase exceptional or unnecessary services, hardware, or software.

Texas has also revised its Civil Rules of Procedure to address discovery of electronic or magnetic data. Amended in 1999, Rule 196.4 requires parties seeking discovery of such data to specify the form in which it should be produced. The responding party must comply if the requested data and form is reasonably available to the responding party in its ordinary course of business. The responding party may object if it cannot, through reasonable efforts, retrieve the information or produce it in the form requested. If the court orders a response, the court must also order the requesting party to pay the reasonable expenses of any extraordinary steps required to retrieve and produce the information.

In addition to Texas and California, Maryland, Illinois, Wyoming, Mississippi, Florida, New Jersey, and Arkansas have adopted rules related to electronic discovery, computer forensics, or technology in litigation. For a detailed list of state statutes and court rules, see the appendix.

EMERGING LAWS: PROPOSALS TO MODIFY EXISTING LAW

In light of the unique characteristics of electronic evidence, state and federal rules committees are considering offering more direction in this area. *See* Richard L. Marcus, *Confronting the Future: Coping With Discovery of Electronic Materials*, 64 Duke L. and Contemporary Problems 253 (2001).

Proposals to modify the Federal Rules of Civil Procedure are mounting, and the advisory committee is seeking input from practitioners, the bench, electronic evidence experts, academics, government researchers, and law and policy think tanks.

One such proposal is to rework Federal Rules of Civil Procedure 26 and 34—the discovery rules containing general provisions—to better define "documents" and "data compilations." While most courts and commentators have interpreted these rules to allow the discovery of electronic materials, the rules could be clarified to address whether metadata, embedded data, cookies, temporary files, and deleted documents are included within the definition of electronic "documents" or "data compilations." *See* Shira A. Scheindlin & Jeffrey Rabkin, *Electronic Discovery in Federal Civil Litigation: Is Rule 34 up to the Task?*, 41 B.C.L. Rev. 327 (2000). These rules could also address exchange of information regarding the parties' storage of electronic data and special problems of identifying privileged items in electronically stored materials. Further, Rule 34(a) could be tailored to include an operating protocol for use by an electronic discovery expert or contain prerequisites for onsite inspection of computerized materials.

Another alteration to the Federal Rules of Civil Procedure could occur in Rule 30—the rule relating to depositions. Within this rule, a special procedure could be developed to depose information systems managers to provide useful and inexpensive technical information on the types of operating systems used, data storage locations, and backup systems, among other things. Further, if a party fails to make disclosures or cooperate in submitting electronic documents, Federal Rule of Civil Procedure 37—the rule addressing sanctions for discovery violations—could be tailored to include a specialized rule about spoliation of electronic materials.

Although it is easy to discuss such improvements, revising the state and federal rules is a daunting and time-consuming task, and changes are not expected for several years. Striking the right statutory balance between too little guidance and too much control is imperative. In fact, some commentators argue that discovery statutes such as those in California and Texas excessively restrict a party's liberty to engage in widespread discovery. Other commentators point out that given the ever-changing nature of technology, detailed statutory protocols could be obsolete in a couple of years, if not a couple of months.

The proliferation of electronic information is the driving force behind these legal developments. As technology continues to evolve and judges and practitioners learn more about electronic evidence, bright-line legal precedent and protocols will develop. As one court noted, "At some point, a party and/or its attorneys must be held responsible for knowing what documents are discoverable and where to find them." *Danis v. USN Communications*, 2000 WL 1694325 (N.D. Ill. Oct. 23, 2000). This axiom has never been more relevant than now.

CHAPTER ❖ 2

Legal Issues

2.1 Discoverability

Contrary to the belief of some lawyers who hold out hope that they will not have to master the universe of issues relating to e-evidence, the simple reality today is that electronic documents are every bit as discoverable as paper documents. Although there is much unsettled law in the area of e-evidence, this is the one inescapable truth: e-evidence is discoverable and practitioners must be prepared to request it, respond to requests for it, and ultimately produce it.

Myriad cases in both state and federal courts have confirmed the principle that e-evidence is discoverable. The oft cited *Linnen* case held that "A discovery request aimed at the production of records retained in some electronic form is no different in principle, from a request for documents contained in any office file cabinet." The court continued, "To permit a corporation such as Wyeth to reap the business benefits of such [computer] technology and simultaneously use that technol-

ogy as a shield in litigation would lead to incongruous and unfair results." *Linnen v. A.H. Robins Co.*, 1999 WL 462015 (Mass. Super. June 16,
1999). This rule has been confirmed by numerous other cases, across all
jurisdictions and in all types of litigation. As stated back in 1985 by the
Utah Federal District Court in *Bills v. Kennecott Corp.*, "[C]ertain propositions will be applicable in virtually all cases, namely, that information stored in computers should be as freely discoverable as information not stored in computers, so parties requesting discovery should
not be prejudiced thereby; and the party responding is usually in the
best and most economical position to call up its own computer stored
data." *Bills v. Kennecott Corp.*, 108 F.R.D. 459 (C.D. Utah 1985). Even
twenty years ago, courts—such as the *Bills* court—could foresee that
computer data was valuable in discovery and could not be overlooked.

Early in the evolution of cases relating to the discoverability of e-
evidence, parties often argued that important evidence had been
printed or that all of the "good" evidence had already been produced
in paper form. Case law demonstrates that these arguments are no
longer successful. "The law is clear that data in computerized form is
discoverable even if paper 'hard copies' of the information have been
produced." *Anti-Monopoly, Inc. v. Hasbro, Inc.*, 1995 WL 649934
(S.D.N.Y. Nov. 3, 1995). Requesting parties in discovery see the value
in receiving electronic documents in an electronic form. Electronic documents are easily transported and imported into existing case management systems. They are searchable, and contain valuable "behind
the scenes" data (also known as metadata) that paper documents do
not contain. Litigants should now be prepared to produce electronic
information and to do so in electronic form in many cases.

That is not to say that litigants are afforded unfettered access to all
electronic evidence in the possession of their opposing parties. To the
contrary, the same rules of proportionality, as embodied in the Federal
Rules of Civil Procedure, apply to electronic evidence. Federal Rule
26(b)(2) imposes general limitations on the scope of discovery in the
form of a "proportionality test":

> The frequency or extent of use of the discovery methods otherwise
> permitted under these rules and by any local rule shall be limited
> by the court if it determines that: (i) the discovery sought is **un-
> reasonably cumulative or duplicative, or is obtainable from
> some other source that is more convenient, less burdensome, or
> less expensive**; ii) the party seeking discovery has had **ample op-
> portunity by discovery in the action to obtain the information**
> sought; or (iii) the **burden or expense of the proposed discovery**

outweighs its likely benefit, taking into account the needs of the case, the amount in controversy, the parties' resources, the importance of the issues at stake in the litigation, and the importance of the proposed discovery in resolving the issues. Fed. R. Civ. P. 26(b)(2) (emphasis added).

These principles apply equally to the discoverability of electronic evidence. As stated by the court in *Rowe Entertainment, Inc. v. The William Morris Agency*, "Rules 26(b) and 34 for the Federal Rules of Civil Procedure instruct that computer-stored information is discoverable under the same rules that pertain to tangible, written materials." *Rowe Entertainment, Inc. v. The William Morris Agency*, 2002 WL 975713 (S.D.N.Y. May 9, 2002). Simply put, electronic data is discoverable, but not *more* discoverable than hard copy. In order to navigate the constraints contained in the Federal Rules of Civil Procedure, lawyers must not only understand the fundamentals of their case and the legal and financial situation of the parties; now litigators must also grasp the technical realities of e-evidence so as to adequately demonstrate burden and expense.

Courts have also increasingly adhered to the fundamental principles of Federal Rule of Civil Procedure 26 in the determination of the scope of discoverability of e-evidence. In particular, the marginal utility test is often employed by courts in this area. For example, in *McPeek v. Ashcroft*, the court stated that "[E]conomic considerations have to be pertinent if the court is to remain faithful to its responsibility to prevent 'undue burden or expense'. . . . If the likelihood of finding something was the only criterion, there is a risk that someone will have to spend hundreds of thousands of dollars to produce a single e-mail. That is an awfully expensive needle to justify searching a haystack." *McPeek v. Ashcroft*, 202 F.R.D. 31 (D.D.C. 2001). Just as in the paper world, the legal and other costs incurred in retrieving and producing electronic evidence must be in proportion to the size of the claim. Generally, it would be unreasonable for a producing party to search all e-mail and documents from every hard drive, server, and backup tape if the claim does not substantiate that need.

Basic consideration of whether electronic evidence is relevant to the claims and defenses in the subject litigation is also very important, as it is with all other forms of evidence. This principle was aptly demonstrated in a recent personal injury suit against the retail giant, Wal-mart. The plaintiff in this case sought discovery of Wal-mart's electronic database containing customer incident reports and employee accident review forms. The district court granted the request without limitation.

The appellate court held that the discovery order was overbroad and should have been restricted to falling-merchandise incidents with geographic and temporal limits set forth by the trial court. *Ex Parte Walmart, Inc.*, 809 So. 2d 818 (Ala. 2001). *See also Wright v. AmSouth Bancorp*, 320 F.3d 1198 (11th Cir. 2003) (denying the plaintiff's motion to compel discovery of computer disks and tapes containing "all word processing files created, modified and/or accessed" by five of the defendant's employees because the request was overly broad and unduly burdensome and made no reasonable showing of relevance). Just because evidence is electronic does not mean that parties have special access to non-relevant or privileged information. So, while litigators are frequently given access to their opponents' electronic documents in discovery, they cannot ask for the moon; e-documents are not *more* accessible to the requesting party than traditional forms of discovery.

Interestingly, one area of evolution in e-discovery that is new and different from the discoverability of paper documents is the ability of litigants to gain access to not just the business data of their opponents and witnesses, but also to personal data on home computers. In the paper world, only in the most *extraordinary* cases would a business litigant have to go to the homes of its employees in search of responsive documents. However, in the electronic world, where employees can and do conduct business at home just as easily as in the office, the exception is becoming the rule.

Arguably, the most important case on the discoverability of personal computer data is *Northwest Airlines v. Local 2000*, C.A. No. 00-08DWF/AJB (D. Minn. Feb. 2, 2000) (Order on Defendants' Motion for Protective Order and Plaintiff's Motion to Compel Discovery); *Northwest Airlines v. Local 2000*, C.A. No. 00-08DWF/AJB (D. Minn. Feb. 29, 2000) (Memorandum Opinion and Order). The case involved a labor dispute between Northwest Airlines and its flight attendant union. Specifically, a dispute arose about an alleged "sick out" organized by a group of flight attendants. In requesting access to the personal computers of the flight attendants, Northwest argued that even though the computers contained personal data, the flight attendants had used those home computers in order to organize the illegal "sick out."

In granting access to the flight attendants' home computers, the court fashioned a protocol designed to protect the personal information contained on their hard drives unless it was relevant to the case. The court ordered plaintiff's electronic evidence expert to act as a neutral third party expert on behalf of the court to accomplish this task. The expert collected and imaged the defendants' personal hard drives and provided the parties with a complete report of all data deemed "responsive."

The Northwest case is not an anomaly. In *Superior Consultant Co. v. Bailey*, the defendant was a former employee of the plaintiff's company who began working for a competitor and engaged in soliciting employees away from the plaintiff's company. Here, the court saw no difficulty in ordering the defendant to create and produce a backup file of his laptop computer, and a backup file of any personal computer hard drive to which he had access. *Superior Consultant Co. v. Bailey*, 2000 WL 1279161 (E.D. Mich. Aug. 22, 2000).

As we enter the "e-everything era," courts are grappling with these issues and more. Litigators should be prepared to understand the computer systems and technology used by both their clients and the opposing party as they argue the discoverability of this information.

2.2 Data Locations

When paper documents comprised the core of a discovery production in years past, the discovery teams focused their efforts on paper—paper in filing cabinets, paper in boxes, paper in warehouses, offshore paper, and even paper that blew off a table and slid behind a bookcase. Counsel needed intricate knowledge of all the locations where paper evidence could be stored, or in some cases, hidden. Similarly, counsel facing discovery of electronic evidence must become well versed in the many places where data resides—desktops, laptops, servers, floppy disks, CD-ROMs, DVDs and backup tapes, just to name a few. The difficulty with electronic evidence is that the storage locations are virtually endless, and with the development of new technologies, e-evidence types are changing almost daily. It goes without saying that this complexity makes finding and retrieving electronic evidence a bit more challenging.

The good news is that a lawyer does not need a technical background or an exhaustive understanding of how computers operate to effectively navigate discovery in today's electronic age. From a data collection perspective, it is easiest to concentrate on the types of media that can store e-evidence. This perspective is more straightforward (especially for non-technical individuals) than analyzing data collection from an Information Technology (I.T.) topography point of view, which focuses on the role that a computer plays in the larger network system. Consider this section a "short course" on media types and data locations.

LAPTOP AND DESKTOP HARD DRIVES

In the world of paper discovery, an individual's most recent (and perhaps most valuable) information would be the papers and files lying directly on their desk. These "active files" are usually a good indication of what an individual has been working on at that point in time. Today, an individual's desktop or laptop computer is usually the best place to begin an electronic evidence investigation when attempting to ascertain an individual's most recent pursuits. Data that can be seen and accessed upon normal booting of the computer is known as active data. The process of collecting, processing, and producing active data is known as electronic discovery. In addition to active data, a laptop or desktop hard drive can contain deleted data, slack data (i.e., fragments of data found in the unused portions of a hard drive) or data created automatically by the computer system, such as swap and temporary files. The process of recovering and analyzing this data, which is not accessible by the common user, is known as computer forensics. Often an electronic evidence production will take on both electronic discovery and computer forensic components in relation to laptop and desktop hard drives.

NETWORKS AND SERVERS

In addition to an individual's paper files, an organization will likely have a common file room where paper documents and other resources can be shared amongst all users. In the information age, this file room concept can be compared to an organization's computer network. Rarely does an individual in a corporate environment operate his or her computer in a stand-alone state. Typically, the single desktop or laptop is connected to a network server. A network allows users to share hardware, software, and files, in addition to having group scheduling and messaging capabilities.

An organization's I.T. department can arrange the network in countless ways; however, most often networks are arranged in a client-server network. In these systems, each individual's computer is a "client" of a centralized server, a large computer infrastructure with a large amount of hard disk space. In this configuration, each individual user has access to information placed on the network, but cannot access the hard drives of other individuals. Just as counsel would examine a central file room for responsive or privileged paper documents, counsel must search an organization's server hard disks when conducting electronic discovery.

BACKUP TAPES

Organizations typically back up data to magnetic tape to archive electronic information in the event of catastrophic loss for disaster recovery. In the pre-computer era, this task would be similar to making copies of important files and storing them offsite in case of a fire or flood at the organization's main center of operations.

Usually, an I.T. staff member is charged with implementing the organization's backup policy and procedures. Backup software programs are used to copy system information to magnetic tape or another removable archival device. Backups are completed according to a backup procedure or calendar. Most organizations create nightly backups, using a different tape for each night's backup which will capture only changes that occurred during that day. Often, an organization's backup policy requires these nightly backup tapes to be recycled or overwritten after one week. In addition to nightly incremental backups, organizations usually conduct full weekly or monthly backups, copying everything that exists on their systems at that time. These backups are stored, sometimes offsite, for longer periods of time, sometimes up to one year or more if the backup tape storage policy goes unchecked.

By and large, organizations are diligent in enforcing their backup polices. But those with less stringent rules or compliance can create a superfluity of potentially discoverable data and have provided great opportunity for case law development in this area. For instance, in the *Murphy Oil* case, the defendant maintained backup tapes long beyond their useful-life time frame, as determined in the defendant's document retention policy. The court stated, "Fluor's e-mail retention policy provided that backup tapes were recycled after 45 days. If Fluor had followed this policy, the e-mail issue would be moot. Fluor does not explain why, but it maintained its backup tapes for the entire fourteen month period." *Murphy Oil USA, Inc. v. Fluor Daniel, Inc.*, 2002 WL 246439 (E.D.La. Feb. 19, 2002). Because these backup tapes containing e-mail relevant to the suit were still in existence, the court carved out a detailed plan for the defendant to restore and produce information contained therein. As noted by the court, if the tapes had been destroyed pursuant to the document retention policy and prior to notice of the plaintiff's suit, this electronic information would have been nonexistent.

Both the courts and parties in litigation are coming to recognize that archival data is valuable in discovery because it provides a complete snapshot of the documents and e-mail communications at a single point in time. Backup data may be most beneficial when comparing it to active hard drive data to detect data deletion, file modifications, evidence tampering, or to reveal a string of e-mail communication that no longer exists in a user's e-mail system. Backup tapes often contain evidence that is no longer available from any other source.

Backup tapes, however, are not always a panacea for gathering electronic evidence from a single point in time. In certain circumstances, data important to a legal proceeding will be missed if backup tapes are the sole source of gathering evidence. For example, a potentially responsive e-mail that is received and deleted on the same day will not reside on the backup tape archives for either the day prior, day of, or day after the e-mail is received and deleted. A forensic investigation of the hard drive of either the sender or the recipient of that e-mail may (depending on the amount of time elapsed since its deletion) yield a copy of the e-mail.

Figure 2.1 Talking Technology: *Boning Up on Backups*

Because backup tape data can be very valuable in litigation, it is advantageous for lawyers to become well-versed in backup tape media. Listed below are some of the common backup tape types, as well as some of the common software formats used to archive data onto backup tapes.

Common Types of Backup Tapes:
- DLT—Type III, IV and V. (May also be referred to as DLT 2000, 4000, 7000, and 8000 or 15/30, 20/40, etc.)
- Super DLT
- 8mm—Including Mammoth and AIT
- 4mm DAT—DDS-1, DDS-2, DDS-3, DDS-4, and DDS-5

Common Backup Software Formats:
- NT Native Backup
- Backup Exec
- ArcServe
- Legato Networker
- Veritas Netbackup
- TAR

REMOVABLE MEDIA

In order to conduct a comprehensive search for all paper evidence, lawyers need to consider whether any documents have been physically removed from the main premises that is the subject of the search for documents. Questions are asked, such as: Did the president take files home? Do the assistants have documents saved in a location away from the main facility? In a search for electronic evidence, lawyers face a similar challenge in the form of removable media.

Today, the most common type of removable media in the 1990's, the 3.5" floppy disk, has virtually gone the way of the dinosaur due to the relatively small amount of data these disks can hold. However, the team conducting discovery might find some 3.5" disks floating around the client's offices. The more likely find is the floppy disk's descendants, the CD-ROM and DVD or their high density counterparts such as mini-disks, Jaz and Zip disks, and PCMCIA memory cards. In this area, technology is constantly pushing the envelope, developing smaller pieces of hardware that can store greater and greater amounts of data. For example, USB drives (also known as thumb-drives, pen-drives, lipstick-drives) are commonplace in many high-tech working environments. These small storage media devices can store more than a gigabyte of information and still fit inconspicuously in a user's pocket.

Because documents can grow legs and travel around via these types of removable media, counsel must pose direct questions to the client or the opposing party about evidence contained on removable media.

- Do the users in question typically store data on floppy disks, CDs, Zip disk, USB drives?
- Has any person downloaded excessively large amounts of data since commencement of the suit?
- Is there a central storage location for archived removable media?

ATYPICAL SOURCES: CELL PHONES, PDAS, BLACKBERRIES

The depth and breadth of this category of electronic evidence sources runs the gambit of technology's latest and greatest developments—personal digital assistants (PDAs) with and without e-mail capabilities, cell phones with e-mail or other computing functions, handheld computers, and electronic tablets just to name a few. The existence of these atypical electronic evidence sources should be explored in discovery and the wording of counsels' discovery requests should be expanded to include relevant evidence stored therein.

ANTIQUATED DATA LOCATIONS

Because technology changes so quickly, today's high-tech gadgets are tomorrow's relics. Yet, the data contained on these antiquated data sources might contain the smoking gun piece of evidence in litigation. As such, it is important that out-of-date media sources are not overlooked, especially if they reside in close proximity to or have some strong connection to other relevant evidence. Such antiquated data locations might include optical disks or older desktops or laptops that have been exchanged for newer models. In addition, do not neglect seemingly "broken" hard drives, computers, or media sources. Oftentimes, qualified computer forensic experts can retrieve data that is outwardly inaccessible to the average person.

THIRD PARTY SOURCES

Whether searching for paper-based evidence or electronic evidence, the last location lawyers should consider when uncovering discoverable information is third parties. In the paper world this means inves-

Figure 2.2 Media Matrix

Where Data Lives	Average Page Count (Without filtering, assumes data and email files)	Ease of Access (5 = Most Difficult)
Back-up Tape Average 40 GB	Approx 3,500,000 Pages	⚷⚷⚷⚷⚷
Hard Drive Average 15 GB	Approx 1,250,000 Pages	⚷⚷
USB Drive Average 80 GB	Approx 2,500,000 Pages	⚷
DVD 4.7 GB	Approx 411,250 Pages	⚷
CD 625 MB	Approx 55,000 Pages	⚷

© Kroll Ontrack Inc. 2004.

tigating whether any documents were mailed or distributed to people outside the company. In the electronic world, the important questions to ask only differ slightly. Were the files e-mailed to someone who might still have them saved on their computer? Did the e-mail travel through an internet service provider (ISP)? Did a third party save a copy to a disk and store it at another location? Is a third party operating a database of information that might be relevant? Oftentimes if data has been destroyed by a party pursuant to a document retention policy or even intentionally in bad faith, the data might reside somewhere in cyberspace with a third party.

Whether looking for one single e-mail or searching for every piece of relevant evidence, it is important that counsel think globally rather than restrict themselves to only the desktop of the key individuals involved. Counsel should ask broad questions that help ascertain how the targeted individuals and their companies use technology on a daily basis. Just as a good forensic scientist would not go straight for the dead body and ignore the blood spatters, fingerprints, and bullets scattered on the ground, an electronic evidence investigator cannot proceed straight for the desktop computer and ignore removable media, servers, and backup tapes. With a little "Perry Mason" creativity, a lawyer can develop a discovery strategy that encompasses the wide range of potential electronic evidence locations.

2.3 Requesting Electronic Evidence in Litigation

There is an art and a science to obtaining all critical electronic documents in litigation. Successful practice of this art involves a complicated dance, using all the traditional tools of discovery available to litigators. The steps, which will be discussed at length in this section include:

- Enforcing initial disclosure requirements;
- Participating in and gaining agreements via the Rule 16 Conference pursuant to the Federal Rules of Civil Procedure;
- Framing initial interrogatories relating to your opponents' management of e-evidence;
- Taking Rule 30(b)(6) depositions of I.T. representatives pursuant to the Federal Rules of Civil Procedure;
- Issuing requests for production and onsite inspections; and
- Enforcing compliance via motions to compel and motions for sanctions.

What follows is a practical, step-by-step guide to help litigators request and obtain the most relevant and complete e-evidence possible. These steps may be expanded upon or otherwise modified to fit one's case strategy, but they are designed to afford practitioners the best odds at obtaining critically important electronic evidence.

STEP ONE: ENFORCE COMPLIANCE WITH RULE 26 DISCLOSURE REQUIREMENTS.

Federal Rule of Civil Procedure 26(a)(1)(B) requires the disclosure of "data compilations" (e.g., electronic files, databases, e-mails) following a full investigation of the case. The subparts of Rule 26(a)(1) provide in relevant part:

> A party must, without awaiting a discovery request, provide to other parties: (B) a copy of, or a description by category and location of, all documents, data compilations, and tangible things that are in the possession, custody, or control of the party and that the disclosing party may use to support its claims or defenses, unless solely for impeachment. FRCP 26(a) (1).

This means that litigators must disclose, at a minimum, all sources and locations of electronic data. Data will commonly be located on individual desktops and laptops, network hard discs, removable media (e.g., floppy discs, tapes and CDs) and, increasingly, personal digital assistants (e.g., Palm Pilots, Blackberries). Data may also be in the possession of third parties, such as Internet service providers, and on the computer systems of other peripherally involved entities. (See Chapter 2, section 2.) Having knowledge of how much, what type and where data exists is essential to effective discussions in the Rule 26(f) and Rule 16 conferences regarding the timing, form, and limitations on discovery. Given the requisite technical expertise necessary to competently evaluate electronic data, it may be in your best interest to consult an experienced electronic discovery expert. Lastly, from an offensive position, enforcing your opposing party's Rule 26 disclosures is critical in helping you frame further document requests later on down the e-discovery road.

STEP TWO: PARTICIPATE IN AND GAIN AGREEMENTS PURSUANT TO THE RULE 16 CONFERENCE.

One of the most useful electronic discovery management tools may be the Federal Rule of Civil Procedure Rule 16 pretrial conference. The subparts of Rule 16 provide in relevant part:

Figure 2.3 Practice Points: Disclosure of E-Evidence Experts

A subtle issue within the broader topic of requesting electronic information is the question of whether a party must disclose its retained electronic evidence experts under the requirements of Rule 26. FRCP 26(a)(2) calls for the disclosure of any person who may be used at trial to present evidence under Federal Rules of Evidence 702, 703 or 705. Counsel must determine whether to disclose any retained electronic evidence experts involved in the case under this rule.

In analyzing the text of the rule and its construing case law as well as the Federal Rules of Evidence relating to experts, some guidance is found. The basic questions which one must ask are:

1) Will any testifying expert rely on computer data provided by either party, or will the expert rely on data obtained through his or her own investigations?
2) Will any testifying expert use custom, proprietary, or publicly-available software to process data, generate a report, or present to the court?
3) Does counsel anticipate requesting discovery of either the underlying data or the software used by any testifying expert?

See Kenneth J. Withers, *"Computer Based Discovery in Federal Civil Litigation"* Federal Courts Law Review, October 2000.

Computer forensic experts likely fall within the gambit of the Rules given their similarity to other types of scientific or technical expert witnesses (e.g., medical experts, engineering experts, fire experts) and therefore should be disclosed under FRCP 26(a)(2). Examples of testimony from a computer forensic expert include opinion testimony regarding the source of a particular data fragment on a hard drive, or the date an electronic file was originally created. Unlike computer forensic experts, the need to disclose e-discovery experts is not so clear. Electronic discovery experts assist with the collection, filtering, and production of electronic evidence,and may possess the kind of "scientific, technical, or other specialized knowledge" contemplated by Federal Rule of Evidence 702. However, a parallel can be drawn between such an expert and a records-custodian who simply retrieves, photocopies and certifies hard copy documents. A discovery expert used in the simple records-custodian capacity should only perform duties that fall squarely within the work product doctrine. To the extent such an expert is necessary to establish chain of custody, he or she becomes a foundational witness and need not be disclosed under Rule 26.

If a party fails to disclose an expert as required, the party could risk a finding by the court that the expert is not able to testify or provide evidence. Overall, the safer approach may be to err on the side of caution and to include such electronic discovery experts in the Rule 26(a)(2) disclosures.

In any action, the court may in its discretion direct the attorneys for the parties and any unrepresented parties to appear before it for a conference or conferences before trial for such purposes as:

(1) expediting the disposition of the action;
(2) establishing early and continuing control so that the case will not be protracted because of lack of management;
(3) discouraging wasteful pretrial activities;
(4) improving the quality of the trial through more thorough preparation; and
(5) facilitating the settlement of the case. FRCP Rule 16(a)(1).

At this conference, as with the FRCP 26(f) meeting, lawyers should be prepared to discuss some realities of their own client's electronic data, as well as take this opportunity to gain good background information about how opposing parties are storing electronic information. Further, the Rule 16 conference may, in some circumstances, afford an opportunity to gain agreement from the opposing parties about what protocols will be used for both parties to discover and produce electronic information.

Topics for discussion at the Rule 16 conference may include:

- preservation of evidence (including whether backup, archival and "deleted" files will be exchanged);
- preliminary disclosures as to the parties' computer systems (including numbers, types, and locations of computers, operating systems in use, and backup schedules);
- e-document processing, review, and production formats and protocols;
- testifying experts; and
- any anticipated evidentiary disputes (including the inadvertent waiver of privilege).

Being adequately prepared to address these topics at the Rule 16 conference will likely assist counsel in limiting the scope of discovery required from one's own client while maximizing the disclosures from opposing parties. In many situations it may be necessary to provide the court with expert testimony as to the nature, location, and volume of electronic data, as well as the time and cost involved in producing it at this time. Lawyers should consider whether a retained e-evidence expert could help them prepare for this conference, or in fact, should attend in order to provide the court and parties with further guidance as to the technical realties of locating, restoring, filtering, reviewing and producing electronic evidence.

STEP THREE: FRAME INTERROGATORIES RELATING TO E-EVIDENCE MANAGEMENT OF OPPONENTS.

Based upon the information gained through the process of the Rule 26(a) initial disclosures, or the Rule 16 conference (or any similar state court mechanisms for conferring with other parties and the court), lawyers should frame a few interrogatory questions (or written deposition questions if one is running short on allocated interrogatories). These probes should be aimed at obtaining information about how one's opponent manages their electronic evidence, in essence helping to clarify the opponent's procedures, systems, and policies. An interrogatory directed at gaining more information about the opponent's e-mail system, might look something like this:

Identify all e-mail systems in use, including but not limited to the following:

(a) *List all e-mail software and versions presently and previously used by you and the dates of use;*

(b) *Identify all hardware that has been used or is currently in use as a server for the e-mail system including its name;*

(c) *Identify the specific type of hardware that was used as terminals into the e-mail system (including home PCs, laptops, desktops, cell phones, personal digital assistants [PDAs], etc.) and its current location;*

(d) *State how many users there have been on each e-mail system (delineate between past and current users);*

(e) *State whether the e-mail is encrypted in any way and list passwords for all users;*

(f) *Identify all users known to you who have generated e-mail related to the subject matter of this litigation; and*

(g) *Identify all e-mail known to you (including creation date, recipient(s) and sender) that relate to, reference or are relevant to the subject matter of this litigation.*

For additional sample interrogatories, see Appendix C5.

A good starting place in formulating these interrogatories is a list of electronic evidence issues generated by Kenneth J. Withers of the Federal Judicial Center. This list provides an exhaustive roadmap of the types of information that might be obtained through your interrogatories. Consider:

- Number, types, and locations of computers currently in use;
- Number, types, and locations of computers no longer in use, but relevant to the facts of the case;
- Operating system and application software currently in use;
- Operating system and application software no longer in use, but relevant to the facts of the case;

- Name and version of network operating system currently in use;
- Names and versions of network operating systems no longer in use, but relevant to the facts of the case;
- File-naming and location-saving conventions;
- Disk or tape labeling conventions;
- Backup and archival disk or tape inventories or schedules;
- Most likely locations of records relevant to the subject matter of the action;
- Backup rotation schedules and archiving procedures, including any backup programs in use at any relevant time;
- Electronic records management policies and procedures;
- Corporate policies regarding employee use of company computers and data; and
- Identities of all current and former personnel who had access to network administration, backup, archiving, or other system operations during any relevant time.

See Kenneth J. Withers, *"Computer Based Discovery in Federal Civil Litigation"* Federal Courts Law Review, October 2000.

You may also desire to inquire about:

- I.T. infrastructure and systems architecture (including organizational charts or network configuration diagrams);
- Password protection and encryption policies;
- Use of data compression mechanisms;
- E-mail mailbox management, including size limitations and retention policies; and
- Litigation response policies, including any response if given notice of a duty to preserve data.

If properly phrased, an opponent's response to these interrogatories should provide direction for a follow-up Federal Rules of Civil Procedure Rule 30(b)(6) deposition and Rule 34 document requests or subpoena *duces tecum,* as discussed in the remaining steps in this section.

Conducting the appropriate inquiry into the realities of an opponent's data management and retention is absolutely critical to the ultimate success of attempts to obtain electronic evidence. In litigation—as in life—you have to walk before you can run. If counsel does not have a basic understanding early in the case of what data and information is in the possession of the opponent, it will be very difficult to adequately enforce requests for production and to ensure that all relevant information has been produced.

STEP FOUR: TAKE 30(B)(6) DEPOSITIONS OF
I.T. REPRESENTATIVES.

Following the receipt of responses to the initial interrogatories, counsel should note the Federal Rule of Civil Procedure Rule 30(b)(6) deposition relating to the opponents' computer systems and e-document management (a.k.a. the "person most knowledgeable" deposition). The subparts of Rule 30(b)(6) provide in relevant part:

> A party may in the party's notice and in a subpoena name as the deponent a public or private corporation or a partnership or association or governmental agency and describe with reasonable particularity the matters on which examination is requested. In that event, the organization so named shall designate one or more officers, directors, or managing agents, or other persons who consent to testify on its behalf, and may set forth, for each person designated, the matters on which the person will testify. A subpoena shall advise a non-party organization of its duty to make such a designation. The persons so designated shall testify as to matters known or reasonably available to the organization. This subdivision (b)(6) does not preclude taking a deposition by any other procedure authorized in these rules. FRCP 30(b)(6).

The real beauty of this type of deposition is most apparent in the e-evidence context. Rule 30(b)(6) requires the opposing party to evaluate the deposition notice and put forth the person or persons within the organization who are truly able to provide full and complete answers on the topics described in the notice. Typically, mid-level Information Technology (I.T.) managers are the most knowledgeable about where and how to find their organization's relevant data. If upon deposition the person is unable to answer key questions, counsel is able to require the opponent to produce another individual who is capable of answering the questions completely.

A distinct advantage in using this discovery mechanism is, as we have found in our experience, that internal I.T. professionals often exhibit a high degree of both knowledge and candor with respect to their employer's computer systems. For example, one of our clients experienced a situation in which she deposed the opponent's Director of I.T. following her receipt of a discovery response indicating that all relevant e-mail had been produced. In the deposition, our client inquired at length about backup tape recycling policies and the existence of archival copies of e-mail. The deponent I.T. Director indicated, quite proudly from his perspective, that his department had indeed suspended backup tape recycling practices in order to ensure that they had a complete copy of all past backups. In fact, he indicated that the company had several hundred additional backup tapes containing e-mail from the target individuals for the target time period. He further went so far as to ask counsel if she would like a copy.

Consider preparing for this type of deposition using an I.T. or e-evidence expert of your own, or actually have your e-evidence expert accompany you to the deposition as an expert resource. We propose closely evaluating each of your opponent's interrogatory responses, as discussed above. These responses will serve well as an outline for inquiry in the Rule 30(b)(6) deposition. Further, in taking the deposition, it is critical that counsel not simply cease questioning after the policies in place are revealed; instead, counsel should determine whether and to what degree the organization is complying with these policies.

Successful completion of one or more Rule 30(b)(6) depositions will be a tremendous help in guiding the future requests for production of documents and interrogatories. Equally important, information gained through these depositions will prepare counsel to formulate a plan for receiving, processing and reviewing the data that will be produced by the opponent.

STEP FIVE: ISSUE RULE 34 REQUESTS FOR PRODUCTION AND ONSITE INSPECTIONS.

Once the groundwork has been laid by completing steps one through four, counsel is ready for the meat of discovery—the Rule 34 request for production of documents and onsite inspections.

The subparts of Rule 34(a) provide in relevant part:

> Any party may serve on any other party a request (1) to produce and permit the party making the request, or someone acting on the requestor's behalf, to inspect and copy, any designated documents (including writings, drawings, graphs, charts, photographs, phonorecords, and other data compilations from which information can be obtained, translated, if necessary, by the respondent through detection devices into reasonably usable form), or to inspect and copy, test, or sample any tangible things which constitute or contain matters within the scope of Rule 26(b) and which are in the possession, custody or control of the party upon whom the request is served; or (2) to permit entry upon designated land

or other property in the possession or control of the party upon whom the request is served for the purpose of inspection and measuring, surveying, photographing, testing, or sampling the property or any designated object or operation thereon, within the scope of Rule 26(b). FRCP 34(a).

Document Requests

We suggest consideration of the following issues when framing FRCP 34(a)(1) requests for production of electronic documents:

1. *Proportionality*: Ensure that the requests are broad enough to cover the required electronic evidence but not so overly broad as to result in legitimate burden and expense objections from your opponent.
2. *Search terms and custodians*: Consider narrowing requests by providing specific keywords to be used in document searches, precise data locations or media types to be searched, key personnel to be focused on, or exact date ranges by which the search for information can be restricted.
3. *Data locations*: Consider all of the various potential locations for relevant evidence, as discussed in detail in Section 2.2 of this text.
4. *Version control*: Be sure to request prior versions and drafts of word processing documents, e-mail, and other important documents so that you can be assured that you have all the relevant information that may be contained in multiple draft documents.
5. *Unique file types*: Request specific information or native copies of files for documents that originate in electronic formats that are unique, or which contain additional valuable information that is not necessarily available on the face of the documents. This typically includes spreadsheet and database files.
6. *Production format*: Specify the format that is preferred for the production of the information. For example, request either .tiff or .pdf images, litigation support load files, native document productions, printed documents, or other formats as appropriate. See Chapter 3.2 on review and production of electronic data.
7. *Forensic analysis for deleted files*: Where appropriate, consider requesting that a complete mirror image of media be produced in order to facilitate a forensic review and analysis. Depending on

the circumstances, this type of production may require the appointment of a third party neutral expert to facilitate the implementation of a protocol for the review and production of this data in order to preserve privilege and relevance objections. See Chapter 3.1 on computer forensic analysis.

8. *Document retention policies*: Request an actual copy of adversary's electronic information retention policy and compare it to that which was learned in the Rule 30(b)(6) depositions of the I.T. staff.

It is important to note here that any Rule 34 document requests must be narrow in scope and closely defined. It is our experience from first-hand conversations with several federal court judges that courts have little difficulty telling a party seeking "all relevant electronic documents" that they need to go back to the drawing board. There is plenty of case law to support a responding party's objections in this regard as well. *See Wright v. AmSouth Bancorp*, 320 F.3d 1198 (11th Cir. 2003).

Onsite Inspections

In addition, consider requesting inspection of your opponent's physical premises and computer infrastructure through a Rule 34(a)(2) onsite inspection. *See e.g., GTFM, Inc., v. Wal-Mart Stores*, 2000 WL 1693615 (S.D.N.Y. Nov. 9, 2000); *Lawyers Title Ins. Co. v. United States Fidelity & Guar. Co.*, 122 F.R.D. 567 (N.D. Cal. 1988).

Onsite inspections will be particularly useful if, for example, the opponent has a unique and proprietary computer system so that the retrieval of the information would be particularly difficult and burdensome. Data stored in a database is often difficult to produce in discovery because of the inherent architecture of databases. Because a database is merely a grouping of data as opposed to a series of actual documents, a simple Rule 34 document request will not typically afford access to the information sought.

The optimum approach to obtaining access to database information is to inspect the database onsite with a qualified database expert who can formulate the proper queries to identify and extract the relevant data in a usable format. Typically, the court or parties will establish detailed protocols for such an inspection so that non-responsive, privileged, and proprietary information is protected.

A recent Kroll Ontrack case provides a practical example of this type of situation. In this matter, a large corporate defendant had a legacy version of a complex database which the plaintiff, a competitive corporation, believed contained relevant and discoverable information. The database was no longer in use in the defendant's business.

Plaintiff made a motion to compel discovery of the information contained in the database. In response to the motion, an electronic evidence expert retained by the defendant indicated that the data in the database was no longer accessible because it was no longer in use and no one within the defendant organization knew or had the technology to make the data available. However, Kroll Ontrack, retained by the plaintiff in this case, believed that it could gain access to the database with one of our database experts. The judge in the case ruled that the database might contain discoverable information and suggested that Kroll Ontrack immediately put its expert on the plane to the defendant's location in order to inspect the database to see what could be done. We did so and recovered discoverable information from the database.

STEP SIX: ENFORCE COMPLIANCE WITH MOTIONS TO COMPEL AND MOTIONS FOR SANCTIONS.

In analyzing your opponent's disclosures and Rule 34 productions, you might be able to determine if your opponent undertook a complete and good faith search for electronic documents. For example, in *Zubulake v. UBS Warburg*, 217 F.R.D. 309 (S.D.N.Y. 2003), it became clear to the plaintiff that the defendant had not searched for and produced all relevant electronic documents. In this case, the defendant responded to the plaintiff's electronic document request by producing approximately 350 pages of documents, including approximately 100 pages of e-mails, and claimed that its production was complete. However, the plaintiff knew there were additional responsive e-mails that the defendant had failed to produce because she herself had produced approximately 450 pages of relevant e-mail correspondence. Clearly, numerous responsive e-mails were not produced by the defendant.

If your opponent's response to your discovery request does not seem adequate, there are plenty of cases to support your motion to compel. *See Commissioner v. Ward*, 580 S.E.2d 432 (N.C. App. June 3, 2003) (Plaintiffs made several motions to compel the defendants to examine, review and copy stored documents and make a good faith search for other documents, including all electronic data on DAT tapes); *Zhou v. Pittsburgh State Univ.*, 2003 WL 1905988 (D.Kan. Feb. 5, 2003) (In an employment discrimination suit, plaintiff sought to compel defendant to produce computer generated documents instead of typewritten documents compiled by hand already produced reflecting the salaries of defendant's faculty); *Concord Boat v. Brunswick Corp.*, 1996 WL 33347247 (E.D.Ark. Dec. 23, 1996) (Plaintiffs filed motions to compel discovery of electronic information and to prevent further destruction of documents, claiming that the defendant's search for and production of relevant information was insufficient because it failed to review all computer documents and e-mail).

In some cases, you should also seek sanctions, most often in the form of lawyer's fees and costs for the opposing party's failure to produce electronic documents. *See Giardina v. Lockheed Martin Corp.*, 2003 WL 1338826 (E.D.La. Mar. 14, 2003); *Illinois Tool Works, Inc. v. Metro Mark Prod. Ltd.*, 43 F. Supp. 2d 951 (N.D. Ill. 1999).

CONCLUSION

The discovery of electronic documents does not change the manner in which discovery practices have been conducted for years. When seeking electronic documents and data compilations, do not stray from the tried and true discovery tools from the paper world. According to the Federal Judicial Center, the most frequently used discovery devices are:

- Document production: 84 percent
- Interrogatories: 81 percent
- Depositions: 67 percent
- Initial disclosures [FRCP 26(a)(1)]: 58 percent
- Expert disclosure [FRCP 26(a)(2)]: 29 percent
- Expert discovery: 20 percent

Source: Federal Judicial Center, *Discovery and Disclosure Practice, Problems and Proposals for Change: A Case-based National Survey of Counsel in Closed Federal Civil Cases.* November 1997.

These same discovery tools should be your best means for securing information in the electronic world. Following the above six steps will assist counsel in navigating the sea of electronic discovery, everything from initial disclosures, through interrogatories, depositions, document production, and onsite inspections. If counsel forgoes one step in the process, he or she might have difficulties evaluating whether the opponent has truly "produced" everything requested.

2.4 Responding to Electronic Evidence Requests in Litigation

Typically, a party issuing a discovery request will also likely need to respond to a discovery request at some point during the lawsuit; it is the proverbial goose and gander phenomenon. In other words, what is demanded of one party may well be eventually requested of the other.

Lawyers facing a discovery request should consult the provisions of Federal Rules of Civil Procedure 26(b) and its subparts. Specifically, the Rule provides that "all discovery is subject to the limitations imposed by Rule 26(b)(2)(i), (ii), and (iii)." FRCP 26(b)(1).

The subparts of Rule 26(b)(2) provide in relevant part:

> The frequency or extent of use of the discovery methods otherwise permitted under these rules and by any local rules shall be limited by the Court if it determines that: (i) the discovery is unreasonably cumulative or duplicative, or obtainable from other source that is more convenient, less burdensome, or less expensive; (ii) the party seeking discovery has had ample opportunity by discovery in the action to obtain the information sought; or (iii) the burden or expense of the proposed discovery outweighs its likely benefit, taking into account the needs of the case, the amount in controversy, the party's resources, the importance of the issues at state in the litigation, and the importance of the proposed discovery in resolving the issues. FRCP 26(b)(2).

Application of this rule to responses to request for discovery of electronic information are governed primarily by the proportionality considerations embodied in subparts (i), (ii), and (iii) of Rule 26(b)(2). The subparts of this rule and their applicability to the evidence issues will be the topic of the remainder of this section.

PROPORTIONALITY

Rule 26(b)(2)(i) provides that discovery may be limited to the extent that it is unreasonably cumulative, duplicative, or obtainable from another source. Historically, parties responding to requests for electronic documents have argued that the request for their documents in electronic form is cumulative to the request for documents in paper form. Due to the special nature of electronic documents (as described at length in other sections of this text) this argument has largely been unsuccessful, particularly in recent years.

Electronic documents contain metadata specific to their creation including information relating to who created documents, when they were created, when they were saved, when they were modified, and to whom they were sent. This and other valuable information is contained only in documents in their electronic form. Therefore, arguments that electronically created documents that have been previously produced in paper should be sufficient often fail. However, as with all discovery, if the party has already produced information in one electronic format or in the electronic format most convenient to it, it is a valid argument to assert that such information should not <u>also</u> be produced in multiple other electronic formats.

Subsection (ii) of FRCP 26(b)(2) permits the court to limit discovery where the requesting party has had the opportunity to obtain the information sought. As stated before, electronic documents are very often the best and only source of some information. The best example of this is e-mail documents. E-mail represents a uniquely accurate source of evidence and information relating to the individual's opinions, thoughts, and actions contemporaneous to the events. Electronic documents also contain a degree of candor, which is not often seen in other forms of communication. Therefore, any argument that a party has had ample opportunity to obtain information may have only marginal success if it is used to defeat the production of electronic records, unique by their very nature.

By far the most used subset of Rule 26(b) is subpart (iii). This subpart provides the meat of all objections to discovery, particularly document discovery in the electronic context. The rule provides an opportunity for advocacy on behalf of one's client and the demonstration of the specific burden or expense associated with the proposed production of electronic records. As known by any party who has engaged in substantial electronic record productions, the task can be both burdensome in time, effort, and expense. Therefore, an objection to the production of one's electronic records has the most chance of success if it is couched in a context of subpart (iii) of this rule.

However, it is of the utmost importance to note that blanket objections of burden and expense have been largely unsuccessful in thwarting the discovery of electronic records. This fact is increasingly true as courts, counsel, and highly litigated organizations become more e-discovery savvy. As players in the civil litigation industry became more educated on how exactly an e-discovery production works, courts will be less receptive to parties claiming that it is plainly too expensive and burdensome to produce the requested data. Any objection to the production of electronic records based on burden and expense must be supported by an accurate and credible demonstration of that burden or that expense.

With respect to the burden and expense of producing electronic records, counsel would be well advised to seek the assistance of an external electronic records production expert to provide an affidavit or testimony as to the extent of the burden and expense associated with a particular production. The expert retained for this purpose should be able to provide concrete specific factual data to support its assertions.

Figure 2.4 Talking Technology: *Understanding Data Accessibility*

The demonstration of burden turns on whether the electronic data is stored in an accessible or inaccessible media format. *Zubulake v. UBS Warburg*, 217 F.R.D. 309 (S.D.N.Y. 2003), identified five categories of data and listed them in what Judge Scheindlin stated as the order from most accessible to least accessible. While many experts debate the labels assigned to these categories, counsel should certainly consult an e-evidence expert with regard to determining the true accessibility of client data. The categories are:

1. <u>Active, online data</u>: Data that can be seen and accessed upon normal booting of the computer is known as active, online data. This data is generally stored on desktop, laptop, and server hard drives. Active data is accessed frequently and quickly by users.
2. <u>Near-line data</u>: Near-line data typically consists of a removable storage device that houses data. Data can be created on and read from the storage device if placed into a computer system. Today, the most common type of removable media, the 3.5" floppy disk, has virtually gone the way of the dinosaur due to the small amount of data these disks can hold. The more likely find is the floppy disk's descendants, the CD-ROM and DVD or their high density counterparts such as the Zip disk and PCMCIA memory cards. Near-line data is easily accessible if already placed in the appropriate read device.
3. <u>Offline storage/archives</u>: Offline storage media is a removable optical disk or magnetic tape, which can be labeled and stored in a shelf or rack. Offline storage of electronic records is traditionally used for making disaster copies of records. Likelihood of retrieval of offline storage is minimal and accessibility is much slower than online or near-line storage.
4. <u>Backup tapes</u>: Backup tape data is created by a device much like a tape recorder that reads data from the computer system and writes it onto a tape. As with offline storage, organizations typically back data up to tape to archive electronic information in the event of catastrophic loss or disaster recovery. Tape drives have data capacities of anywhere from a few hundred kilobytes to several gigabytes. Data contained on backup tapes is not very accessible because the lack of data organization on the tape and the special restoration software needed to restore the tape.
5. <u>Erased, fragmented, or damaged data</u>: Media storage devices may contain deleted data contained in temporary files or damaged data. This data is not accessible to the common computer user. Instead, skilled computer forensic engineers are needed recover and analyze the data in order to make it accessible.

As seen above, information deemed "accessible" is stored in a readily usable format and does not need to be restored or manipulated to be usable. "Inaccessible" data, on the other hand, is not readily usable and must be restored, recovered, or repaired to be usable. Most litigators are finding that their cases involve more than one category of media, for example, active user e-mail and documents stored on laptops and desktops, near-line data on removable media, and archived data on backup tape.

Consider a request for production of e-mail from several company executives relating to customer accidents for a two-year period in a product liability litigation. This is not an uncommon request. The expert, who provides the demonstration of burden and expense related to the production of electronic records, should at a minimum include statements in their affidavit or testimony which specifically address:

1. The type of e-mail package used by the executives or users in question and the technological tools available to access that e-mail.
2. If archival media (i.e. backup tapes) must be accessed in order to obtain e-mail for a past time period, the expert affidavit or testimony should specifically address any technological limitations in accessing data from the software and hardware platform used to create the backup tape. The expert statement should specifically state the amount of time necessary to restore each of the backup tapes as well as a mathematical calculation of the number of backup tapes that must be restored in order to gain access to the subject e-mail.
3. The expert's statement should specifically include reference to the structure of the data on any backup tapes or media regarding the time period at issue in the case. If the two-year time period in question spans several tapes, the expert's statement should calculate any additional time or effort required to restore those tapes individually, as well as any other technological hurdles in the production of the data, including whether the target individual's e-mail is maintained on separate servers and separate locations, thus necessitating additional tape restoration.
4. The expert's statement used to demonstrate the burden and expense should specifically state whether any keyword terms will be applied to the data set in order to extract information relevant to the case.

The expert report should provide an accounting for the costs of the production based on its expertise. A party can then rely on the specific statements of its retained e-evidence expert in order to make recommendations to the court and opposing parties regarding specific limitations on its duty to produce electronic records.

This premise was amply demonstrated in *Ex Parte Wal-mart, Inc.,* 809 So. 2d 818 (Ala. 2001). In this case, an individual was struck by a falling 19-inch television set in a Wal-Mart store a few days after Christmas. In his personal injury action against Wal-Mart, the plaintiff requested that Wal-Mart produce a wide variety of electronic documents maintained in its corporate database. Wal-Mart objected to the request for production on the ground that the requests were overly broad, unduly burdensome, and not relevant to the case. The plaintiff moved the trial judge to compel Wal-Mart to answer the questions and produce the documents. The trial court entered an order requiring Wal-Mart to produce all of its customer incident reports and employee accident review forms, limiting the production to stores within the state of Alabama and to a five-year period prior to the incident. Wal-Mart vigorously opposed this order including making motions at the trial court and appellate level. On appeal to the Supreme Court of Alabama, the court held that the trial judge was authorized to order discovery of all of the falling merchandise incidents within the geographical and temporal limits he imposed. In so holding, the court confirmed that within the context of the electronic document production it was appropriate to place these geographic and temporal limits.

Going beyond *Ex Parte Wal-mart, Inc.*, we propose that any objection to the production of electronic records be specific in requesting the following limitations:

1. Time;
2. Geography of incidents or locations within an organization;
3. Specific individuals and organizational elements relevant to the case;
4. Specific issues of the case, including the potential inclusion of keyword terms (inclusion of these elements in one's objection or response to discovery of electronic records will significantly advance the probability that the argument will be successful in placing limits on discovery).

Further, it is always critically important to provide specifically supported arguments with regard to the remainder of Rule 26(b)(2)(iii) dealing with matters addressing the marginal utility of a request such as the needs of the case, the amount in controversy, the parties' resources, and the importance of the issues at stake in litigation. These specific factors were again confirmed as important to the production of electronic records in the recent decision by Judge Shira Ann Scheindlin from the Southern District of New York in *Zubulake v. UBS Warburg*, 217 F.R.D. 309 (S.D.N.Y. 2003).

RELATED ISSUES

Aside from the specific proportionality limitations within the text of Rule 26(b) and its construing case law, there are other procedures and tactics that should be considered and employed in the context of responding to requests for electronic records. Discussion of these issues follows.

Consider Data Sampling.

When faced with a request for production of electronic records that seems overly broad in scope, one should consider proposing that the client first provide a sample of representative electronic data for review and evaluation. Then the court can determine whether additional data should be produced. The concept of sampling has gained particular popularity and momentum in the context of electronic discovery. One of the first cases in which the data sampling protocol was explored and used extensively was *McPeek v. Ashcroft*, 202 F.R.D. 31 (D.C. 2001). A "must read" e-evidence case, *McPeek* contains a succinct analysis of the realities of backup tape procedures within organizations and comments on the proportionality issues specific to this type of evidence. It also addresses this concept of data sampling discussed herein.

McPeek involved a suit by a Department of Justice employee who alleged discrimination while employed by the Department. In the context of his suit, the plaintiff requested e-mail and other electronic documents be produced from backup tapes of the department's e-mail system. In evaluating the request and response, the court engaged in an important discussion of the nature of backup tape data. The court stated that:

> "Using traditional search methods to locate paper records in a digital world presents unique problems. In a traditional "paper" case, the producing party searches where she thinks appropriate for the documents requested under Fed.R.Civ.P. 34. She is aided by the fact that files are traditionally organized by subject or chronology . . . , such as all the files of a particular person, independent of subject. Backup tapes are by their nature indiscriminate. They capture all information at a given time and from a given server but do not catalogue it by subject matter." *McPeek v. Ashcroft*, 202 F.R.D. 31 at 32-33.

This random nature of data storage on backup tapes creates problems unique to electronic evidence. Backup tapes from multiple locations and time periods must be restored and searched in order to obtain relevant e-mail even if it is requested for a specific person and time. In order to properly address the competing needs of the plaintiff to obtain critical evidence that may only exist in e-mail form on the backup tapes, and the needs of the department to control costs in alignment with the case issues, the *McPeek* court ordered the use of a data sampling protocol. Specifically, the *McPeek* court ordered the department to perform a backup restoration of e-mails attributable to a specific department individual during a specific time period—July 1, 1998 to July 1, 1999. The court ordered that the Department should pay for the restoration of the backup tapes necessary to retrieve information for the sample. The court stated that the Department should then search and produce the sample data for e-mails responsive to the plaintiff's request.

Importantly, the court required that the Department "carefully document the time and money spent in doing the search" and the results of the search. Upon completion of the search, the court stated that it would permit the parties an opportunity to argue why the results did or did not justify a further search for e-mail evidence.

The *McPeek* decision was followed by an additional *McPeek II* opinion in 2003, *McPeek v. Ashcroft*, 212 F.R.D. 33 (D.D.C. 2003). In this opinion, the court analyzed the arguments of both plaintiff and defendant as it related to the production of additional e-mail evidence following the evaluation of the sample. The court specifically considered the issues relevant to the case, for which contemporaneous information may have been recorded via e-mail, and the time periods for which backup tapes still existed. The court ordered the search and production of some information while denying the plaintiff's request for search and production of other information.

Other courts have expanded upon the protocols discussed in *McPeek* when determining the extent to which electronic records should be produced. Two notable cases employing the data sampling protocols are *Murphy Oil USA, Inc. v. Fluor Daniel, Inc.*, 2002 WL 246439 (E.D. La. Feb. 19, 2002) and *Zubulake v. UBS Warburg*, 217 F.R.D. 309 (S.D.N.Y. 2003). In sum, these cases indicate that data sampling represents an important mechanism at the counsel's disposal in responding to requests for electronic records. With data sampling, counsel can attempt to limit its duty to restore backup tapes. First, the issues in the case should be translated into actionable technology tasks, such as restoring backup tapes for specific time periods, individuals, and topics. The results of these sample searches should then be used to advocate on behalf of one's client concerning the scope of any additional search and production, which is warranted.

Spoliation Concerns.

For better or for worse, a common tactic used by counsel engaged in complex litigation involving electronic discovery is setting up the other party for potential sanctions relating to spoliation of evidence. This topic will be discussed in more detail in Section 2.6 of this text. At this point, it is important to note that when responding to requests, one should consider whether the requesting party has sought the particular information with the intent of establishing that the opposing party has not retained or preserved all relevant e-evidence.

It is important when responding to requests that counsel attempt to limit the discussion and production to those individuals, time periods, dates, and matters that are relevant to the case. In doing so, one can attempt to ensure that one's duty to avoid spoliation is limited to data which is truly discoverable. In reality, a surprisingly large number of cases have turned on sanctions issued for the negligent or intentional spoliation of electronic records. In some of those cases, the discovery sanctions were issued irrespective of whether the data contained on those tapes ultimately would have contained discoverable information.

Inadvertent Waiver of Privilege.

In responding to the requests for production of electronic records, counsel should consider the potential dangers associated with inadvertent production of privileged documents. Electronic records present the problem of extreme volume that was previously unseen in the paper world. Any lawyer who has engaged in large scale document review understands that the task of reviewing every single piece of paper to determine whether it contains privilege is Herculean.

Every plan for responding to electronic discovery requests must include a strategy for the potential inadvertent waiver of privileged documents. Having a plan is of particular importance when teams of temporary attorneys and paralegals are assisting in the review of tens of thousands, or even millions, of documents. With so many reviewers, there is bound to be differences in judgment as to whether a particular document is privileged or responsive. The sheer volume of documents reviewed in a certain day can allow privileged documents to slip by unnoticed into the production set. Furthermore, even when the review team has a heightened awareness of inadvertent disclosure and privilege waiver, given the ease with which electronic documents can be copied and distributed, the client can run the risk of waiving privilege. For example, in *United States v. Stewart*, 2003 WL 22384751 (S.D.N.Y. Oct. 20, 2003), the defendant, Martha Stewart, prepared an e-mail in response to her attorneys' requests for factual information in the furtherance of their legal representation and then a day later accessed the e-mail and forwarded it to her daughter. The court held that the e-mail was protected work product and that the defendant did not waive its immunity by forwarding the document to her daughter.

Depending on the jurisdiction, the attorney-client privilege or work product doctrine can be waived if a party voluntarily discloses the confidential matter to a third person, either explicitly or implicitly through actions inconsistent with the reasonable maintenance of confidentiality. This waiver may occur inadvertently through documents produced in litigation. The implications of the inadvertent waiver of privilege can be significant. For example:

1. You cannot put the toothpaste back into the tube. Even if a document is returned to a producing party, the likelihood that it has been seen by the opposing party in this context is great. You cannot erase that information from the memory or minds of counsel despite a court order to disregard the contents.
2. If a court deems that a waiver has occurred, it is possible that this confidential information or work product may be used in other contexts throughout the litigation, and in some cases even in other proceedings.
3. There is a real danger in some jurisdictions that the waiver of privilege will extend to all documents pertaining to the subject matter disclosed by the inadvertently produced document. This could have catastrophic results to one's client.
4. Counsel may be subject to litigation in a second context by one's client if it is determined that the lawyer has acted negligently in inadvertently producing privileged documents.

Depending on the jurisdiction, different rules have been applied to the topic of an inadvertent waiver. There are three main approaches. In the first approach, taken by the D.C. Circuit, nearly any disclosure of the communication or document, even inadvertent, waives the privilege. *See, e.g., In re Sealed Case*, 877 F.2d 976 (D.C. Cir. 1989). In the second approach, taken by a minority of courts, the unintentional disclosure does not waive the privilege. *See, e.g., Helman v. Murry's Steaks, Inc.*, 728 F. Supp. 1099 (D. Del. 1990). The growing trend of cases across the country, however, favors the third approach, a balancing test to determine whether waiver has occurred. Using this approach, courts consider five factors to determine whether waiver has occurred:

1. The reasonableness of precautions taken to prevent the inadvertent disclosure;
2. The time taken to rectify the error;

3. The scope of the discovery;
4. The extent of the disclosures; and
5. Overriding issues of fairness.

See, e.g., Simon Property Group L.P. v. mySimon, Inc., 194 F.R.D. 639 (S.D. Ind. 2000).

Despite the daunting task of ensuring that no privileged documents are produced to opposing counsel, there are several tactics that counsel can take to minimize the probability that inadvertent documents will be produced or to mitigate the consequences of the disclosure.

First, act proactively by gaining the advanced agreement of opposing counsel regarding any inadvertent disclosure or securing a court order. This should include an agreement that the inadvertent disclosure of a privileged document does not constitute a waiver of privilege, that the privileged document should be returned (or there will be a certification that it has been deleted), and that any notes or copies will be destroyed or deleted. Ideally, an agreement or order should be obtained prior to any production.

An illustrative example is in the Bridgestone/Firestone/Ford multi-district litigation currently pending in the Southern District of Indiana. The pertinent provision of the January 30, 2001 Case Management Order states:

> In the event that a privileged document is inadvertently produced by any party to this proceeding, the party may request that the document be returned. In the event that such a request is made, all parties to the litigation and their counsel shall promptly return all copies of the document in their possession, custody, or control to the producing party and shall not retain or make any [copies]. Such inadvertent disclosure of a privileged document shall not be deemed a waiver with respect to that document or other documents involving similar subject matter. http://www.insd.uscourts.gov/Firestone/default.htm.

Second, examine the scope of the requests and potential production to see if there are ways to limit the production either by objection or by agreement, especially in terms of electronic files. Certainly a large volume of electronic documents, such as e-mail, exists in many organizations. But, is a complete review and production necessary when weighed against the costs and burdens?

Third, ensure that your production system has the requisite checks and balances that can withstand the light of judicial scrutiny for reasonableness. Do your procedures for human review assure the necessary inspection of documents to identify and assert privilege claims? Are the review and production systems well organized? Is there a final review of the production set before shipment? You will need to work closely with your electronic discovery consultants and experts on this step, for even if you have an agreed "no waiver" provision, a court can still find that the inadvertent production of privileged documents was so inexcusable that waiver is nonetheless appropriate. *See In re Bridgestone/Firestone, Inc. Tires Prods. Liab. Litig.*, No. MDL 1373 (S.D. Ind. Oct. 10, 2001) (Entry regarding inadvertently disclosed document: "To produce the document once was inadvertence; to produce it again while at the same time vigorously asserting in court the importance of keeping it confidential, was something entirely else"; magistrate found that "failure to maintain the confidentiality of the document after the first inadvertent production was discovered was inexcusable and constituted a waiver of any privilege that may have originally attached to the document"). http://www.insd.uscourts.gov/Firestone/default.htm. *See also Murphy Oil USA v. Fluor Daniel*, No. 2:99-cv-03564 (E.D. La. Dec. 3, 2002). (The defendant waived the attorney-client privilege by voluntarily producing the contents of an e-mail, where specifically two copies of the e-mail in question existed on the defendant's backup tapes: (1) the e-mail attached to a message from the mail system administrator stating that the attached e-mail was not deliverable due to an error in the mail address and (2) a copy of the same e-mail sent to the correct e-mail address.)

Fourth, new evolutions in technology can also assist in reducing the risk of inadvertent disclosure by segregating potentially privileged data for review. For example, if a firm engages an electronic discovery expert to assist in the collection, processing and production of e-mail and other electronic evidence, that expert may be able to set aside potentially privileged documents so that a reviewer is able to be "on guard" that certain documents he or she reviews on a particular occasion may be privileged. This is accomplished through the use of key word searching through electronic documents to find words such as "privileged" or "confidential" as well as setting aside data that is created or received by, or which mentions a corporation's in-house and outside counsel by name. The overall goal of this technology is to avoid the most common type of inadvertent disclosure: that which results from fatigue or inattention to detail in a large scale document review in which reviewers spend long days looking at a myriad of documents.

Fifth, develop a plan to react in the event you determine that a privileged document has been inadvertently produced. People (and computers) make mistakes. You need to be able to assert the claim in a timely manner and effectively invoke your rights under any agreement, or if there is no such creature, take proper judicial action to obtain return of the documents. Knowing the law of your particular jurisdiction will be critical here.

Sixth, ensure that clients are aware of the risks and the decisions made in the production process so that there are "no surprises" even in the event of an inadvertent disclosure. Involve the client in each step so that the client understands the attorney-client privilege and privilege waiver issues.

2.5 Retention, Preservation, & Spoliation

The topics of preservation, spoliation, and sanctions associated with electronic evidence are of critical importance. Attorneys practicing in this area of law must be aware of the unique spoliation hazards that are particular to electronic evidence. Further, lawyers representing organizations with significant electronic records collections should keep abreast of the quickly evolving law relating to a party's duties to preserve electronic evidence and the potential sanctions for failure to properly preserve such evidence. This section will give practitioners step-by-step advice on how to manage the potential pitfalls specific to spoliation of electronic evidence.

Counsel can assist organizations in protecting themselves against a potential spoliation accusation and its consequences as discussed in the following chapter. Doing so requires striking a balance between appropriate destruction of stale documents, known as document retention, and adequate safeguarding of documents potentially significant to a pending or impending litigation, better known as document preservation. Such balance is the key to effective electronic document management and the protection of an organization's informational assets.

One need not look any further than the corporate scandals of 2002 to see what an organization should *not* do with regards to electronic document management. Throughout 2002 and well into 2003, the most prominent newspapers across America headlined stories of companies encouraging their employees to delete their files in the wake of a lawsuit or government investigation. Two e-mails more heard around the world:

- "Shut up and delete this e-mail" wrote bank staffers at JP Morgan. In 2002 several thousand e-mails were located which seemed to indicate that officials at many of America's top banks knew details of the Enron scandal. http://news.bbc.co.uk/2/hi/business/2148534.stm.

- "We strongly suggest that before you leave for the holidays, you should catch up on file cleaning." This e-mail was sent December 5, 2000 by Frank Quattrone to hundreds of workers in Credit Suisse First Boston's technology group in the wake of a pending federal investigation into how the company allocated shares of initial public stock offerings. http://www.cincypost.com/2003/05/13/quat051303.html. In late 2003, Mr. Quattrone's criminal prosecution for obstruction of justice and witness tampering went to trial. Mr. Quattrone faced 25 years in jail; however, given the jury's failure to reach a verdict, the judge declared a mistrial.

Electronic data management should not be seen as a once-a-year "spring cleaning" but rather a business initiative that is continually reviewed, updated, and audited. Because of the threat of sanction for non-compliance with retention and preservation laws, this topic should garner top-priority for corporate leadership and counsel in today's digital workplace. However, statistics reveal that electronic document retention is not garnering the attention it needs. A 2003 survey revealed that only 34 percent of U.S. companies polled have a written e-mail retention and deletion policy in place. http://www.informationweek.com/story/showArticle.jhtml;jsessionid=UJQ2IS4D5IX4KQSNDBCCKHSCJUMEYJVN?articleID=10700336. What organizations need to know about electronic document retention and preservation is not as complicated as one thinks.

RETENTION

One cannot successfully address the issue of document retention without the development and implementation of a thorough and thoughtful electronic document retention policy tailored to the organization's particular needs. This involves the systematic review, retention, and destruction of documents received or created in the course of business.

The bulk of the retention policy should include a method for determining retention periods, the retention schedule, the retention procedures, and a records custodian. However, the best place to start is to create an electronic information inventory, including records of:

- all electronic hardware and software in use throughout the company (including, cell phones, PDA's, laptops, etc.);
- all locations and storage formats of archived electronic data; and
- all methods in which data can be transferred to/from the company.

This inventory provides a "table of contents" for the document retention policy—supplying an outline of the company's electronic framework.

Next, every organization should define specific classifications of business records. Differing types of business records have different purposes and different "useful life" periods—a period of time when the record is important for business decisions. Rae N. Cogar, *Records Retention Programs*, Digital Discovery & e-Evidence, April 2002. After the document's useful life period expires, the document should be destroyed and recorded in a destroyed records log book. Setting up record classifications and the corresponding usefulness periods will streamline record-keeping decisions after the record retention policy is in place.

In determining appropriate retention periods, there are two guidelines. First, many records (such as tax documents and SEC filings) have state or federal statutory/regulatory retention requirements. These vary by jurisdiction and can differ for each company. The standard for all other records is based on reasonableness. What is reasonable is determined according to individual business practices, industry standards, and relevant statute of limitations periods. All categories of records do not have to be treated equal. Some data (such as e-mail) can be retained for relatively short time periods (i.e., 30-90 days), whereas other categories of data (such as financial records or legal documents) should be permanently preserved, depending on their contents. The majority of routine business correspondence and project files can be retained anywhere from one to five years depending on the document's useful life period as defined above (i.e., purchase orders, human resource files, vendor reports, sales reports, inventory/production schedules, etc.).

The policy should also include appointing a records custodian for each department. Similar to a company's main organizational chart, the company should set up a records management reporting structure that determines which individuals in the company are directly responsible for developing and enforcing records management policies. In addition, the organization should appoint a discovery response team to handle records management issues in the event of pending or impending litigation. Such litigation response teams should be comprised of outside counsel, corporate counsel, human resource supervisors, business line managers, and I.T. staff. This team should be officially authorized to quickly alter any document retention policy in the event of an emergency and ensure compliance with record preservation duties.

Figure 2.5 Model Corporate Records Retention Plan

The objective of this guideline is to establish a requirement for corporations and each of their subsidiaries and divisions to develop and implement an appropriate records retention program that meets the following criteria:

1. All records are retained for the period required by applicable state and federal laws and regulations.
2. Adequate records will be developed and maintained to document the company's compliance with all relevant laws and regulations.
3. All records necessary for business reasons are retained for a period of time that will reasonably assure the availability of those records when needed.
4. Vital records will be identified and appropriately safeguarded.
5. All records not necessary for legal and business reasons can be destroyed in order to reduce the high cost of storing, indexing and handling the vast amount of documents and paper which would otherwise accumulate.
6. Destruction of records shall take place only in compliance with a standard policy that has been developed for business reasons in order to avoid the inference that any document was destroyed in anticipation of a specific problem.
7. Documents that are not subject to retention may need to be retained due to otherwise unusual circumstances, such as litigation or government investigation. If for any reason it is felt that a document should be retained due to an unforeseen circumstance, the Corporate Legal Department must be consulted. When litigation or investigations occur, the Corporate Legal Department will notify the appropriate departments and direct that relevant categories of documents be labeled for retention until further notice.
8. The privacy and security of records shall be appropriately assured.
9. Records maintained on microfilm and microfiche, magnetic tape or other electronic data processing storage media are legally acceptable media for records retention and are governed by the same guidelines as other records.
10. It is imperative that the corporation knows which documents have been retained and which documents have been discarded. Therefore, extra files including correspondence, notes, memoranda, computer discs, tapes, etc. that are maintained in individual offices, at home or any other offsite location are subject to these guidelines and shall not be retained in excess of these guidelines.

Delegation
The responsibility for seeing that an appropriate records retention program is established and implemented at each of the divisions is delegated to the Division Controller.

Final Approval

Each records-retention program shall be in written form and must be approved by the Corporate Controller and General Counsel. The Corporate Records Retention Plan has already been approved by the Corporate Controller and General Counsel and if used without change, does not require further approvals. Changes must be approved by the Corporate Controller and General Counsel.

Audit

The Corporate Controller and General Counsel shall be responsible for auditing the existence and content of all written records retention programs. Each Division Controller shall be responsible for auditing the actual implementation of such programs at the various operating units.

Exceptions

Requests for exceptions from this policy should be submitted first to the Corporate Controller and General Counsel. In order to obtain an exception from this policy, there must be a program that will assure compliance with the basic objectives stated above at least as effectively as the Corporate Records Retention Plan.

Review

The Corporate Controller and General Counsel will review this policy and the Corporate Records Retention Plan annually. Suggested changes should be submitted to the Corporate Controller. Changes in the records retention plan made necessary by changes or additions to the law will be communicated directly by the Corporate Controller to each of the Division Controllers who will cause appropriate changes to be made in the records retention plans of the divisions.

Interpretation

The Corporate Controller and General Counsel will be responsible for interpreting any portions of this management guideline or the records retention plans as they may apply to specific situations.

Reprinted with the permission of the Association of Corporate Counsel (formerly known as the American Corporate Counsel Association) www.acca.com. Copyright © 2003.

Once the document retention policy is established, the company should clearly document and regularly train employees regarding how the policy impacts the day-to-day operations of their work. For example, how often are employees allowed to delete e-mail and under what circumstances should e-mail files must be retained? One must work closely with the I.T. and human resources departments to post the policy and a "frequently asked questions" brochure on the company's Intranet site.

Figure 2.6 Model Corporate Records Retention Guidelines

General correspondence and internal memoranda should normally be retained according to the following guidelines:

A. **Letters to be Destroyed Within One Year.**
   1. Routine letters and notes that require no acknowledgment or follow-up, such as notes of appreciation, congratulations, letters of transmittal and plans for meetings
   2. Form letters that require no follow-up
   3. Copies of inter-departmental or other company correspondence that have a copy retained in the originating department's file
   4. Letters of general inquiry and replies that complete a cycle of correspondence
   5. Letters or complaints requesting specific action that have no further value after changes have been made or the appropriate action has been taken, such as name or address change
   6. Other letters of inconsequential subject matter or which no further reference will be required
   7. Chronological correspondence files

B. **Letters Retained from One to Five Years.**
   The following are examples yet the specific retention periods should be defined in the appropriate functional category or department.
   1. Letters explaining but not establishing company policy
   2. Letters establishing credit
   3. Collection letters after the account is paid
   4. Quotation letters where no contract results

C. **Letters Retained for the Life of the Principal Document that It Supports or Retained Indefinitely.**
   The following are examples yet specific retention periods should be defined in the appropriate functional category or department.
   1. Letters pertaining to patents, copyrights, bills of sale, permits, etc.
   2. Letters which constitute all or a part of a contract or which are important in the clarification of certain points in a contract
   3. Letters denying liability of the company

D. **General Corporate Records.**
   The office of General Counsel shall be responsible for establishing adequate record retention programs and policies for all documents normally handled by that office. The office of General Counsel shall keep all legally required documents and documents of business significance and, in addition, shall keep or provide for the retention of such other documents as may have historical value.
   1. Records of incorporation, by-laws and amendments thereto for the corporation and subsidiaries
   2. Qualification to do business in states and related records

3. Corporate seals
4. Stock transfer and stockholder records
5. Dividend records
6. Minute books of Corporate and Subsidiary Boards (Board committees and stockholder meetings)
7. Annual reports, quarterly reports and proxy material
8. Shareholder proxies except for those related solely to the election of directors
9. Proxies for election of directors
10. Acquisition files
11. All financing documents, credit agreements, loan agreements, commitments, etc.
12. Divestiture files
13. Cancelled stock certificates

E. **Legal Files and Papers.**
1. Requests for departure from records-retention plan
2. Litigation files including correspondence, depositions, discovery, responses and pleadings:
   a. Major litigation
   b. Other litigation
3. Legal memoranda and opinions subject matter files

F. **Contracts.**
1. Contracts and related correspondence and documents—commercial
2. Contracts—government
3. Licensing and distribution agreements including production and royalty data

G. **Pension Documents and the Supporting Employee Data.**
Pension documents and supporting employee data shall be kept in such manner and for such periods that the company can establish at all times whether or not any pension is payable to any person and if so, the amount of such pension.
1. Pension plans and all amendments thereto
2. Pension plan determination letters
3. Records of employee service and eligibility for pension (including hours worked and any breaks in service)
4. Required personal information on employees and former employees. (Name, address, social security number, period of employment, pay type, either hourly or salary)
5. Records of plan administrator setting forth authority to pay
6. Records of pension paid to employees or their beneficiaries
7. Reports of pensions or pension, plans filed with the Department of Labor or the Internal Revenue Service

H. **Personnel.**
1. Original union agreements
2. Invention assignment forms

3. Records showing employee exposure to potentially hazardous substances
4. Medical histories or health data
5. Earnings records (general)
6. Employees' personnel records, including individual attendance records, application forms, performance evaluations, termination papers, exit interview records, withholding information, garnishments, test results (individual), etc.
7. Individual contracts of employment (seven after termination)
8. Commissions, bonuses, incentives, awards, etc.
9. Attendance records (general)
10. Job descriptions
11. Safety or injury frequency reports
12. Affirmative action programs
13. EEO-I and EEO-2 Employer information reports
14. Applications, resumes, results of pre-employment physicals, and related correspondence (non-hired applicants)
    a. Advertised job openings
    b. Unsolicited applications and resumes
15. Correspondence with employment agencies and advertisements for job openings
16. Wage and salary surveys
17. Census reports and headcount comparisons
18. Employee handbooks

I.   Insurance Records.
1. Policies:
   a. Workers compensation
   b. Product liability
   c. Umbrella
   d. Property
   e. Fidelity & crime
   f. General liability
   g. Other 3rd party
2. Certificates
   a. Issued on behalf of Company
   b. Issued to Company
3. Group insurance plans:
   a. Active employees
   b. Retirees
4. Audits or adjustments
5. Claims files (including correspondence, medical records, injury documentation, etc.):
   a. Workers compensation
   b. Product liability
   c. 1st party
   d. Other 3rd party

   e. Long term disability

   f. Group life

  6. Release/settlements

  7. Inspections

  8. Loss runs

  9. Annual loss summaries

  10. Journal entry support data

J. Accounting and Finance.

  1. Annual audited financial statements

  2. General ledgers

  3. General journals and other posting & control media subsidiary to the general ledgers

  4. Annual audit work-paper package

  5. Monthly financial statements

  6. Bank statements and cancelled checks

  7. Original copies of accounts payable invoices and employee expense reports: Normal trade payables

  8. Freight bills

  9. Accounts receivable invoices

  10. Accounts receivable cash receipts files

  11. Annual plans and budgets

  12. Strategic plans

  13. Census bureau and other government surveys

  14. Physical inventory records

  15. Appropriation requests

  16. The Corporate Controller will annually issue a directive outlining the specific years to be destroyed

K. Tax Records.

All corporations required to file a tax return of any kind must keep books of account or records, including inventories, as are sufficient to establish the amount of gross income, deductions, credits or other matters required to be shown in any such return. These documents and records shall be kept for as long as the contents thereof may become material in the administration of federal, state, and local income, franchise, and property tax laws. The corporation shall keep sufficient records to prove its cost basis and to compute its earnings and profits permanently.

  1. Tax returns (income, franchise, property)

  2. Tax bills, receipts and statements

  3. Tax work-paper packages originals

  4. Payroll tax records

  5. Sales and use tax records

  6. Excise tax records

  7. Represents the estimated retention period for storage planning purposes. Actual retention will be based on the specific statute of limitations governing each return and the necessity to keep documents for years which remain open pending settlement

with the taxing authorities. The Corporate Controller will annually issue a directive outlining the specific years to be destroyed.

L. **Payroll Documents.**

Payroll documents and supporting data shall be kept in such a manner that the company can prove that it has fulfilled its responsibilities under the Wage and Hour Rules of the Department of Labor, as well as the Walsh-Heasley Act. Also, payroll records must be such as to enable the company to compute the payment of any pension. (See section G above.)

1. Employee earnings record
2. Labor distribution cost records
3. Payroll registers (gross and net)
4. Unclaimed wage records
5. Employee deduction authorizations
6. Assignments, attachments and garnishments
7. Time cards and sheets

M. **Plant and Property Records.**

1. Original purchase, sale or lease agreement of plant facility
2. Correspondence, property deeds, easements, licenses, rights of way and miscellaneous documents pertaining to sold plant facilities
3. Property insurance policies
4. Fixed asset ledgers
5. Mortgages
6. Records relating to disposal of plant waste
7. Plant inspection and safety audit reports

N. **Research and Development.**

1. Original patents, trademarks and copyrights
2. Minutes of all technical meetings
3. Invention notebooks and invention records
4. Laboratory notebooks, supporting data and test data
5. Outside submissions of new product ideas
6. Quality control data
7. Production batch data
8. Pilot run data and related research
9. Inspection and test reports on new or proposed products

O. **Safety and Environmental Documents.**

The company must keep all documents in relation to employee and public health and safety for such periods as will enable it to demonstrate compliance with an applicable regulation or standard. These standards and regulations are in a state of continual expansion and change. Following is a current list of widely applicable rules:

1. Records relating to each occupational injury or illness, including the annual summary and other OSHA forms
2. Companies subject to asbestos standards:
   a. Personnel or environmental monitoring
   b. Employee medical examinations

3. Companies subject to ionized radiation standard, employee radiation exposure tests
4. Companies subject to vinyl chloride standard:
    a. Monitoring and measuring records and authorized personal rosters
    a. Medical records
    a. Monitoring and inspection reports
5. Companies subject to mechanical power press standard, records of periodic regulation inspection
6. Companies subject to industrial slings standards, inspection records and repair records
7. Companies subject to carcinogen standards:
    a. Authorized personnel rosters
    a. Medical records
    a. Monitoring or inspection reports
8. Companies subject to ground fault standards, testing records
9. Companies subject to ethylene oxide standard 29 CFR 1910.1047 Testing records
10. Environmental site files including insurance claims
11. Records relating to disposal of hazardous waste

P. Manufacturing.
1. Lab test reports
2. Product tooling, design, specifications and research data
3. Engineering change requests
4. Engineering change notices
5. Work orders
6. Bills of material
7. Safety related tests and inspection reports for existing products
8. Records showing quantities, sources, costs, shipment dates and related information for products assembled abroad with U.S. components

Q. Quality Control and Inspection.
1. Inspection and test records
2. Customer service records
3. Equipment and instrument calibration records
4. Material substitution records
5. Supplier quality data
6. Returned goods records
7. Consumer complaints
8. Summary of consumer complaints

R. Traffic and Transportation.
1. Freight bills
2. Bills of lading, waybills
3. Freight claims
4. Household moves
5. Rates and tariffs

S. Sales and Marketing.
1. Catalogs and price lists
2. Advertising copy and marketing programs
3. Copies of packaging materials and instructions
4. Customer order files
5. Customer correspondence files
6. Salesmen's reports
7. Sales department copies of invoices
8. Rebate and co-op advertising payments
9. Export certificate of origin and information necessary to prepare certificate for exports to or imports from Canada
10. Records relating to duty drawbacks on exports

T. Credit Relating to Customers.
1. Application for credit, approval forms, qualification reports
2. Collection litigation files
3. Correspondence, collection
4. Customer financial statements
5. Guarantees and subordination agreements
6. Security agreements & financing statements

U. Procurement Material Control.
1. Purchase order register
2. Vendor files (requisitions, purchase orders, quotations, correspondence)
3. Inventory control reports
4. Production schedules

V. General.
1. Books, professional periodicals, published reports, etc.
2. Charitable contribution records
3. Consultants reports
4. Departmental budgets and related work sheets
5. Major corporate and division policy and procedure manuals
6. Major speeches by corporate officers
7. Material of historic value (pictures, publications. etc)
8. Project files not otherwise classified
9. Trade association materials

As one author stated, "The existence of a document policy may under certain circumstances be deemed a mitigating factor in litigation when documents are destroyed pursuant to it, while a company's failure to have a coherent policy may be an aggravating factor." *See* Ian C. Ballon, *How Companies Can Reduce the Costs and Risks Associated with*

Electronic Discovery, 15 Computer L. 8 (1998). Courts see destruction of e-documents according to a policy or plan as permissible, while on the other hand, digital document destruction occurring haphazardly or contrary to a policy or plan is suspect. In addition to meeting legal obligations, several business and technical advantages exist for implementing and enforcing document retention policies. If stale documents are destroyed, computer storage space is conserved and system efficiency is improved, just to name a few.

Figure 2.7 Kroll Ontrack's Top Ten Tips for Effective Electronic
Data Management

Kroll Ontrack has created the following ten tips that should be considered when developing and maintaining rules for electronic record retention:

1. Make electronic data management a business initiative, supported by corporate leadership.
2. Keep records of all types of hardware/software in use and the locations of all electronic data.
3. Create a document review, retention, and destruction policy, which includes consideration of: backup and archival procedures, any online storage repositories, record custodians, and a destroyed documents "log book."
4. Create an employee technology use program, including procedures for: written communication protocols, data security, employee electronic data storage, and employee termination/transfer.
5. Clearly document all company data retention polices.
6. Document all ways in which data can be transferred to/from the company.
7. Regularly train employees on your data retention policies. Make a practice of conducting routine audits of policies and enforcing violations.
8. Implement a litigation response team, comprised of outside counsel, corporate counsel, human resources department, business line managers, and IT staff, that can quickly alter any document destruction policy.
9. Be aware of electronic "footprints"—delete does not always mean delete, and metadata is a fertile source of information and evidence.
10. Cease document destruction policies at first notice of suit or reasonable anticipation of suit.

PRESERVATION

Before the invention of the computer and other techno-gadgets, document preservation was rather straightforward. Counsel gathered the important documents contained in the client's filing cabinets and informed them not to put any documents through the paper shredder until the suit was resolved. With electronic evidence, data preservation is slightly more challenging because of the fragile nature of e-mail, electronic documents, metadata, and more. Destruction can occur by simply maintaining the status quo.

Initial Considerations

The initiation of a lawsuit or investigation against one's client should immediately trigger consideration of the client's electronic records retention policy. This is true for one important reason: unlike paper documents, which must be physically placed in a shredder or otherwise discarded in order to be destroyed, electronic records may be inadvertently destroyed by simply maintaining the status quo.

Most businesses employ a backup tape procedure in order to create a copy of all the data created by an organization and to retain it for purposes of disaster recovery. This task is often completed by the organization's I.T. department, which employs backup tape recycling protocols in order to save on the cost of the media on which the data is stored. In many cases, this backup tape recycling is an automated or automatic process, taking place at various locations on multiple servers throughout an organization. If an organization is of substantial size and complexity, the web of servers being archived and recycled can be immense.

When an investigation or litigation ensues, an organization's duty to preserve electronic evidence relevant to the case is triggered. As stated by the court in *Lewy v. Remington Arms*, 836 F.2d 1104 (1988), "A corporation cannot blindly destroy documents and expect to be shielded by a seemingly innocuous document retention policy." At this point, most organizations are unprepared and unable to quickly suspend automated document destruction, which regularly occurs due to the tape recycling procedures. The potential consequences of this automated destruction are severe. Therefore, it is very important for counsel representing organizations with electronic records collections (which is virtually every organization doing business) to advise clients to evaluate their automated tape recycling protocols. Similarly, the initiation of litigation should prompt an attorney to notify all of its opponents, potential opponents, and third parties relevant to the litigation of their preservation duty. This should occur at the earliest possible point in time.

Finally, at this early stage of litigation counsel should engage in prompt discussions with the client's I.T. manager or director as well as an external electronic discovery expert in order to formulate a plan for both preservation of all relevant electronic evidence and its probable production. Until appropriate copies or backups are created, a party under a duty to preserve should work with their I.T. team to ensure that (1) all document destruction policies are halted, including recycling of backup tapes; (2) any automated destruction protocols or system maintenance such as defragmentation are stopped; (3) new software that might overwrite relevant data is not installed; (4) virus protection software and techniques are up to date and properly working to protect from data loss; and (5) website content and links are preserved. These considerations are only a few of the items that a party and its counsel should consider when looking to preserve data commonly destroyed in the ordinary course of business. A party should investigate all systems and data storage locations on an individual basis to ensure that all appropriate steps are being taken to preserve data.

In order to avoid unintentional spoliation due to everyday computer use, a complete bit by bit copy (also known as a mirror image) of the hard drives in question should be created. However, all well-intentioned preservationists beware: failure to use computer forensic best practices when copying files that are potential targets of a suit can destroy valuable data. Most commercially available software used for these purposes only copies specific identified files or only targets the hard drive's active data. Deleted files and remnants of older files left on the computer (both of which are potentially recoverable) will not be preserved. Case law indicates that instead counsel should ensure that all data on potentially relevant hard drives is preserved by creating a complete bit by bit copy of the hard drive in question. See *Gates Rubber Co. v. Bando Chem. Ind.*, 167 F.R.D. 90 (D. Colo. 1996).

Secondary Considerations

Early in litigation, but before substantial discovery occurs, counsel should also consider other tactics for insuring that all electronic evidence relevant to litigation is properly preserved. First, a party may seek a court order for preservation of the opponent's data. In some instances, these orders may be maintained on an ex-parte basis. When requesting a preservation order for an opponent's electronic data, a practitioner should be certain to make the request with specific dates, places, individuals, and topics to prefect a reasonable request to the court. Requests that are overbroad or do not define data that can be visibly segregated by one's opponent are unlikely to be granted.

Similarly, when faced with the challenge of advising a client regarding the proper preservation of relevant electronic evidence, while at the same time ensuring that the business of the client is not unduly interrupted, practitioners should consider seeking an order from the court defining the scope of their duty to preserve electronic records. This motion to the court can include suggested date ranges, lists of individual electronic documents, custodians, and keywords to narrow the duty to preserve.

Additionally, at this stage of litigation parties may consider seeking stipulations with their opponents concerning the scope of both parties' document retention duties. Again, these stipulations can and should be specific with regard to date ranges, individuals, or organizational groups within each party engaged in the litigation. These stipulations will provide a framework for each organization to adequately preserve the electronic evidence relevant to the case while avoiding any undue business interruption, which would certainly occur if each party were required to suspend all backup tape recycling organization-wide.

Finally, the early stages of litigation provide a good opportunity for parties to consider the appointment of a third party neutral electronic evidence expert. Such an expert can help the parties define a mutual protocol for the retention, preservation, collection, processing, review, and ultimate production of electronic documents.

2.6 Sanctions for Spoliation of E-Evidence

Courts have granted very severe sanctions against parties for committing electronic document spoliation, whether intentionally or unintentionally. These spoliation sanctions include default judgments, monetary sanctions, and adverse inferences and jury instructions.

The *William T. Thompson Co.* case is an example where the most severe sanction, that of default judgment, was granted for electronic document destruction. In this case, an electronic document preservation order was issued by the court. In contravention of the order, executives within the organization directed their employees to continue with backup tape recycling procedures, indicating that this was permissible under the order. *William T. Thompson Co. v. General Nutrition Corp.*, 593 F. Supp. 1443 (C.D. Cal. 1984). The court disagreed, ordering default judgment against the party and individually sanctioning the executive issuing the memo in the amount of $450,000. This decision is of particular note for a couple reasons. First, it is not an isolated incident. There are a number of cases where default judgment was granted against a party for negligent spoliation of electronic documents. *Zubulake v. UBS Warburg*, 2003 WL 22410619 (S.D.N.Y. Oct. 22, 2003); *Computer Assocs. Int'l, Inc. v. American Fundware, Inc.*, 133 F.R.D. 166 (D. Colo. 1990); *Cabinetware, Inc. v. Sullivan*, 1991 WL 327959 (E.D. Cal. July 15, 1991). Second, the *William T. Thompson* case is of particular interest in that it is not a new case. This decision dates back to 1984, providing sanctions for electronic document destruction that actually occurred in 1979. Thus, this is not a new proposition and parties should heed the lessons learned from *Thompson* and similar cases.

Another decision of particular note can be found in *Linnen v. A.H. Robins Co.*, 1999 WL 462015 (Mass. Super. June 16, 1999). *Linnen* was one of the product liability cases involving the diet drug Phen-Fen. In this case, the plaintiff took the drug in order to lose weight in preparation for her upcoming wedding. The plaintiff died and her relatives sued the manufacturer of the diet drug. There were several interesting electronic evidence components to this case referenced elsewhere in this text. However, in the context of spoliation, this case is of particular interest. In the case, the court issued an e-document preservation order, defining the scope of the diet drug manufacturer's duty to preserve relevant e-mail. Although the party had produced a large volume of e-mail to the plaintiffs, a small subset of e-mail was destroyed in the context of backup tape recycling procedures. In the case, the court ordered that an "inexcusable conduct" instruction be given to the jury in the case. Further, the court allowed plaintiff's counsel to reference the document destruction at length in his opening statement. The opening statement was quite powerful and strongly suggested that crucial evidence was not available to be produced to the jury, specifically because of the defendant's conduct. *See* Alicia Mundy, *Dispensing with the Truth*, St. Martin's Press, Inc. (April 2001). The combination of this inexcusable conduct jury instruction and the opening statement of plaintiff's counsel resulted in a swift settlement. The matter was reportedly settled for one of the largest personal injury awards, if not the largest personal injury award, in Massachusetts' state history.

Lastly, a more recent case where the court harshly sanctioned a party for data spoliation is *Metropolitan Opera Assoc., Inc. v. Local 100*, 212 F.R.D. 178 (S.D.N.Y. 2003). In this labor dispute, the defendants failed to search for, preserve, or produce electronic documents. The court stated:

> "[C]ounsel (1) never gave adequate instructions to their clients about the clients' overall discovery obligations, what constitutes a

'document' . . . ; (2) knew the Union to have no document retention or filing systems and yet never implemented a systematic procedure for document production or for retention of documents, including electronic documents; (3) delegated document production
to a layperson who (at least until July 2001) did not even understand himself (and was not instructed by counsel) that a document
included a draft or other non-identical copy, a computer file and
an e-mail; (4) never went back to the layperson designated to assure that he had 'establish[ed] a coherent and effective system to
faithfully and effectively respond to discovery requests,'. . . and (5)
in the face of the Met's persistent questioning and showings that
the production was faulty and incomplete, ridiculed the inquiries,
failed to take any action to remedy the situation or supplement the
demonstrably false responses, failed to ask important witnesses
for documents until the night before their depositions and, instead, made repeated, baseless representations that all documents
had been produced."

The court granted severe sanctions, finding liability on the part of the
defendants and ordering the defendants to pay plaintiff's attorneys'
fees necessitated by the discovery abuse by defendants and their counsel. The court found that lesser sanctions, such as an adverse inference
or preclusion, would not be effective in this case "because it is impossible to know what the Met would have found if the Union and its
counsel had complied with their discovery obligations from the commencement of the action."

WINNING CASE STRATEGIES

All these consequences beg the question: "How can one avoid sanction
for destruction of electronic evidence?" Practitioners can avoid the se-
rious consequences of electronic document spoliation by employing a
few key case strategies. First, seek an order from the court defining the
scope of your client's duty to preserve electronic documents. Second,
confirm that you have suspended any policy that regularly destroys or
overwrites data. A simple instruction to a client's executives to suspend such policies is not sufficient. Counsel should engage with the
leadership within its client's organization to ensure that document destruction is ceased in accordance with the preservation duty. Third, review all the current case decisions and statutes on the topic of electronic document preservation, and remain up-to-date on this quickly
evolving area of law. Further, notify your client's general counsel and
other management personnel of the duties defined by the current case

law. Finally, ensure that mirror imaging technology is employed where individual hard drives may be at issue in a suit.

2.7 Cost Bearing and Shifting Rules

Depending on the circumstances of the case, the price tag connected to the electronic investigation and production can be significant. Not surprisingly, some of the most intense arguments ensue over which party should bear the costs associated with electronic discovery. As Judge Shira Ann Scheindlin in *Zubulake v. UBS Warburg*, 217 F.R.D. 309 (S.D.N.Y. 2003) noted,

> "The more information there is to discover, the more expensive it is to discover all the relevant information until, in the end, 'discovery is not just about uncovering the truth, but also about how much of the truth the parties can afford to disinter' [quoting Judge Francis in *Rowe Entertainment, Inc. v. The William Morris Agency*, 205 F.R.D. 421 (S.D.N.Y. 2002)]."

Case law has established three cost allocation protocols: the traditional rule, the cost-shifting approach, and the balancing test approach.

THE TRADITIONAL RULE

The traditional discovery rule is that each side bears its own costs. *See* Kenneth J. Withers, *Computer-Based Discovery in Federal Civil Litigation*, 2000 Fed. Cts. L. Rev. 2 (2000). This tradition is based on Federal Rule of Civil Procedure 34(a), which states that "Any party may serve on any other party a request (1) to produce . . . any tangible things which constitute or contain matters within the scope of Rule 26(b) and which are in the possession, custody or control of the party upon whom the request is served." Furthermore, FRCP 34(b) designates that "A party who produces documents for inspection shall produce them as they are kept in the usual course of business or shall organize and label them to correspond with the categories in the request." Based upon this language, courts employing the traditional cost allocation approach find that costs associated with reviewing documents for responsiveness or privilege and then organizing, printing, and shipping them for production are costs to be borne by the producing party.

These rules limit the universe of data that must be generated by the producing party to things that are in its possession, custody, or control in the ordinary course of business. Producing parties cannot be forced to bear the costs of anything outside their "possession." From this, many litigators advocate that electronic documents, files, and emails that have been deleted, archived, or are simply too burdensome to produce are not within their "possession" and should not have to be produced.

However, courts tend to be unsympathetic to such arguments. For example, in *Delozier v. First Nat'l Bank of Gatlinburg*, 109 F.R.D. 161 (E.D. Tenn. 1986), the court stated, "A court will not shift the burden of discovery onto the discovering party where the costliness of the discovery procedure involved is entirely a product of the defendant's record-keeping scheme over which the plaintiff has no control." If a party chooses to maintain records in a relatively inaccessible format, that party must bear the financial consequences of producing any potentially relevant data contained therein. Other courts have made similar determinations regarding the costs associated with electronic data productions. *See e.g., In re Brand Name Prescription Drugs Antitrust Litig.*, 1995 WL 360526 (N.D. Ill. June 15, 1995) (requiring defendant to produce its responsive, computer-stored e-mail at its own expense where the expense of retrieving electronic data was mainly due to defendant's own record-keeping scheme); *Toledo Fair Hous. Ctr. v. Nationwide Mut. Ins. Co.*, 703 N.E.2d 340 (Ohio C.P. 1996) (stating that the defendant cannot avoid discovery simply because their own record keeping scheme makes discovery burdensome), Super Film of Am., Inc. v. UCB Films, Inc., 219 F.R.D. 649 (D. Kan. 2004) (ordering plaintiff to produce e-documents within its control).

COST-SHIFTING METHOD

Courts using a cost-shifting method aim to fairly and economically allocate electronic evidence costs between the parties. Rule 26 of the Federal Rules of Civil Procedure has long provided the opportunity to shift costs to protect from "undue burden or expense." With regard to e-mail and other electronic data, a significant line of authorities exist which take the polar opposite approach to the traditional rule described above.

Courts have based electronic evidence cost-shifting rulings on several key findings. Two decades ago, in *Oppenheimer Fund, Inc. v. Sanders*, 437 U.S. 340 (1982), the Supreme Court of the United States first addressed the issue. The court wrote, "We do not think a defendant should be penalized for not maintaining his records in the form most convenient to some potential future litigants whose identity and perceived needs could not have been anticipated." The Court focused on the fact that the expense of creating computer programs that would locate the desired data was the same for both parties and ultimately ordered that the party seeking the information must bear the cost of production.

Several years later, in *Zonaras v. General Motors Corp.*, 1996 WL 1671236 (S.D. Ohio Oct. 17, 1996), the issue was addressed again. There the court held that, because admissibility of the electronic evidence in question was still undecided, the requesting party should pay half of the production costs incurred by the producing party. This represents a line of reasoning which focuses on the utility of the evidence and the effort and expense involved in obtaining it—a burden versus benefit analysis. This proportionality test provides the court with the ability to shift costs when it deems the economic burden on the producing party too great relative to the potential probative value derived from it.

Some states have taken an affirmative step in addressing the issue of cost allocation. For example, Texas Rule of Civil Procedure 196.4 provides that parties must specifically request electronic data where it is desired and must designate the form in which it is to be produced. Where the requested data is "reasonably available . . . in the ordinary course of business," the associated costs will be borne by the producing party. However, where the data can be accessed only via extraordinary efforts and the court orders production, the court must order the requesting party to pay the "reasonable expenses" incurred in the extraordinary steps that are required.

THE BALANCING TEST APPROACH

Recent decisions have set forth a more formal cost-shifting approach, a balancing test that mandates consideration of several separate factors when determining the cost allocation of electronic data. The factors that counsel need rely upon depend on two significant cases in this area, an eight-factor test set forth in the *Rowe* case and a seven-factor test modifying *Rowe* set forth in the *Zubulake* opinions. *See Rowe Entertainment, Inc. v. The William Morris Agency*, 205 F.R.D. 421 (S.D.N.Y. 2002); *Zubulake v. UBS Warburg*, 217 F.R.D. 309 (S.D.N.Y. 2003); *Zubulake v. UBS Warburg*, 216 F.R.D. 280 (S.D.N.Y. 2003). All three decisions come out of the Southern District of New York.

As stated above, the traditional rule regarding the costs of producing data in discovery is that the producing party must bear the costs. In contrast, the *Rowe* court points out that: "[E]ven if this principle is unassailable in the context of paper records, it does not translate well into the realm of electronic data. The underlying assumption is that the party retaining information does so because that information is useful to it, as demonstrated by the fact that it is willing to bear the costs of retention. That party may therefore be expected to locate specific data, whether for its own needs or in response to a discovery request. With electronic media, however, the syllogism breaks down because the costs of storage are virtually nil. Information is retained not because it is expected to be used, but because there is no compelling reason to discard it. And, even if data is retained for limited purposes, it is not necessarily amenable to discovery."

The *Rowe* court held that consideration of the following eight factors would dictate "who pays" for electronic discovery:

(1) the specificity of the discovery requests (the less specific, the more appropriate it is to shift costs);

(2) the likelihood of discovering critical information (the more likely it is that critical information will be found, the more fair it is to force a producing party to pay);

(3) the availability of such information from other sources (if equivalent information is available from another source, the requesting party should pay for the electronic production);

(4) the purposes for which the responding party maintains the requested data (if a party maintains data for use in current activities, it is fair to make them pay for its production in litigation);

(5) the relative benefit to the parties of obtaining the information (where the responding party benefits from the production, there is less rationale to shift costs);

(6) the total cost associated with production (if the total cost of the requested discovery is not substantial, there is no cause to deviate from the presumption that the responding party will bear the expense);

(7) the relative ability of each party to control costs and its incentive to do so (where the discovery process is going to be incremental, it is more efficient to place the burden on the party who will decide how expansive the discovery will be); and

(8) The resources available to each party (the ability of each party to bear the costs of discovery may be an appropriate consideration).

The court stated that each of these factors was relevant in determining whether discovery costs should be shifted to the party requesting the information.

In the year after publication, *Rowe* unquestionably became the "gold standard" for courts resolving electronic discovery cost allocation disputes. *See Murphy Oil USA, Inc. v. Fluor Daniel, Inc.*, 2002 WL 246439 (E.D. La. Feb. 19, 2002); *In re Livent, Inc. Noteholders Sec. Litig.*, 2003 WL 23254 (S.D.N.Y. Jan. 2, 2003); *Gambale v. Deutsche Bank*, 2002

WL 31655326 (S.D.N.Y. Nov. 21, 2002); *Computer Assocs. Int'l, Inc. v. Quest Software, Inc.*, 2003 WL 21277129 (N.D. Ill. June 3, 2002); *Medtronic v. Michelson*, 2003 WL 21212601 (W.D. Tenn. May 13, 2003). As such, it was not unfounded for the parties in the *Zubulake* case to agree that the eight-factor *Rowe* test should be used to determine whether cost-shifting is appropriate. Seeing an opportunity to re-dress perceptions of imbalance in the decisions that followed *Rowe*, Judge Scheindlin issued an opinion modifying the eight-factor *Rowe* test to seven factors. Judge Scheindlin stated, "Indeed, of the handful of reported opinions that apply *Rowe* or some modification thereof, all of them have ordered the cost of discovery to be shifted to the requesting party. In order to maintain the presumption that the responding party pays, the cost-shifting analysis must be neutral; close calls should be resolved in favor of the presumption." To form the new seven-factor test, Judge Scheindlin eliminated one of the *Rowe* factors, combined two *Rowe* factors, and added a new factor:

(1) the extent to which the request is specifically tailored to discover relevant information;
(2) the availability of such information from other sources;
(3) the total cost of production compared to the amount in controversy;
(4) the total cost of production compared to the resources available to each party;
(5) the relative ability of each party to control costs and its incentive to do so;
(6) the importance of the issue at stake in the litigation; and
(7) the relative benefits to the parties of obtaining the information.

Unlike *Rowe*, Judge Scheindlin opined that each of the seven factors should not be treated equally. "Whenever a court applies a multifactor test, there is a temptation to treat the factors as a check-list, resolving the issue in favor of whichever column has the most checks. But 'we do not just add up the factors' " stated Judge Scheindlin. Instead, the *Zubulake* factors are weighted in descending order of importance, with the first two factors holding the most importance.

Why has the advent of electronic evidence caused judges around the country to take a closer look at the traditional way in which discovery costs are allocated? Perhaps it is the perceived high cost of conducting electronic discovery. Perhaps it is the relative unfamiliarity most courts have with electronic evidence (or, more appropriately, counsel's failure to use industry experts to properly educate the bench as on the key technological issues involved). Perhaps, it is even the fundamentally flawed view that e-discovery is somehow a luxury that the propounding party should not enjoy without some responsibility for costs. Regardless of the reason, today's practitioner must be prepared to address the issue of cost allocation for electronic records. In fact, in some cases, collecting, sorting, and producing electronic evidence may be cheaper and easier to address than its paper counterparts. As Judge Scheindlin asserted, "Electronic evidence is frequently cheaper and easier to produce than paper evidence because it can be searched automatically, key words can be run for privilege checks, and the production can be made in electronic form obviating the need for mass photocopying." As the electronic evidence cost allocation jurisprudence continues to develop, time will dictate which viewpoint will prevail.

2.8 Trial Issues

The issues relating to the admissibility of evidence at trial are as old as the practice of law itself. Lawyers in today's digital age need to adapt their evidentiary motion practice (motions *in limine*) and trial objection handling practices to consider the changes brought by technology. This adaptation will allow the tech-savvy lawyer to presente a larger body of more convincing evidence in today's digital age.

This section will address the following issues pertaining to admissibility of electronic evidence:

- How can counsel lay foundation and properly authenticate electronic evidence? (Federal Rule of Evidence 901)
- Does the best evidence rule apply to electronic evidence? (Federal Rule of Evidence 1001–1006)
- Is electronic evidence subject to the hearsay rules? Do any exceptions apply? (Federal Rule of Evidence 801-803)

FOUNDATION AND AUTHENTICATION

All of the applicable rules of evidence that apply in the paper world apply when dealing with electronic evidence, and it is now settled law in many jurisdictions that computer produced evidence is admissible at trial. To lay a foundation for a computer-printed document, counsel must engage in the same protocols used for laying foundation of a paper document. This includes testimony about who created the document, when it was created, who received the document, where it was located, how it pertains to the relevant legal issues in the case, etc. For database documents, case law has held that the testimony of the company employee who prepared the databases was sufficient foundation for admission of the electronic records. *See People v. Markowitz*, 721 N.Y.S. 2d 758 (N.Y. Sup. Ct. 2001).

Electronic data must also be properly authenticated pursuant to Federal Rule of Evidence 901, just like other forms of evidence. This rule requires that the evidence is "sufficient to support a finding that the matter in question is what its proponent claims," or in other words, counsel must show that the document is true and accurate.

Authentication provides a particular challenge when dealing with electronic documents because they can be edited or altered easily, often without leaving a trace. Thus, the danger is that the identity of the document's originator or the contents of the original document may appear to be true and accurate, when in fact they were altered, making the document impossible to authenticate. When challenging authenticity, counsel should ask about steps taken to ensure that the e-document has not been falsified, how the contents of the e-evidence were retrieved, stored, and processed during discovery; who handled the evidence during discovery, and whether there is a chain of custody for the e-evidence.

In most cases, the authentication hurdles have not stopped courts from admitting computer-based evidence. For example, in *Perfect Ten, Inc. v. Cybernet Ventures, Inc.*, 213 F. Supp. 2d 1146 (C.D. Cal. April 22, 2002), the court found that printouts of computer-based documents were properly authenticated under Federal Rule of Evidence 901(a) where the plaintiff's CEO adequately established that the exhibits attached to his declaration were true and that correct copies of papers printed from the Internet were printed by him or under his discretion. Other cases have held that this similar logic also applies to the printing of e-mails and other computer-based documents.

CHAIN OF CUSTODY

As mentioned above, chain of custody is a crucial issue when addressing the authentication of electronic evidence. (See Chapter 3, in the Computer Forensics section for further discussion.) Litigators will want to closely guard the chain of custody of evidence they are seeking to admit while at the same time question the chain of custody of their opponent's evidence.

Because of the high susceptibility for tampering, electronic evidence must be handled in unique ways to ensure that no damage occurs. This often requires a detailed presentation to the court outlining processes used to copy and investigate the data. For example, in *State v. Cook*, 777 N.E.2d 882 (Ohio Ct. App. 2002), the defendant objected to admission of any materials connected with the mirror image of the hard drive in question on the basis that the state did not establish the reliability of the mirror image. In particular, the defendant objected to the lack of testimony regarding the computer forensic expert's qualifications and the failure to check the time on the computer when the first image was made and questioned the protective measures taken to prevent physical damage to the computer. The trial court admitted the evidence over the defendant's objections, stating that trial courts normally "have broad discretion in determining the admissibility of evidence in any particular case, so long as such discretion is exercised in line with the rules of procedure and evidence." Relying upon Ohio Rules of Evidence 901(a) and 901(b), the state counterparts to the Federal Rules of Evidence with the same number, the appellate court determined that all computer evidence was properly authenticated, and that there was no doubt that the mirror image of the computer hard drive was not an authentic copy of what was present on the defendant's computer.

The bottom line is that litigators seeking to admit electronic evidence must be concerned with the procedure and environment to which the computer evidence has been subjected. Pay particular attention to entries noting the time and individual handling of the evidence, as well as entries addressing the physical location where the evidence was stored. Physical conditions such as extreme temperatures, dust, light, water, or any other elements could cause physical media damage to the digital evidence in question. Lastly, make sure that best practice protocols were used in imaging and investigating all computer evidence.

THE BEST EVIDENCE RULE

The Best Evidence Rule, Federal Rule of Evidence 1002, bears mentioning at this point. This rule, at first glance, appears to require the production of the original computer files. Thankfully, this rule does not require counsel to bring the original custodian's computer, monitor, and other equipment into the courtroom to display the document in question. Federal Rule of Evidence 1001(3) specifically states that data stored on a computer or any similar device constitutes an original piece of evidence. Consequently, hard copy printouts of documents, e-mails and other digital data stored on computer hard drives qualify as originals under the Rules of Evidence. In addition, Federal Rule of Evidence 1006 provides that voluminous writings and recordings may be presented in a chart, summary, or calculation. This rule also helps computerized data contained in large databases overcome the limitations of the Best Evidence Rules. Not surprisingly, the Best Evidence Rule has diminished in importance today and is something upon which litigators seeking admission of computer evidence at trial need not focus.

HEARSAY

Last, a litigator seeking admission of electronic evidence at trial will likely encounter hearsay objections. Simply because the evidence is computer-based does not give it any special status when it comes to hearsay. Under Federal Rule of Evidence 801, hearsay is any out of court statement that is offered to prove the truth of the matter asserted. As with any other paper document, electronic documents are not hearsay if they are merely used to establish an operative fact or not being used to prove the truth of the matter. However, in most cases, the electronic evidence will be offered to prove the truth of the matter and will need to fall under an exception in order to be admitted.

The typical hearsay exception used for e-mail and other electronic files is the business records exception under Federal Rules of Evidence 803(6). As with its paper evidence counterparts, the record must have been made in the course of a regularly conducted business activity, by a person with knowledge of the information contained in it, at or near the time the information was obtained. Other typical exceptions to the hearsay rule used when admitting electronic evidence include: admission of party opponent (Federal Rule of Evidence 801(d)), present sense impression (Federal Rule of Evidence 803(1)), and excited utterance (Federal Rule of Evidence 803(2)).

CHAPTER ❖ 3

Technology Issues

Electronic evidence has united the legal world with the world of technology. For many practitioners, the technological aspects of electronic discovery and computer forensics bring either excitement or headache. It is our experience that lawyers can either embrace the technology issues in their cases, using technology to gain strategic advantages, or shun the high-tech details, causing further pain for both parties and the judge involved in the matter. The good news is that lawyers do not need a technical background to understand e-evidence issues.

What follows is a discussion of the technology behind computer forensics and electronic discovery. As stated before, many legal and technical professionals incorrectly use these terms interchangeably. As you will see, the technology and processes behind each differ greatly.

Perhaps the main reason computer forensics and electronic discovery are so frequently confused is because they go hand-in-hand in the legal arena. With the notion of "delete does not mean delete" becoming more mainstream, judges are more frequently ordering parties to produce recoverable deleted data in discovery. Thus, a single case or matter typically has both computer forensics and electronic discovery components.

3.1 Computer Forensics

It has been reiterated many times throughout this text that computers play a pervasive role in our modern society. As a federal district court judge wrote almost two decades ago, "From the largest corporations to the smallest families, people are using computers to cut costs, improve production, enhance communication, store countless data and improve capabilities in every aspect of human and technological development." *See Bills v. Kennecott Corp.*, 108 F.R.D. 459 (C.D. Utah 1985).

It takes little imagination for lawyers to see how computers and a plethora of other high-tech gadgets are impacting criminal and civil cases across the country. While these devices purportedly simplify our daily lives, they also make it easier to commit crimes, and in some cases, they memorialize evidence of individuals' wrong-doings. For instance, stalkers have been known to store victims' schedules on their computer or PDA calendars. Small micro-drives make it effortless for disgruntled employees to download proprietary information, conceal the drive, and walk out the front door. E-mail and instant message logs track off-the-cuff communications that would never be memorialized with a paper and pen.

All of these high-tech transactions generate millions of electronic "footprints." With each computer keystroke, individuals create trails of electronic information. Whenever data is transferred between computers, more "footprints" are created. Even deleting a file creates a "footprint" that in all likelihood is not gone for good. Because of the way most computer systems save information, when a file is deleted, it *is not actually deleted*. Instead, when a user deletes a file, the computer simply de-allocates the space occupied by the file, making it available for another file to be stored. Until additional information is saved in the precise and entire space occupied by the deleted file, it can still be recovered by skilled computer forensics experts. Furthermore, even if data is deleted and overwritten from the hard drive, this still does not mean that it is gone for good. Documents that have been copied to other media, saved in a routine system backup, or e-mailed to anyone else, have been copied over and over again creating numerous replicas of the "electronic footprints."

Computer forensic investigations provide insight into the virtual world, telling you what computer events transpired, who was involved, and when things happened. While the average non-technical person may use the terms "computer forensics" and "electronic discovery" interchangeably, these concepts differ greatly. Computer forensic protocols are investigative in nature, examining and piecing together computer-related conduct and technology use. Often, these investigations focus on a small number of hard drives or backup tapes from a single individual or a targeted group of individuals. The investigator will usually need to recover and analyze deleted information, break passwords or encryption algorithms, and capture time-critical computer events.

COMPUTER FORENSIC INVESTIGATORS

For litigators, working with a computer forensic expert is really no different than working with any other type of expert. Like arson investigators or medical experts, computer forensic investigators are another arrow in your quiver to help you hit the bulls-eye in your case. As with choosing any other expert, it is crucial that counsel scrutinizes the computer forensic expert's qualifications and experiences.

Lawyers should not be alarmed if the individual does not have a computer forensics degree from an accredited college or university. Only in the very recent past have colleges and universities started offering courses, degrees, and specializations in computer forensics-related areas. Most computer forensic investigators have learned their skills on the job as lawyers, police officers, or computer software engineers.

While an advanced degree in computer forensics is not imperative, computer forensic investigators must have advanced computer knowledge, with specialized data recovery and computer investigation analysis skills. Specifically, look for someone with formalized training, particularly in law enforcement courses offered by large departments and agencies, and certification courses offered by recognized private sector companies. Some of the common computer forensics and related certifications are described below.

- **EnCase Certified Examiner (EnCE)**—This program certifies both public and private sector professionals in the use of Guidance Software's EnCase computer forensic software. EnCE certification acknowledges that professionals have mastered computer investigation methodology as well as the use of EnCase during complex computer examinations. Recognized by both the law enforcement and corporate communities as a symbol of in-depth computer forensics knowledge, EnCE certification illustrates that an investigator is a skilled computer examiner.
- **Certified Information System Security Professional (CISSP)**— This certification reflects the qualifications of information sys-

Figure 3.1 Talking Technology: *Colleges and Universities Offering Computer Forensic Training*

Anne Arundel Community College, Arnold, MD **Cyber Crime Studies Institute**
Arapahoe Community College, Littleton, CO **Computer Crime Investigations and Forensic Examination Certficate Programs**
Blue Ridge Community College, NC **Cyber Crime Investigations**
Bridgewater State College Center for Technical Education, Bridgewater, MASS **Certified Digital Forensic Specialist Program**
British Columbia Institute of Technology **Bachelor of Technology in Forensic Investigation**
Bryant College, Smithfield, RI **Digital Forensics Program**
Butler County Community College, Butler, PA **Computer Forensics Program (AAS)**
Canadian Police College, Ottawa, Ontario **Technological Crime Learning Institute**
Canyon College, Caldwell, Idaho **Introduction to Computer Forensics (Online course); Law Enforcement: Breaking the Technological Barrier Certificate Program**
Capitol College, Laurel, MD **Master of Science in Network Security**
Champlain College, Burlington, VT **Digital Forensics Technology Program**
Cleveland State University, OH **CyberForensics Course**
Cranfield University, Wiltshire, UK **Postgraduate Diploma/Postgraduate Certificate in Forensic Computing**
Curry College, Milton, MA **Certificate in Computer Crime Investigations & Computer Forensics**
Eastern Michigan University, Ypsilanti, MI **School of Cybercrime Investigation**
Fleming College, Ontario, Canada **Computer Security and Investigations (CSI)**
George Washington University **Graduate Certificate in Computer Fraud Investigation**
Glouster County College Police Academy, Sewell, NJ **High Technology Investigations**
Hong Kong University of Science & Technology **Professional Diploma in Computer Forensics**
Iowa State University, Ames, IA **Advanced Topics on Computer Forensics and Cyberspace Camouflaging Course**
James Madison University, Harrisonburg, VA **Computer-Related Law and Computer Forensics Course**
John Jay College of Criminal Justice, The Stephen E. Smith Center for Cyber Crime, New York, NY **Certified Electronic Evidence Collection Specialist Training Course (LE Only)**
Kennesaw State University's Southeast Cybercrime Institute, Kennesaw, GA **Computer Forensics Training & Certification**
Medaille College, Buffalo, NY **CJ Concentration in Computer Crime Investigation (BS)**
North Carolina Wesleyan College, Rocky Mount, NC **Course in Computer Forensics**
Northeastern University, Boston, Mass. **Graduate Certificate in Network Security Management—System Forensics—Incident Response Handling**
Norwich University, Northfield, VT **Introduction to Computer Forensics**
Oregon State University **Computer Forensics Certificate**
Polk Community College, FL **Internet Course in Internet Investigation & Intro. to Computer Crime; Additional information about the Certificate in Computer Related Crime Investigations**

Portland State University, OR **Introduction to Computer Forensics; Malicious Code and Forensics**
Quinnipiac University, Hamden, Connecticut **Introduction to Computer Forensics**
Redlands Community College, El Reno, OK **Criminal Justice/Forensic Computer Science Emphasis**
Rochester Institute of Technology (RIT), Rochester, NY **Series of online courses in cybercrime, including Computer Forensics and Investigations**
Sandia National Laboratories, CA **College Cyber Defenders Institute (CCD)**
Southwestern Community College, NC **Cyber Crime Technology (AAS)**
Spokane Falls Community College, WA **Computer Forensics/Network Security Certificate Program**
St. Ambrose University, Davenport, IA **Minor in Computer and Network Security**
Stark State College of Technology, Canton, Ohio **Computer Network Administration and Security Technology Security & Forensics Option**
State University of New York (SUNY) Farmingdale **B.S. degree program in Security Systems; SUNY Learning Network Online (Distance) Learning—Courses in Computer Forensics (Fall 2003 Schedule)**
Tompkins Cortland Community College, Dryden, NY **Computer Forensics (AAS)**
University of California **Computer Forensics Courses/Basic and Intensive**
University of Central Florida, Orlando **Graduate Certificate Program in Computer Forensics (GCCF)**
University of New Haven, CT **Forensic Computer Investigation Program (Undergraduate & Graduate Certificates)**
University of Southern California, Center for Information Assurance Studies, Los Angeles, CA **Computer and Data Forensics Course**
University of Texas at Austin **Digital Evidence: Investigation, Computer Systems Audits & Forensics Class**
Utica College, Utica, NY **Undergraduate program in Criminal Justice-Economic Crime Investigation, and Graduate Program in Economic Crime Management**
West Virginia University, Morgantown, WV **Certificate in Computer Forensics**
Wilbur Wright College, Chicago, IL **Forensics Computer Investigation Certificate**

See The Electronic Evidence Information Center, http://www.e-evidence.info/education.html. Reprinted with Permission.

tems security practitioners. The CISSP examination consists of 250 multiple choice questions, covering topics such as Access Control Systems, Cryptography, and Security Management Practices and is administered by the International Information Systems Security Certification Consortium or (ISC) .2.

- **International Association of Computer Investigation Specialists (IACIS)**—This association offers training programs that certify only public sector (law enforcement) professionals. It is widely recognized as a good certification program in computer forensic and investigative techniques, but it is not open to the public, and therefore its methods and techniques are difficult to verify from a legal perspective.

- **National White Collar Crime Center (NWCCC or NW3C)—** This federally funded non-profit corporation offers training only to public sector (law enforcement) professionals. It does not offer certification in computer forensics but is recognized as offering good training sessions in computer forensic and investigative techniques. Its training sessions are not open to the general public, and therefore its methods, techniques, etc. are difficult to verify from a legal perspective.
- **The National Consortium for Justice Information and Statistics (SEARCH)—**This non-profit organization offers training only to public sector (law enforcement) professionals. It does not offer certification in computer forensics but is recognized as offering good training sessions in computer forensic and investigative techniques. Its training sessions are not open to the general public, and therefore its methods and techniques are difficult to verify from a legal perspective.
- **Federal Law Enforcement Training Center (FLETC)—**This is the training center for most federal agencies other than the FBI, which has its own training academy. FLETC offers a Seized Computer Evidence Recovery Specialist (SCERS) training course/certification but only to public sector (law enforcement) professionals. It is widely recognized as a good certification program in computer forensic and investigative techniques, but it is not open to the public; therefore, its methods and techniques are difficult to verify from a legal perspective.

Lastly, seek experts who have extensive computer forensic experience. When interviewing potential experts, request information on how many cases they have worked on in the past. Ask about the processes they use and the results they typically achieve. Obtain a list of the cases in which they have provided deposition testimony and a list of the cases in which they have provided courtroom testimony to gain insight into how the experts' credentials will withstand the scrutiny of expert vaire dire. In short, acquire a complete copy of the expert *curriculum vitae*, including citations for any articles they have written and a listing all memberships in computer forensic organizations such as:

- High Technology Crime Investigation Association (HTCIA)
- International Association of Computer Investigative Specialists (IACIS)
- American Society for Industrial Security (ASIS)

Most importantly, do not assume that any computer techie is a computer forensic expert. Information Technology (I.T.) staff, computer consultants, software developers, and network administrators are not computer forensic experts and should not be relied upon to issue expert opinions in court. Several cases have been won or lost because one of the lawyers in the litigation failed to hire a qualified and experienced computer forensic expert. Instead, they hired someone who seemed to know something about computers, and the individual was unable to give solid opinions about the who, what, when, where, and why of certain computer activity when deposed or placed on the stand.

DEFINING COMPUTER FORENSIC TERMINOLOGY

Many industry specific terms are used within computer forensic science. Understanding the technology lingo is half the battle in demystifying computer forensics.

- Metadata—Metadata is best described as data about data—the who, what, where, why and how about a file. Most software programs and operating systems store metadata, such as the last modified dates, creation dates, last access dates, size, etc., for each file. However, each program or system stores different metadata fields differently.
- Active Data—This term describes the data that is accessible to a typical user from a hard drive, backup tape, or other like media. This is the data that was accessible to the particular user working with the computer, as distinguished from unallocated recovered (deleted), and "slack" data.
- Unallocated Space—Areas of the hard drive to which data has never been written.
- Recovered (Deleted) Data—This term refers to files and directories that were recovered after being deleted from the active data. As stated above, when a file is deleted, it is merely marked as available for overwriting. If new data has not overwritten the area occupied by the previously deleted data, the deleted data can be recovered by computer forensic investigators. Due to the way computers store data, some of the files may be recovered completely and are easily identifiable, while some may just be fragments of the original data.
- Slack Data—When saving a file to a drive, the computer assigns it to a sector where the file will be stored, even if the file is not

Figure 3.2 Sample Metadata

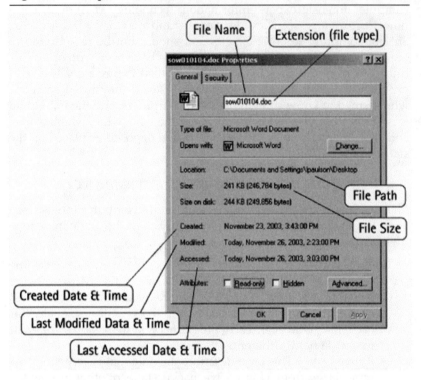

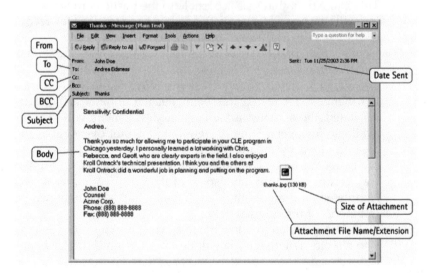

Figure 3.3 Delete Does Not Mean Delete

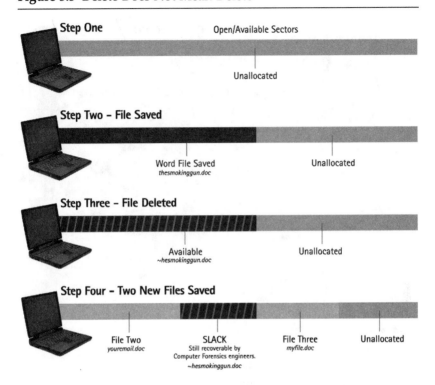

big enough to fill up the entire sector. Slack space is the space between the end of the file and the end of the sector. Sometimes,
when a file is marked as available for deletion and a new file is
overwritten to that sector, that new file does not overwrite the
entire file. Thus, bits and pieces of the old file reside in the slack
space in the sector or sectors. Computer forensic engineers
search this space for remnant data when conducting computer
forensic investigations. *Note: This is a simplified definition of slack
data. There are additional concepts like "RAM slack" that will not be
explored here.*

Consulting

The most effective place to begin a computer forensic investigation is
to work with the computer forensic expert in creating a strategy for
collecting, analyzing and processing the data. The strategy should include analysis of where the critical information might reside, as well as

Figure 3.4 The Computer Forensics Process

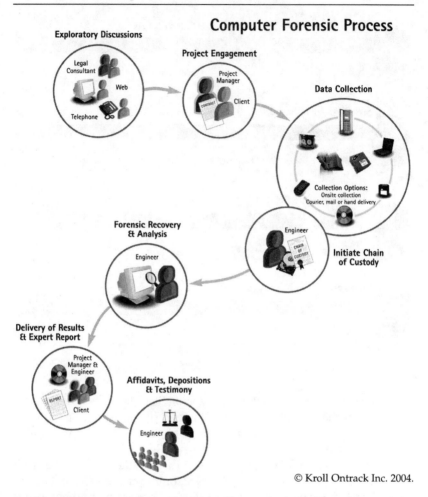

© Kroll Ontrack Inc. 2004.

the identification of protocols that will ensure the admissibility of the data into evidence in a court of law should it become necessary.

Counsel should convey to the computer forensic expert information about the case and the desired outcomes of the investigation. Best practices dictate that the investigator identify where key evidence is likely to be located and then piece together user and system information in order to obtain a comprehensive and thorough account of the technological landscape. Understanding where data resides, what conduct is at issue, and what output is sought should occur before any digital data is ever examined.

Data Preservation and Collection

Electronic evidence, like other types of evidence, is fragile. Entering data, loading software, performing routine system maintenance or simply booting a computer can destroy certain files or metadata that is stored on the hard drive. Just as a medical examiner takes extreme caution to ensure that the body, blood evidence, fingerprints, and hair follicles are preserved in a murder case, computer forensic examiners must take extreme caution to ensure that data is not damaged, computer viruses are not introduced, and a proper chain of custody is maintained. Failure to adhere to strict industry standards regarding data collection may not only result in the loss of critical data, but may also impinge upon the reliability of any data that is recovered, potentially rendering it inadmissible in a court of law.

Once the location of the relevant data is identified, it must be retrieved. Computer forensic experts can retrieve data from virtually any storage device or computer operating systems, including many antiquated systems. Counsel should not assume that simply because the computer, disk drive or other storage media is old or damaged that the data is therefore inaccessible.

Figure 3.5 Talking Technology: *Standards for Handling Digital Evidence*

At the International Hi-Tech Crime and Forensics Conference in October 1999, the International Principles for Computer Evidence were promulgated by the International Organization on Computer Evidence (IOCE). They are as follows:

- Upon seizing digital evidence, actions taken should not change that evidence.
- When it is necessary for a person to access original digital evidence, that person must be forensically competent.
- All activity relating to the seizure, access, storage, or transfer of digital evidence must be fully documented, preserved, and available for review.
- An individual is responsible for all actions taken with respect to digital evidence while the digital evidence is in their possession.
- Any agency that is responsible for seizing, accessing, storing, or transferring digital evidence is responsible for compliance with these principles.

Implementation of these requirements requires that a computer forensic expert have in place best practices polices and procedures for preserving the evidence in its custody. See FBI Laboratories publication Forensic Science Communications, Vol. 2 No. 2, April 2000.

Also, maintaining data integrity at this stage is crucial. Counsel should be certain that the computer forensics expert maintains a complete chain of custody for all data that is collected. This means adhering to the following chain of custody procedures:

1. Uniquely identify each item of property to be placed under chain-of-custody control. This means that the investigator should be able to examine the item and be able to tell that it is the same one described on the chain of custody form. Some items will have a manufacturer's name, model number, and serial number, but others (such as tapes or removable media) may have no intrinsic unique identifier.
2. Document who the media was received from or who authorized its removal, the location where the media was received, and the date and time at which the investigator took control of the media. If an item is received by mail or other courier service, document this transaction as well.
3. Keep a continuous record of custody of the item, from the time the item is acquired, until it is transferred out of the investigator's control.

Performing analysis work on original media is undesirable and can be a grave mistake in the electronic evidence industry given the spoliation concerns addressed above. Instead, best practices provide for the making of an "image" whenever possible so that the forensic examiner can work on an exact duplicate of the media rather than the original. Most often two copies of the original media are made. A copy of the media is made for archival purposes and a copy of the copy is made for the investigator to use in his or her recovery and analysis. This imaging process utilizes proprietary or commercial imaging software to provide an exact duplication or "image" of the data contained on the media. The "image" is a perfect bit by bit copy of the drive, including all of the unused and partially overwritten spaces—the nooks and crannies where important evidence may reside.

The imaging process is non-destructive to the data and does not require the operating system to be turned on, ensuring that the system is not altered in any way during the imaging process, thus preserving its evidentiary value. It is not commonly understood that the mere act of booting a computer may damage critical evidence and may change metadata. Also, booting the system may overwrite the startup data on the hard drive that would have remained more accessible if the boot did not occur.

Figure 3.6 Data Collection

There are several methods for gathering the target data, depending on the specifics of the situation. This section applies to both computer forensics and electronic discovery.

Onsite Data Collection—For large organizations with multiple office locations, many targeted custodians, complex cases, or simply as a precautionary measure, consider bringing an electronic evidence expert onsite to collect the data. The individual collecting the data should be specially trained to understand various topologies of Information Technology systems to ensure that the data gathering process is efficient and conforms to forensic standards. When data is collected onsite, the expert uses hard drive cloning technology that transfers the target data to a portable device. The target computer is not booted, thus preserving valuable metadata, but instead power is provided to the drive to copy the data. Oftentimes, data collection can be completed during non-business hours so that business operations are affected only for a limited time (if affected at all) or so that the target of an investigation is not even aware that anything has occurred.

Do-It-Yourself Data Collection—Many software products exist on the market, allowing the client to collect the data on their own. While these software products make data collection relatively straightforward, untrained individuals should not attempt to perform this work. The risks associated with damaging or deleting data are high if proper data collection procedures are not followed. Above all, the individual gathering the data should under no circumstances boot the computer and copy the subject data. As discussed in this chapter, this may change valuable metadata associated with the files and may overwrite otherwise recoverable, previously deleted data.

Mail or Courier—If the computer or media is not needed on a day-to-day basis, the client can mail or courier the media to the electronic evidence expert's laboratory. It is important to reiterate that files, slack space and metadata are at risk to be modified or lost through continued use of the computer or media.

Forensic Recovery & Analysis

The computer forensic recovery and analysis begins once the data collection phase is complete. In the data recovery phase, computer forensic investigators attempt to recover active data as well as physically or logically damaged data that may be crucial to the case. Some of the most common reasons that data becomes inaccessible include: hardware or system malfunction, human error or destruction, software corruption or program malfunction, computer viruses, and natural disasters. If required, a handful of computer forensic experts have access to special "clean room" facilities where engineers can disassemble a drive to diagnose and remediate problems prior to beginning the computer forensic investigation. A clean room is an environment where precision parts can be assembled without contaminating sensitive components such as the physical magnetic surface of the media (i.e., hard drive platters). Clean rooms have a rating system indicating the number of contaminating particles per square inch. For example, a class100 clean room environment contains fewer than 100 particles of contaminants per square inch. A clean room environment should be used to minimize the risk of further damaging a hard drive when it becomes necessary to open it to repair or replace damaged internal components. Examples of this include damage to internal circuits, a damaged motor or bearings, platters that are out of alignment, fire and/or water damage. In computer forensics investigations, a clean room must be used, for example, if circuit boards or cable connectors have been damaged or destroyed or if pieces of the drive need to be replaced to make it readable again.

Data recovery is not necessary in every computer forensic matter. If the device has not suffered any physical or logical damage, the first step in the computer forensic investigation is to examine the image of the media. This commonly includes:

- *Accessing active data files.* Active files are data files readily available to the user upon accessing the media.
- *Accessing and recovering e-mail data.* E-mail is often a primary piece of the project and requires separate handling and processing.
- *Recovering deleted data files.* Deleted files are files and directories that were recovered after being deleted from the active data. Some files are recovered completely and are easily identifiable, while in other instances, only fragments of files (i.e., slack and unallocated data) may be recoverable. Factors influencing the recovery of deleted files include: how the files were deleted, the amount of time passage and computer usage since deletion, the use of file deletion/destruction programs, etc.
- *Accessing password protected and encrypted files.* Most computer forensic engineers should be able to scan data to determine if any security features have been placed on the data. They then attempt to "break" password protection or encryption to access the contents of the file. This can be done by using propriety technology tools which "work" on breaking the passwords or en-

cryption for a specified period of time or by human intervention using passwords discovered in other portions of a data set. For example, if software is run on number of files on a hard drive, it is common to discover a pattern of password use. Those passwords can then be used to look at data files in another location, or on other media utilized by the same person. In password and encryption breaking scenarios, this issue is more often *not* whether the encryption can be broken, but how much time is reasonable to spend in the attempt.

Beyond retrieving files, computer forensic investigators often can determine whether computer evidence was tampered with, altered, damaged or removed. They examine hidden information associated with recovered files (including deleted data or data from unused storage areas on the media) and provide a historical ledger of the content contained in the files. In essence, they reveal evidence of the conduct of those who had access to the drive. Computer forensic engineering analysis may include:

- Recreating a specific chain of events or user activity, including Internet activity and e-mail communication;
- Searching for key words and key dates;
- Searching for copies of previous document drafts;
- Searching for privileged information;
- Authenticating data files and the date and time stamps of those files;
- Comparing and contrasting computer codes to determine whether a particular program is original or copied from a similar program; and
- Advising on what evidence is likely to be found on the computer media and identifying the most effective methods to search for relevant data.

The amount of information that is recoverable through the computer forensic recovery and analysis processes varies on a case-by-case basis; however, the possible results are endless.

Expert Testimony and Reporting

Once the data analysis is complete, computer forensic engineers can help support the lawyer and client's court case by customizing reports about the data collected and produced, providing data for affidavits or other pleadings, and giving expert testimony and Rule 26 expert reports.

DATA DESTRUCTION

Some of the most common questions litigators ask electronic evidence experts are "How much data is recoverable if my client redeployed the computer and the new user has been overwriting data that is relevant to our investigation?" "How much data is recoverable if my client reformatted, defragmented, or wiped the hard drive?" "How much data is recoverable if the hard drive was damaged due to fire, water, or other physical damage?"

Figure 3.7 Talking Technology: *Destroying Computer Evidence*

The common ways that computer data is permanently destroyed include:

- **Overwriting**—Overwriting old data with new data during everyday computer use or using overwriting software to write a pattern to every addressable location of a hard drive, essentially returning the drive to a factory (blank) condition.
- **Physical Destruction**—Shredding the hard drive platters by manually breaking them into several small pieces or utilizing a drive shredder.
- **Heat**—Exposing the media to extreme heat, usually in excess of 300 degrees Fahrenheit.
- **Magnetic Destruction**—Using a degaussing device with a magnetic field strong enough to disrupt the magnetic orientation of the data on the platters.

Destroying Data By Overwriting

Every time a computer is used, the user inevitably overwrites something. Thus, when a computer is redeployed, the new user may unintentionally overwrite the old user's previously deleted data through continued use of the computer. In a simplistic view, every computer storage device contains files (used space) and free space (unused space). Each time the computer is used, it may modify the metadata of the files in the used space and may overwrite previously deleted data that exists in the unused space.

- Modification of metadata of existing files. As the operating system starts up, it accesses several files during the boot process and may modify temporary cache files (e.g., Windows swap files) that may contain clues to the computer's past environment. Also, if any files are "touched" by the user, the file's "last accessed date" may change.
- Modification of free space. When the computer needs to create new files or grow existing files, it requests a new block of space

(a "sector" or "cluster") from the free space pool. Different computer systems manage free space reuse in different ways. Some may contain intelligence to use the "least recently used" free space block when requesting new blocks. In this manner, the oldest free space block will be used first and only when all free space blocks have been used at least once, will it begin to reuse (overwrite) old free space blocks. Other operating systems may respond to free space requests by writing data to the closest available free space block in an attempt to optimize the data writing process. Regardless of the operating system, there is a risk of overwriting free space. The more the computer is in use or the less free space there is available on the drive, the probability of overwriting old (free space) data increases.

Standard computer maintenance and routine computer use overwrite data, often without the knowledge of the user. But there are also instances where users employ formatting, defragmenting, wiping and other techniques to intentionally destroy all traces of electronic evidence.

Formatting
Formatting a drive is a quick and easy housekeeping task that eliminates the document indexes and file/folder pointers on a computer hard drive. Many I.T. departments format a user's hard drive to give the computer a fresh start when it is deployed to a new user. In most cases, the formatting does not actually get rid of the pre-existing data on the hard drive. The contents of the documents, files, and folders still physically exist on the drive and are fully recoverable by computer forensic experts using best practice industry standards. If a drive looks blank or the operating system looks empty upon booting, the files and folders may still be present on the drive. Shut off the computer immediately and consult a computer forensics expert to inquire whether data may be recoverable based on what has been done to it.

Defragmentation
Defragmentation can be compared to a reorganization of the computer's filing cabinet. To make the computer run more efficiently, all of the files are condensed to the smallest space possible, reorganized, and placed at the front of the drive. This is another I.T. tool to keep the computer functioning at peak performance. Defragmenting a computer will not harm the active data (the data that a user can access on their own from the desktop) but may render normally recoverable deleted data (the data that only a forensic investigator can recover) vir-

tually unrecoverable. This depends on the size of the drive, amount of data, and order of operations. Sometimes, defragmentation can even create additional copies of computer evidence on the hard drive. A complete computer forensic investigation will help identify what is recoverable after defragmentation.

Wiping

Wiping utilities are frequently used by I.T. staff when a computer is going to be redeployed within the company (for example after an employee leaves the company) or sold or donated outside of the company. In addition, it is our experience that individuals attempting to destroy bad acts committed on the computer will purchase and run wiping utilities. When a drive or portion of a drive is wiped, a software program is used to overwrite data with a specific or randomly generated pattern of data. If run properly, a wiping utility will make the data unrecoverable by commercial computer forensic experts. (The government does purport to have some tools to drill deeper into a hard drive that has been wiped, but these processes are time-consuming, extremely expensive, and highly confidential.) Depending on the software utility that was run, computer forensic experts might be able to tell the date, time, and specific program used to conduct the wiping.

A Northern District of Illinois case directly on point is *Kucala Enters., Ltd. v. Auto Wax Co.*, 2003 WL 21230605 (N.D.Ill. May 27, 2003). In this patent suit, the district court ordered the inspection of the plaintiff's computer. The defendant hired a computer forensic investigator to create a forensic image of the computer hard drive and analyze the results. The computer forensic expert was able to identify that the night before the computer image was created, a wiping utility called "Evidence Eliminator" was used to delete and overwrite over 12,000 files. The expert further determined that 3,000 additional files had been deleted and overwritten three days earlier. Even though there was no clear indication that relevant evidence was among the destroyed files, the court described the plaintiff's actions as "egregious conduct" and emphasized the plaintiff's apparent intent to destroy evidence that it had a duty to maintain. The magistrate judge recommended to the district court that the plaintiff's case be dismissed with prejudice and that the plaintiff be ordered to pay the defendant's lawyer fees and costs incurred in defending the motion.

Other less sophisticated ways to intentionally destroy computer data include saving "garbage files" to the hard drive in attempts to fill the entire hard drive space thus removing all traces of data on the drive. A specific example of this tactic occurred in *Minnesota Mining & Mfg. v. Pribyl*, 259 F.3d 587 (7th Cir. 2001). In this case, the plaintiff brought suit against three former employees for misappropriation of trade secrets. The appellate court affirmed the trial court's negative inference instruction to the jury where the one defendant committed spoliation of evidence by downloading six gigabytes of music files onto his laptop. This act, which occurred the night before the defendant was to turn over his computer pursuant to the discovery request, destroyed numerous files sought by the plaintiff. The lesson learned from this decision is that spoliation can be found not only when a party has deleted data but also when they have simply downloaded data in what is typically thought to be the open space of a computer hard drive.

Destroying Data by Physical Damage or Heat Exposure

Some individuals will try to cause physical damage to the media or set the media on fire in attempt to destroy the data contained therein; for example, slamming a drive (sometimes still in the PC or laptop) onto a concrete floor, setting the drive on fire, submerging it in water (or other liquids), or even shooting a hole through it. In one case, a perpetrator squirted charcoal lighter fluid into the cooling slots of a PC case and then ignited the fumes. They fried the majority of the PC, but computer forensic experts were still able to recover data from the hard drive for analysis. These attempts are typically unsuccessful because computer data is not easily destroyed in this manner. Only if the media is exposed to heat at least 300 degrees Fahrenheit or is shred into many pieces is the data gone for good.

Destroying Data By Magnetization

Another common way to destroy computer data is by magnetization. Using a degaussing device with a magnetic field strong enough to disrupt the magnetic orientation of the data on the platters will permanently destroy computer evidence. Holding a strong magnet up to a hard drive, however, will not erase any data. Hard disk assemblies are designed to shield the drive from disruptive magnetic fields during the normal course of a hard drive's life. It takes a very powerful commercial grade magnetic field to penetrate the hard drive enclosure to actually impact the platters inside. Some people may be successful in destroying computer evidence by opening the drive and placing a strong magnet next to the exposed platters.

Conclusion

Lawyers and judges are quickly realizing the importance of understanding how computer data is stored and destroyed. In many cases,

Figure 3.8 In the News: *Destroying Computer Evidence*

Overwriting, physical destruction, heat, or magnetizing computer media are not the only ways to permanently destroy computer evidence. This story from the *New York Times*, reveals the lengths some people will take to obliterate all record of computer activity. What these individuals might have forgotten is that even if the computer is gone, there might be a record of the fraud contained on network shared drives or company backup tapes. . .

Rite Aid Ex-Lawyer Said to Toss Evidence
By THE ASSOCIATED PRESS
October 2, 2003

http://www.nytimes.com/2003/10/02/business/02RITE.html?dlbk

HARRISBURG, Pa., Oct. 1 (AP)—A former chief counsel of the Rite Aid Corporation told a colleague that a computer used to create backdated letters that inflated benefits for some executives was dumped in the ocean, according to testimony Wednesday.

Timothy J. Noonan, former chief operating officer, testified that the former chief counsel, Franklin C. Brown, made the claim in March 2001 after Mr. Noonan began cooperating in an inquiry that led to conspiracy and fraud charges against Mr. Brown.

Mr. Noonan testified that Mr. Brown reassured him that investigators could not examine the computer of a secretary who reportedly helped the former chief executive, Martin L. Grass, create false documents leading to millions in benefits.

"He said they'll never get her computer now, it's in the Atlantic," Mr. Noonan said that Mr. Brown told him. Mr. Noonan allowed the F.B.I. to record the conversation, but noise rendered it unintelligible so he described it for the jury.

Mr. Brown is accused of conspiring to inflate income falsely at Rite Aid in the 1990s, then misleading investigators. He also faces charges of obstruction of justice, witness tampering and lying to authorities.

---

even if data is rendered unrecoverable, a computer forensic expert often can provide counsel with significant details about how and when the data was destroyed, which may be deemed more damaging to the defendant than the actual evidence destroyed.

3.2 Electronic Discovery

The other discipline within electronic evidence is the large-scale gathering, searching, filtering, and producing of relevant electronic data in legal discovery—electronic discovery. This has been a very hot topic in most complex litigation matters in the last few years. In an average case, the electronic discovery process involves gathering media from multiple sources including, desktop, laptop and server hard drives, network shared drives, and backup tapes. Active data (data readily available on the hard drive) and archival data (data contained on backup tape for disaster recovery purposes) are included as a part of the production but are not analyzed by the e-evidence expert processing the data. Electronic discovery does not typically include the collection or processing of any discarded, hidden, or deleted data, although as mentioned previously, a single case can have both electronic discovery and computer forensics aspects. Instead, electronic discovery is a very close cousin to traditional paper discovery. It involves the gathering, review and ultimate production of document responsive to requests under the rules of civil procedure. The new variable is simply that the documents were created and are maintained only electronically.

DATA COLLECTION

Data collection for electronic discovery is similar to data collection for computer forensics. Clients can have the e-evidence expert come onsite to collect the data, gather the data themselves with data cloning software and ship it to the e-evidence expert on CDs and DVDs, or send the original media to the e-evidence expert if it is not imminently needed. The main difference in collecting data for electronic discovery is that a complete mirror image is not needed if only the active data will be col-

Figure 3.9 Mapping a Timeline for Electronic Discovery

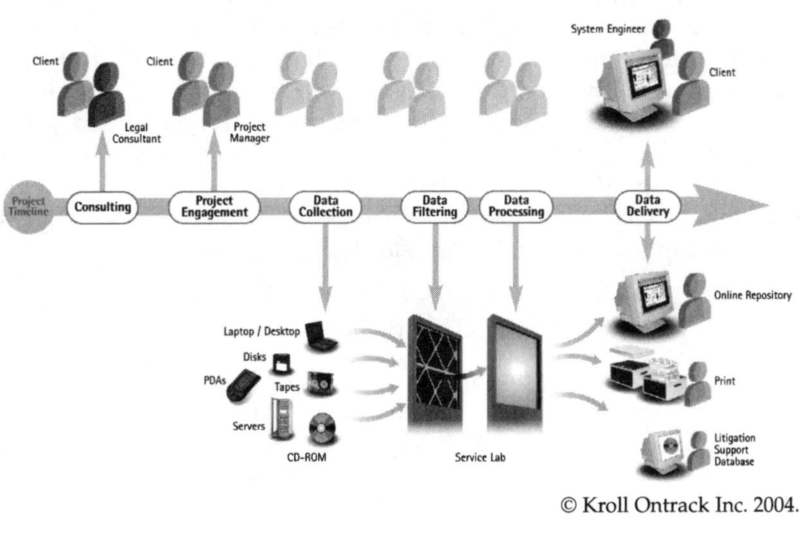

© Kroll Ontrack Inc. 2004.

lected. Computer forensics best practices require a complete bit-by-bit copy of the media so that all activity occurring on the media is available in the investigation. Because data in electronic discovery is merely gathered and not analyzed, only the active data needs to be captured. However, counsel should carefully consider imaging all media for purposes of presentation, even if it may not be produced in disvovery. An active data capture takes less time and physical storage space than a complete image. Despite this, as mentioned in the computer forensics section, untrained individuals should not attempt to capture data.

DESK-SIDE COLLECTION AND REVIEW

At this juncture, the client needs to determine whether to conduct the electronic discovery in-house or consult an e-evidence expert. Many lawyers and corporate executives falsely believe that when electronic data is included in a discovery request, all they need to do is direct the target employees to boot their computers and print any relevant documents and e-mail. Another dangerous "deskside collection" plan is to request that employees drag and drop relevant files and e-mail into folders set aside for data collection.

There are many risks associated with these procedures. If the collection of evidence is left to employees, they may leave out relevant documents either because they do not realize the importance of the data, or they are afraid it will be embarrassing, inappropriate or libelous.

Also, if an employee simply presses "print" when trying to collect electronic documents, the metadata might not be included or could be altered. While the law is silent as to whether metadata is considered part of the document, many lawyers are beginning to specifically ask for metadata in their document requests. In addition, the employees might be committing spoliation in that metadata can be altered when a computer is booted and files are opened or dragged and dropped into collection folders. Lastly, the opposition may question the completeness or accuracy of the data collection and target these employees through depositions or subpoenas for testimony.

DATA FILTERING

As we state repeatedly throughout this text, electronic evidence, while providing a wealth of important evidence, can present challenges of volume. If left "untreated," this problem of volume can cause pandemic pain to the lawyer and to the document review team. Imagine how much data one creates in the average day, week, or month, and how much relates to any one specific topic. It is estimated that workers in corporate America will send 9.3 billion e-mails every day in 2004. *See* IDC Email Usage Forecast and Analysis. http://www.business leader.com/bl/nov02/techtools.html. According to a 2003 study, the average worker receives more than 50 e-mail messages a day, and about one in six e-mail users receive more than 100 messages daily. http://www.nwfusion.com/newsletters/gwm/2003/0421msg1.html.

With electronic evidence, the problem is often not as much, "how can the e-discovery team find relevant information," but rather, "how can the e-discovery team avoid information patently *not* relevant." How many company picnic, birthday, and out-of-the office e-mails do you receive each day? Not to mention the amount of SPAM e-mail circulating the World Wide Web!

Luckily, the e-discovery industry has developed a host of technology solutions that can greatly ease the pain of volume by culling the vast e-document universe down to that which is most likely to be relevant to a particular case or issue. The scope of the volume problem and the mitigating impact of technology are demonstrated in the chart below.

Figure 3.10 Filtering Data

Type of storage medium	Approximate number of pages before filtering (assuming media is full to capacity with a mixture of file and email data)	Approximate number of pages after filtering
3.5" Diskette (1.44 Megabytes)	108 – 144	27 – 36
CD-Rom (625 Megabytes)	46,875 – 62,500	11,719 – 15,625
Hard Drive (15 Gig)	1,250,000 – 1,500,000	37,500 – 50,000
Network Hard Drive (36 Gig)	2,700,000 – 3,600,000	675,000 – 900,000
Backup Tape (40 Gig)	3,000,000 – 4,000,000	750,000 – 1,000,000

© Kroll Ontrack Inc. 2004.

The e-discovery expert you choose can employ state-of-the art technology to filter the entire set of data and narrow the information to a relevant subset, saving time in the review process and money for your clients. With most sophisticated e-discovery experts, you can elect to use one or all of the following filtering options to narrow down the universe of data for review:

- **File Type Filtering**: Technology can be used to either include or exclude certain electronic files based on their type. For example, if a lawyer thinks that e-mail and word processing files will be important for a particular case, he or she can elect to include only those file types in the review set. More common is the use of file type identification to exclude files. In an average case, operating file types, such as program or system files, by their very nature will not contain any responsive information. These are files associated with the software applications and operating systems installed on the particular piece of equipment. These and other non-responsive file types can take up a significant amount of space on a hard drive or other media and can easily be filtered from the production using e-discovery technology.

Figure 3.11 Talking Technology: *File Type Filtering*

It is very important to ensure that the e-discovery expert that you choose is able to filter file types based on the *actual data* contained within the file, not just based upon its file extension (i.e., .doc, .xls, .exe, .dll, etc). This is true because while all files are automatically "assigned" a three letter file extension to their names to identify the file types, these extensions can be altered by someone who is trying to hide information, or by someone who changes this file extension for any reason at all. The technology used to achieve this filtering (for most experts) relies upon specific "tags" which are internal to the applications used to create files. Important information could be lost if the selected e-discovery vendor is not able to ensure that file types are filtered appropriately.

- **Custodian Filtering:** When paper documents are at the heart of discovery, lawyers begin by counseling their clients to segregate the paper files of individuals who are relevant to the case. In this respect, electronic discovery is no different than paper discovery. It is important to not lose sight of the fact that some of the traditional document collection mechanisms from the paper discovery world are equally applicable to electronic discovery. Instead of finding documents located in paper files and file cabinets, the relevant electronic documents are located in key computer systems such as desktop and laptop computers, backup tapes or other archival storage media. Once the documents are located, experts should employ electronic filtering techniques to isolate files of key custodians who are relevant to the case. Lawyers should further identify which of these custodians should be afforded priority handling by the electronic discovery experts. These can either be individuals who are most likely to have relevant information to the case, or they can be a subset of custodians believed to be representative of a larger group for purposes of data sampling. Employing these tactics will result in a substantially smaller document universe for processing, and thus a reduced cost for the electronic discovery project. Additional custodians can be added at a later date if the electronic evidence expert has captured an entire backup of the e-mail server and maintains that data live on its servers for processing. If this is required, lawyers should consult with their electronic evidence expert to identify whether any potential deduplication issues arise and to determine the impact they may have on the total volume of data for review. (See deduplication section below for further information.)

- **Keyword Filtering:** One of the distinct advantages of employing electronic evidence technology is the availability of keyword and term searching in order to segregate potentially responsive and potentially privileged information for further review and scrutiny. Unlike in the paper world where documents are stored according to illogical formats such as date or topic, or filed alphabetically, electronic information is stored according to the realities of the software used to create the information. This is often due to media storage constraints or the particular setup of the software. Applying keyword filtering to a broad universe of documents provides an excellent mechanism for getting around this problem. Electronic evidence experts are able to run keyword searches across all the data and are not limited to searching in individual files or application types only. This type of searching provides lawyers with a comprehensive view of the makeup of the data that is subject to litigation. Depending on the capabilities of the individual electronic discovery expert retained, keyword searching may be very complex or very simple. In other words, the searching may be "Boolean" type searching involving "and/or" connectors, or it may be simple keyword lists applying "or" against the universe. One key point to remember when applying keyword term searching across the document universe is that "or" is not necessarily better. Conversely, the axiom of "less is more" applies to this situation. In our experience, a list of 30 to 50 keyword terms is recommended in most situations to grab potentially responsive information without including too much irrelevant data. Often electronic discovery experts also have a list of "noise words" that they recommend you not include in your keyword list to avoid an unreasonably high number of "hits." Examples of noise words are, "it," "and," and "the." (See Appendix D for noise word list.) Additionally, most e-discovery experts also recommend that no initials, acronyms, or two to three character words are applied against the document universe unless special care is given to in-sure that these terms are handled properly and return results as intended. You can also use keyword searching to segregate po-tentially privileged data for further review and scrutiny by lawyers and paralegals. This type of search is accomplished by identifiying data from custodians likely to create and maintain privileged information (such as in-house and outside counsel) and then applying keyword term searches aimed at identifying potentially privileged information. Such terms may include words such as "privileged, confidential, attorney, work prod-uct" and other similar words, depending on the circumstances of the case. Employing this type of technology may speed the identification of privileged information and may help avoid the pitfalls of the inadvertent waiver of privilege. As indicated in other sections of this text, segregating potentially privileged documents may assist with the automated or manual creation of a privilege and redaction log as necessitated by the case.

- **Time Frame Filtering:** Another filtering technique that can be applied in the context of the discovery project, and which prac-titioners are unable to take advantage of in the paper document discovery world, is the date and time filter. This filter allows lawyers to target discrete periods of time that are particularly relevant to a case, or time periods that must be produced in ac-cordance with a document request or court order. Most elec-tronic discovery experts can target periods very specifically de-pending upon the way the data is stored. If archival backup tapes are at issue in the case, practitioners may segregate tapes for particular time periods according to the backup schedule of the client's archival tape procedure. Tapes are often created or maintained by year, month, week, or day. Therefore, lawyers can request their client's I.T. department to turn over tapes repre-senting backups for time periods of particular interest in a given case. Once data is restored from backup tapes or other media, the electronic discovery expert can apply date filters in order to include only documents that are created, modified, or, in the case of e-mail, sent or received within a particular date range. An excellent example of the date filtering approach is the *Keir v. UnumProvident Corporation*, 2003 W.L. 21997747 (S.D.N.Y. Au-gust 22, 2003). In this case, the court specifically addressed the availability of backup tapes for a particular time period relevant to the case. Specifically, the court referenced several investiga-tive journalism TV programs that targeted the topic at issue in the case. The court noted the likelihood that individuals involved in the case would have sent e-mails to one another during times close to the airing of the TV programs. The court took these air-dates for the investigative journalism TV programs and cross-referenced them against the available backup tapes. The court then ordered the filtering according to the availability of information in this context.

Figure 3.12 Talking Technology: *Time and Date Filtering*

For practitioners attempting to find specific documents, note the key occurrences and dates within the case fact pattern and compare it against the backup tape periods. Use this cross-reference as the highest priority for electronic evidence processing.

- **Deduplication:** There are bound to be duplicate documents when electronic data is gathered across time periods and from multiple individuals' files. Consider how frequently in corporate America, individuals send "company wide" e-mail on topics both mission-critical and mundane. These e-mail messages are then duplicated, not only in the mailbox of each individual throughout the company, but also on daily, weekly, monthly and quarterly backup tapes! This explosion of data can be enormous. For the lawyer conducting e-discovery, this duplication adds unnecessary risk and cost to the review and production of electronic information. When employing large teams of lawyers or paralegals to conduct review without "deduplication" of electronic data, there is a great risk that individual reviewers will make decisions as to the responsiveness or privileged nature of documents that are not consistent with each other. This problem can be solved through the use of e-discovery industry technology, known as deduplication, which involves identifying duplicate documents, and the "special-handling" or elimination of these duplicate documents from either or both the review and production set of documents. Deduplication can decrease the number of documents that need to be reviewed by as much as 90 percent, with 30 to 40 percent in the average case. E-discovery experts have varying levels of expertise and capabilities with respect to deduplication. Practitioners should be wary of claims of "deduplication" capabilities and should ask specific questions relating to the process that will be applied to the document universe. Some types of deduplication use simple technology,

Figure 3.13 Talking Technology: *Illustrating DeDuplication*

Deduplication is one of the most complex technological topics in e-discovery.

In this graphic, three custodians had separate document sets loaded into the e-discovery filtering tool in the following sequence—Bob, Joe, and then Cam.

If global deduplication is selected, only the original documents (yellow) would be produced, thus reducing the number of produced documents from twelve to seven.

If per custodian deduplication is selected, eleven of the twelve documents would be produced. The only document not to be produced would be Bob's duplicate message "Subject: Ontrack," because that is the only duplicate document that is within one custodian.

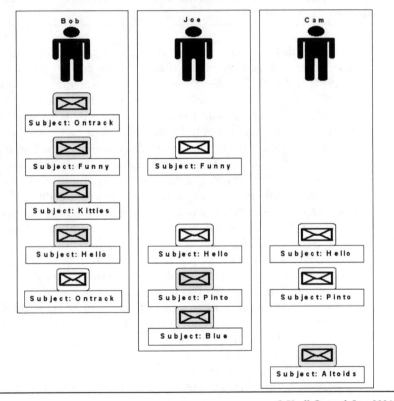

such as filenames or e-mail subject lines to identify duplicates. This type of technology is highly inaccurate and ineffective. It may either "over-dupe," eliminating very different documents both of which may contain contrary information, or "under-dupe" by failing to identify duplicates as such. Sophisticated e-discovery experts should employ true deduplication technology in order to identify redundant documents. Industry-leading technology creates an electronic fingerprint at the bit level (using the "1's" and "0's" in the file) for the document, which can be used to determine if a document is an exact duplicate of another document. This fingerprint changes any time the document is modified in any way (including the insertion of additional spaces, or other items which *may not* be seen if the document is printed). This fingerprint is compared against the fingerprints of all other documents in the data universe in order to determine if it has already been produced. Duplicate documents are flagged appropriately so they can be removed from the initial review and can then be repopulated for the production to the opposing party upon the request of the lawyer. Also, it is usually not sufficient to simply remove duplicate documents from the universe of documents. If this is done, the lawyer can lose the value of some important information such as who received an important e-mail, or who had access to it. Instead, the deduplication process employed should include a mechanism for accounting for all of the original locations of the document so that the lawyers handling the matter can evaluate the importance of the context of each incidence of a document. Advanced e-discovery experts offer lawyers several deduplication options depending on the needs of the case:

1. **No Deduplication**—All duplicate documents are produced, reviewed, and categorized. This results in the largest number of documents for review.

2. **Global Deduplication**—As each file is processed, it is compared against the entire database for the e-discovery project. Only the first instance of each unique document is produced for review and categorization. This type of deduplication results in the fewest documents for review. Care should be taken when carrying this type of deduplication over to the production of documents because only one copy of a document will be produced and not necessarily in the context most relevant to the case.

3. **Per Custodian or "Data Slice" Deduplication**—As each file is processed, it is compared to a limited database of documents from one document custodian, time period, or other "data slice" segment of documents. Only the first instance of

each unique document per custodian or "data slice" will be produced. However, the same document may exist in other custodians or "data slices" and be produced in those slices for independent review. This type of deduplication is useful when processing multiple backup tapes for the same e-mail custodians over time.

If deduplication is chosen, matters are further complicated by the choice of whether to employ the following additional technologies:

1. **E-mail attachment deduplication:** Counsel has the option to produce all duplicate attachments for messages that are part of the case.
2. **Re-population of duplicates for final production:** Depending on the case requirements experts can re-populate all duplicates for production to the opposing party.

The moral of the story of deduplication is that when processing electronic data, deduplication can create tremendous cost savings, but it can be fraught with complexity and pitfalls associated with a particular election. The technology is highly cost-effective; however, it is critical that practitioners engage an expert that they can trust to evaluate all of the potential implications of any deduplication decision.

- **Large File Handling:** Many electronic discovery experts also have the ability to either flag or filter very large files in a processing phase of electronic discovery. This mechanism reduces the amount of data for initial review and can also avoid the unnecessary review and production of documents. Practitioners may work with their electronic evidence expert to identify a pre-defined size at which files will be flagged as very large.
- **Removal of Blank Pages:** Lawyers should also consider using blank page removal technology. Sophisticated electronic discovery venders have the ability to apply technology that examines files behind the scenes to determine whether there is printed text or information on a given page. This technology should not be a manual process, but rather should employ filtering technology that can examine individual pages within a file. If pages are completely blank, they can be eliminated from further processing, thus saving review time as well as the ultimate cost of e-discovery productions.

To review, lawyers should consider filtering the data associated with an e-discovery production by:

- Limiting the processing of data to relevant file types;
- Limiting the universe of data to only those key custodians or individuals involved in the case;
- Limiting the universe of data to specified date ranges;
- Removing or flagging documents, e-mail, and attachments by keyword searching for relevancy and privilege;
- Removing duplicate documents from the initial review and then repopulating for the final production;
- Removing extremely large files and review for relevancy in the file's native format.
- Eliminating blank pages; and
- Limiting spreadsheet and database files to a certain number of pages per tab or table.

Figure 3.14

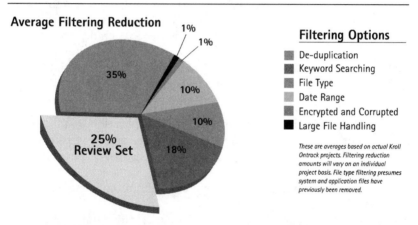

Average Filtering Reduction

Filtering Options

- De-duplication
- Keyword Searching
- File Type
- Date Range
- Encrypted and Corrupted
- Large File Handling

These are averages based on actual Kroll Ontrack projects. Filtering reduction amounts will vary on an individual project basis. File type filtering presumes system and application files have previously been removed.

75% of the document universe can be eliminated through data filtering.

PROCESSING & CONVERSION SPECIAL CHALLENGES

In recent years, the technology behind e-discovery processing and complex document searches has improved by leaps and bounds, as it has in virtually every industry. Today, almost any document search and production effort will need to address many special issues, forcing lawyers to make decisions on how to handle electronic documents. Some of these issues will be discussed in this section. They include:

1. File format selection
2. Spreadsheet Handling
3. Password Protected and Encrypted Files

4. Corrupt File Handling
5. Parent-Child Relationship

File Format Selection

As a practitioner facing electronic discovery review and production, you have the option to keep electronic documents in their native state or convert them to a standard file format. Native data refers to documents in their native format, i.e. the specific software applications used to create each individual document. For example, a native MS Word file with a ".doc" extension is in a word processing format. This MS Word file can only be opened, viewed, or modified in MS Word or a compatible program. A native document has not been processed or converted to a standard file type, such as .tiff or .pdf. in order to facilitate viewing or review and production. Users can review native data in two ways: (1) locally, on a CD or hard drive full of loose native files (sometimes with a directory structure that organizes the files), or (2) online, in a Web-based tool that either launches each document's native application as the document is opened or uses a "viewer" technology to display the documents. There are several potential limitations to reviewing data in a native format, either online or locally, which should be considered when evaluating a review tool:

- Must native data be viewed using the application that the document was created in (sometimes even the proper version of the software is required) on every machine used for document viewing?
- Can a user overlay redactions, bates, brandings, etc. on native documents?
- Can a user search across the universe of native data without assistance of a text-extraction database or similar tool?
- Can a user search metadata of native documents, or view metadata of individual files using the native applications or online tool?
- Be aware that opening a document natively can change the metadata associated with a file.
- Can a user categorize native documents in the tool, or must they drag and drop documents into specific folders, or otherwise group them using a document management system.
- Be aware that it is easy to make changes/overwrite content of documents during the review process with documents in their native format.

- Does native review eliminate the ability to report on the review and categorization process by removing the "birds-eye view" that is possible with traditional litigation support and online review document repositories (as well as all other repository advantages)? Does the tool you are evaluating solve this problem?

In recent months, companies have deployed new tools that overcome many of these native file review limitations. These tools allow the reviewer to keep the documents in a native format while at the same time search extracted text, categorize, and annotate. These tools offer a great first step in e-discovery, eliminating the need for tiffing an overly broad set of documents. Some of the newest tools allow you to combine the advantages of native review with converted document imaging, allowing the reviewer to redact, highlight, bates stamp and perform other functions reserved for tiffed documents. We suggest that you evaluate these cutting edge options and make case appropriate selections.

The other option for reviewing electronic documents is a standard file format. Here, the electronic documents are converted to a standard file format for storing, transporting, and most importantly, viewing online via one of the Web repository tools. Discussions in this regard center on whether TIFF (Tagged Image File Format) or PDF (Portable Document Format) is better for this task. The most common choice today is TIFF, but the argument for and against is raging in a separate adversarial process of its own.

It is easiest to think of TIFF and PDF images as photographs of native electronic files, e-mails or databases. Once uniform "pictures" are made of the native data, they can be printed or imported into an electronic data review system. TIFF is the most widely used format for storing image data and is currently the industry standard for transferring files between scanning, imaging, and litigation support programs.

There are various types of TIFFs that fall into two categories: unlicensed and licensed. An unlicensed TIFF is an open source file format, meaning the source code is freely available. Over the years, however, technology gurus have modified TIFF's open source code and created licensed adaptations that improve segments of TIFF's functionality, allowing them to be highlighted, redacted, and searched—all of the necessary document review functions.

The PDF was developed by the Adobe Corporation to allow efficient electronic viewing and distribution of formatted documents. Licensed Adobe Writer software is required to create PDF files, but for simple document viewing there is no licensing fee for Adobe Reader software. For complex document searching and redaction capabilities, licensed Adobe Reader software is required on each workstation. Software engineers are currently working on expanding the functionality of both TIFFs and PDFs.

The technical reality is that TIFFs and PDFs have similar features. The features, functionality, and underlying technology of the e-evidence expert's proprietary processes and repository tool should enter the evaluation, not the specific features of the file format alone. Issues such as file size, image transmission speed, document clarity, compatibility, searchability, security, and cost are at the center of the debate. These issues arise not primarily at the document level (i.e., whether the data is in the TIFF or PDF format) but rather at the repository architecture level—the operating capabilities of the electronic repository software. Hence, lawyers should leave the TIFF v. PDF debate to the techies and give close scrutiny to features of the online repository tool. The question at the end of the day should be, "Who cares about TIFF or PDF; what I need to know is can the expert's process and tools do what I need them to do?"

Handling Spreadsheet Files

Unlike most data types, which lend themselves well to the e-discovery process, spreadsheets are a unique animal requiring special handling. This uniqueness is due in large part to the multi-dimensional nature of spreadsheet files. Other document types display, organize, and print information based on a standard "page," while spreadsheets by design are a wide open landscape for information creation and storage. There are a lot of capabilities built into these file types that enable the user to do complex calculations, show and hide certain fields in a worksheet, and to create and manage interdependencies in data. This flexibility adds up to a big challenge for the e-discovery process which is predicated largely on the processing of two dimensional file types, such as word processing files or e-mail.

Many of the experienced e-discovery experts have considered all of the complexities associated with spreadsheet files and developed technology to effectively handle spreadsheet files. Using specialized technology, spreadsheet files can be processed and converted just as any other file type (Word, PPT, etc). E-discovery experts can "expose" several aspects of spreadsheet files for further handling in order to display all of the text. Some of these techniques include:

- Revealing all hidden columns or rows, producing them as if they were not hidden;

- Showing all worksheets and tabs within a workbook;
- Producing all data or text contained in a spreadsheet file, not just what is in a defined print area; and
- Removing all blank or empty pages in spreadsheets that have been inadvertently added as a result of formatting. This can be a large cost savings. Often, users of spreadsheet applications will inadvertently "click" or enter data in a spreadsheet field that is well beyond those fields that actually contain data, therefore making the application believe that the spreadsheet is much larger than it really is. If this error is not accounted for in the e-discovery process, myriad blank pages can be unnecessarily produced for review, adding cost to the production.

Most e-discovery experts will work with lawyers to determine the best method for handling spreadsheets.

Password Protected and Encrypted Files

In almost every case, the electronic evidence expert will encounter password protected or encrypted files. Techniques to crack the password or encryption can be used on virtually any file type, and the time required to successfully access the protected data is dependant upon the complexity of the password or encryption algorithm. Most passwords and encryption algorithms can be cracked in less than five minutes, while strong security measures can take days or weeks to decipher. In password and encryption breaking scenarios, the issue is more often *not* whether the encryption can be broken, but how much time is reasonable to spend in the attempt.

Corrupt File Handling

Another potential roadblock e-evidence experts can encounter is corrupt files. Files can become corrupt through a variety of means: normal use, network issues, application errors, etc. Before the data can be accessed, a file repair utility needs to be run to restore the data.

Parent-Child Relationships

In the e-evidence arena, "parent-child relationship" most commonly refers to an e-mail and its associated attachments (i.e., the e-mail message is the "parent" and the attachment is the "child"). Parent-child relationship can also refer to: (1) e-mails within a PST, which is a container file for e-mail messenger, in which the e-mails are the children, and the PST is the parent or (2) files contained in a ZIP file (a compressed file or files), where the files are the children and the ZIP file is the parent. It is very likely that one will encounter multiple layers of parent-child relationships such as a PST with an e-mail message or a ZIP file that is an attachment to an e-mail message.

The decisions that counsel makes about parent-child relationship handling can affect an entire electronic document production. For example, should all child attachments and e-mail be categorized and produced exactly as the parent e-mail? Should you review the entire "family" of documents if one member takes a keyword hit or only the attachment containing the hit and the associated parent? It is critical that the e-evidence expert processing the data maintain all levels of parent-child relationship throughout the process so that each document can be considered in the context of its "document family." For example, in the multiple layer example above, if the relationship of files to the parent ZIP are not maintained and the ZIP is the child of an e-mail, then the relationship of the files to the "grandparent" e-mail would not be maintained. This information might be important to counsel if the question of what documents certain people received or sent is at issue.

E-DOCUMENT REVIEW

Now that electronic discovery is becoming a mainstream litigation tool, it is starting to impact many new areas of practice. Beyond e-data collection and filtering, lawyers have a host of options for conducting the review of electronic documents. As with all other aspects of e-discovery, the review process is complicated by the vast volume of electronic documents that exist.

This sheer volume presents additional challenges and problems with the traditional methods of document review, such as paper review, or even the local (meaning not online) litigation support databases. While these tools are still widely employed by practitioners, they are not always the best choice. Lawyers should evaluate all of their document review options and make a case-by-case decision as to which review method makes the most sense.

Paper Document Review

Despite all of the advances in the technology used to collect, filter, and process electronic information from their native file applications to a uniform file format for review, many lawyers still prefer to conduct their document review for privilege and responsiveness in paper form. Sophisticated e-discovery vendors are able to print electronic documents for review by lawyers while preserving and presenting critical information about the data. For example, if a practitioner elects paper review of the electronic information, care should be taken to insure that the process by which the documents are printed includes a mechanism for preserving and presenting the unique file characteristics inherent in electronic data, such as metadata. Many electronic discovery vendors will preserve and present this information by creating overlays to the electronic documents so that certain components of metadata are printed directly on the documents, or "burned" onto an electronic document. Some examples of metadata, which might be printed directly on the document, include the document creator's name or the control number associated with the document. Other types of metadata may be included in a document "slip sheet," which is a piece of paper (usually colored) printed and placed on top of the actual document in order to present the document reviewer with many key facts about the document, adding additional context to the review process. Some of these additional facts include the creation date of the document, the creator's name, the date it was last modified, and the location where it was retrieved.

There are distinct advantages to reviewing electronic information in paper form. First, everyone is familiar with and able to use paper. There is no training required, other than the substantive training as to whether certain categories of information will be responsive or important in the context of a particular piece of litigation. Further, paper documents are imminently portable. They can be taken from the document review "war room" to a deposition, copied for attachment as an exhibit, or produced at trial with relative ease. Further, paper documents are always available if the human being seeking access to them is in the same physical location as the document. There are no technological issues to overcome.

Despite the seemingly simple nature of a paper document review, there are also good reasons why it is no longer the most appealing option. One of the major limitations of paper document review is that you do not know what you cannot see. In conducting paper reviews, even if metadata is preserved and presented via a slip sheet, you lose much of the valuable context of the document that can be preserved through other means of electronic document review, such as the online repository discussed below. Another major limitation inherent to paper document review is the logistical challenges associated with the review of large volumes of electronic documents. It is not uncommon for an electronic document review on a large piece of litigation to entail millions, or even tens of millions of documents. Most law firms and corporations are not equipped to handle the staging of a review site for hundreds of reviewers and thousands of boxes of documents.

When opting for a paper review of electronic documents, you should consider the additional costs associated with the shipping and storage of paper documents. Reviewing documents in paper will also add time to the total time frame associated with the electronic discovery process. This is primarily attributable to the fact that documents originating electronically must be migrated to paper for a manual review and then returned back to the electronic discovery expert for further manual handling in order to segregate them and copy them for ultimate production. Even if reviewed in paper, some cases require that the documents be produced to the other party electronically. All of this translation in and out of the electronic realm increases the time and cost required to complete the process. Most electronic discovery experts can make this process as seamless as possible. However, it adds unneeded complexity to the endeavor.

Litigation Support Databases

Another alternative for reviewing electronically-based documents is the local litigation support database. Some examples of these types of data bases include Concordance™, Summation™, DBTextWorks™, JFS Litigators Notebook™, Steelpoint Technology's Introspect™ and others. Some of these products now offer web versions of their tools as well.

This type of litigation support database, or document repository, gained popularity in the 1990's as the advent of technology began to impact the practice of law. These databases are designed to house documents that originate both in paper and electronically. They must be maintained locally at a law firm or corporate site and require the law firm or corporation to maintain adequate information technology infrastructure in order to support the database. These databases are used primarily to find known documents by their document control or reference number and to ease the portability of these documents among lawyers by allowing them to be e-mailed or burned to a CD or some other form of media.

The use of old-fashioned litigation support database technology for purposes of electronic document review has both advantages and disadvantages. This type of technology is generally familiar to litigation support managers within large law firms and is somewhat familiar to lawyers or paralegals who have used this technology for the past decade or so. The technology is also, as stated above, local to the law firm or corporation and therefore does not require the firm to be reliant upon technology hosted on the Worldwide Web. This lack of Web hosting also can enhance the security of the documents, particularly when compared to some of the less secure online document repositories. Finally, these types of databases do present a cost advantage in many situations. Many Web-hosted electronic document repositories discussed in the next section of this text require practitioners to pay monthly hosting charges to maintain their electronic documents in their repository. The use of a local litigation support database avoids these hosting charges; however, the cost to house this data internally sometimes offsets these savings.

On the other side, there are limitations to the capabilities of the local litigation support database in handling electronic document discovery. These software databases were not created with electronic document discovery in mind. While they generally allow for the manual coding of paper documents with biographic information, they may or may not have room for metadata. Practitioners should take care to ensure that the most important metadata extracted from their electronic documents are appropriately mapped to corresponding fields in the local litigation support database. Practitioners should also evaluate the functionality of individual litigation support databases in order to determine whether they meet the unique properties of electronic documents and requirements of an electronic document review. A retained electronic discovery expert can assist the practitioner when considering various local litigation support databases and the unique characteristics of the electronic documents. Another limitation of the litigation support database is the actual database size and constraints. Most of these databases were designed to house scanned imagines of paper documents. Therefore, when using them for a greater volume of electronic documents one may run into a storage limitation ceiling. Further, the commercially available litigation support database products were largely developed to function as mere repositories for documents and therefore do not have robust document review capabilities and categorization options. They also do not all have robust and elegant reporting features allowing practitioners to understand precisely the status of the document review.

Online Document Repositories

One hot new piece of litigation technology that emerged at the turn of the new century is the online electronic document review repository. E-discovery experts have led the way with the development of these advanced tools for legal document review categorization, production, and collaboration. Some examples of these tools are: Kroll Ontrack's ElectronicDataViewer™, Fios' Prevail™, Applied Discovery's Online Review tool, and Electronic Evidence Discovery's DiscoveryPartner™.

These tools employ a variety of Web-based products and technology to allow lawyers and paralegals to conduct document review from remote locations, resulting in quick and cost effective document review. Many, if not all, of the e-discovery experts offering this type of review tool provide price breaks or incentives for using this technology. In fact, many of the above-mentioned products are currently being offered at "no charge" for a period of time when the company is used for the processing component of the e-discovery project.

What is an online repository? Why is electronic review superior to paper review? What should you consider when selecting an online repository? These topics are discussed below.

WHAT IS AN ONLINE DOCUMENT REVIEW TOOL?

An online review repository is, as the name implies, a Web-based tool for lawyers to conduct document reviews in the context of litigation and regulatory compliance. It can be contrasted with the traditional litigation support database; these databases "locally" store information at a law firm or corporate site and require the reviewing entity to manage all of the technology aspects of maintaining the document database and production.

After the data on the hard drives, backup tapes, and servers has been gathered and searched, clients have several output options for reviewing the potentially relevant e-mails and documents, as stated above. Using an online electronic reviewing option is becoming more appealing for litigators faced with electronic document productions. In pre-online repository days, electronic document review involved the following steps: the electronic documents and e-mail were gathered from the targeted custodians and then printed; the documents were boxed and shipped to the review team; and the review team sorted through the pages of paper for responsiveness and privilege. With an online repository, the electronic documents and e-mail are first gathered and processed as described in previous chapters. Then, the data is uploaded to the e-evidence expert's proprietary database where reviewers can remotely access the documents via a secure Internet connection. The review team can categorize, redact, and search for documents within the tool. Only after all of the documents have been reviewed are the documents printed to paper or loaded to CDs for production to the opposing party.

WHAT ARE THE BENEFITS?

There are many advantages to using an online review tool. Perhaps the most obvious is efficiency. Studies show that searching, viewing, classifying, and marking data electronically simply saves time and money. In addition, using an electronic review system is more accurate than traditional paper review because a computerized database catalogues each document, ensuring that no documents are overlooked or misplaced.

Managing the logistics of the review is also simplified with an online review repository. Paper review costs additional money to bring the documents to the review team or bring the review team to the documents. With an online electronic repository, however, the documents can be viewed by multiple review lawyers in multiple physical locations with the click of a mouse. Further, litigation support managers have access to elaborate reporting options to monitor the progress of the review. Most electronic review systems run reports to inventory things such as what has been reviewed, what data is left to be reviewed, and how much data each reviewer has evaluated in a certain time frame.

Depending on the characteristics of the review tool, there are also many technological benefits. For example, most repositories store the documents in a uniform format (e.g., .tiff images) regardless of the program the file was created in. They may also provide access to the native file for reference or review. Also, most online repositories allow for sophisticated searching and categorization capabilities. Lawyers or paralegals reviewing the documents can easily mark the document as responsive, non-responsive, privileged, hot, etc. Sophisticated online review tools also have highlighting, annotation, and redaction features.

Finally, reviewing electronically created documents in an electronic repository ensures that all computer-based evidence is evaluated. Reviewing only printed documents results in an incomplete body of evidence because the metadata (i.e., data about the data) is not displayed. Using an online electronic document review tool keeps the metadata with the document and allows the reviewer to search this important information.

CONSIDERATIONS WHEN CHOOSING AN ONLINE REVIEW TOOL

Despite the potential advantages to using an online document review tool, the features and functionality of the products available on the market vary greatly. When selecting an online review tool, the following factors should be considered.

1. **How quickly can reviewers navigate between documents? How long does an average search take?** Look for a software package that provides document viewing and searching in real time. Tools that take several seconds to access the next document or several minutes or hours to run a search can result in hundreds of hours of wasted reviewer time. Avoid software packages that transmit entire documents over the Internet as this protocol is slow and unwieldy. Instead, to facilitate faster transmission, only screen shots should be sent across the Internet. This technology allows the reviewer to approximate the page-turning speed of a paper review, while capitalizing on all of the other benefits of online review.

2. **What security protocols are in place?** The review tool should maintain the highest degree of security for documents managed online. Any data transmitted on the Web, including keystrokes, should be protected with 128 bit encryption. This is the industry-standard security level for online data transmission. In addition, a secure and efficient repository solution should not transfer image file data (.pdf, .tiff, or otherwise) across the Internet where it has the chance of being unlawfully intercepted. A better option is to transmit screen shots of the data. The tool should also include flexibility for managing the document review with varying levels of "reviewer security." This flexibility will permit the lawyers or other individuals managing the review to determine the degree of access and authority that will be given to particular people. For example, only certain people can be allowed to view sensitive information, or users can restrict access to certain features, such as the ability to redact.

3. **How easily can the review team learn to use the software?** The software's graphical user interface (GUI) should be easy to use. The layout should be familiar (i.e., similar to a common word processing or e-mail system such as Microsoft Office) and simple to navigate to the commonly used functionalities. Using the system should be virtually instinctive so that minimal training is required.

4. **What is the tool's functionality?** Search for a sophisticated tool that offers redaction capabilities, document level note-taking, highlighting, deduplication, Bates numbering, custom branding, and visual clarity. Ask whether the tool allows you to view and/or download native files from within the tool. Each of

these features should have high-level functionality that supports the attorney review process. For example, the viewer should accelerate the review process by highlighting key search terms and enabling the user to quickly jump to each instance of a keyword. Users should also be able to assign a "reason-code" to particular document categorizations or redactions in order to facilitate the privilege log generation process.

5. **How is the review administered?** Beware of repository tools that do not provide for self administration by the review team leader. Some software packages require the manager of the review to call the vendor for simple tasks such as adding new reviewer profiles, assigning or reassigning data sets, creating new categories, or running reports or, they require you to pay the provider on an hourly basis for these services. Instead, the tool should provide the review manager with the capability of organizing and administering the data without having to continuously contact the vendor. As the review progresses, the manager should be able to generate a variety of reports to monitor the review's progress.

6. **What software requirements are needed to access the repository?** Most tools require a high speed internet connection and Web browser (usually Internet Explorer) to run the tool. Some tools require other computer programs to be purchased and installed at each data reviewing workstation in order to operate the review tool, or to perform certain functions, such as redaction or note taking. To keep the costs associated with the review to a minimum, look for a tool that does not require downloading additional software before documents can be reviewed.

7. **How is the data organized?** Pay careful attention to the file organization system which houses the captured data. The review tool should not merely dump the data into one large file. Instead, the software should allow a manager to classify the data into logical file sets (i.e., user, date, size, etc.) that can be easily broken up into assignments for the review team.

8. **What are the tool's searching capabilities?** The tool should provide for sophisticated Boolean searching capabilities that search across the text of the e-mail messages, metadata, and all attachments. Also, investigate whether concept searching, sophisticated technology that defines the meaning behind the search terms by identifying word patterns and occurrences in documents, would be beneficial to your case; if necessary, seek a tool that offers this feature.

9. **What output options are available during and after the review?** During the review, it is important that the review team can batch print documents to a local printer from the repository. Once the review is completed, the tool should also allow for quick and easy printing of the responsive documents for production. If the responsive documents must be produced electronically, look for a tool that can output documents in a native format or in load file format compatible with a litigation support database.

10. **What type of training is available for the review team? Does the vendor provide a project manager for the duration of the project?** The vendor should provide project management, in-house training, and continuing service and support. Look for a vendor that assigns a dedicated project manager to your case.

CONCEPT SEARCHING IN ONLINE REPOSITORIES

An up-and-coming feature in the online repository market is concept searching, also known as fuzzy searching or advanced searching. Concept searching uses sophisticated technology to define the meaning behind search terms by identifying word patterns and occurrences in documents and translating them into "concepts." Because concept searching operates on concepts—not keywords—search and retrieval is not constrained by the language used in the query. Instead, advanced mathematics is used to retrieve relevant documents, even if the concept search text does not share many words or objects in common. The concept searching engine first counts the number of occurrences of each concept both in the individual document and in the entire database. Then, the engine examines the relationships between the concept and every other word in the data set, returning top-ranked documents with the strongest conceptual relationship to the word.

With concept searching, lawyers are more likely to find documents relating to the issues in their cases because the search is not limited by the words entered in the query box. For example, if you run a search on "broken bone" your concept results would be narrowed to issues in your personal injury case, such as accident, disease, fracture, femur, injury, hospital, and orthopedic. You can avoid unnecessary review of documents containing unrelated concepts, such as dog bone, dinosaur bone, boning a fish, skull and crossbones, and archeology bones.

Figure 3.15 Talking Technology: *Will concept searching revolutionize document review?*

When combined with traditional terms and connector searching, concept searching gives lawyers the best of both worlds, allowing them to identify relevant documents more quickly and accurately. Even though this feature is only beginning to be implemented into online repositories, its value is anticipated to assist lawyers in the following ways:

- Allows lawyers to learn more about their case before ever reviewing a document.
- Reduces the risk of missing important documents that would not appear in a traditional search.
- Provides lawyers with the ability to learn code words for issues or projects that might not be readily associated with standard search terms, particularly useful for off-the-cuff e-mail or IM conversations.
- Gives counsel a "behind the scenes" tool to find related documents after they agree to a set of search terms.
- Pinpoints similar documents once a valuable document is located.
- Helps lawyers screen and exclude superfluous "junk" documents—such as jokes, recipes, and company picnic notices—that took a hit under traditional keyword searching.

Only time will tell if this new technology feature will truly revolutionize electronic document review; however, one notion is solid. With the volume of e-documents skyrocketing, technology will continue to assist lawyers in their attempts to more quickly and easily locate the needle in the e-haystack!

PRODUCTION OPTIONS

Once the process of reviewing the documents is complete, the practitioner should not lose sight of the final decision that must be made in the context of any discovery project—production. Practitioners have the same basic options for production of electronic information as they do for the review of the information: paper, local litigation support database, Web-based document repository, and native format. Each of these options will be discussed below, paying particular attention to the additional considerations that must be noted in a production context.

The first option, paper production, is the most simple and traditional method of electronic document production. Once a subset of documents has been selected for production, one can return to the discovery expert who conducted the processing and request that they print or "blow back" a document set. The other option is for the practitioner to seek the assistance of a traditional paper scanning and coding company, in order to produce the information. The option that is selected should depend upon the skills and expertise of the e-discovery expert and the associated costs. Typically, if an electronic online document repository is used for the review phase of the process, it makes sense to return to the expert who loaded the documents into the repository to conduct the final production.

The second production option is the local litigation support database. Litigation support databases are a convenient option in that one can send a number of CDs or DVDs containing the responsive documents directly to the opposition to load for their review. The advantage for the receiving party is that they have the ability to search the responsive documents and can easily manage the review of this information. One complicating consideration when producing a litigation support database is whether your electronic evidence expert has adequately eliminated the text of any redacted information and has otherwise protected any privilege or work product from production. Because these database tools were not designed as production tools, but rather local review and repository tools, there are many considerations to evaluate when putting a product to a use for which it was not intended.

The next option for production of electronic information is to consider the online document repository. There are situations in which sharing information via a Web-based tool is convenient and useful. This technology has been employed successfully in the past; for example, it can be used to produce information for a government agency or a number of parties in disparate geographic locations who can access the document repository via the Web. As with the local litigation support database, however, many of the online repository tools were not initially intended for production, but rather for the purposes of review. Therefore, work closely with the software's creator and your electronic discovery expert in order to ensure that any features or functionality inherent in the tool that may compromise privileged or other confidential or work product information are restricted for use by the opponent. These considerations will vary greatly when evaluated in the context of the individual products.

The last option for the production of electronic documents is native production. For reviewing documents, the advantages and disadvantages of using the native documents and the native software tools were discussed above. Similar considerations exist when using native file formats for production.

First, if documents are produced natively, the document appears exactly as it appeared to the user from whose files the document was taken. To open and view the documents, the requesting party must obtain copies of the individual software. The requesting party will not be able to search across the entire universe of native data without using another review database or bearing the cost of conversion. Reviewers have access to hidden data such as formulas behind spreadsheet data.

Despite these advantages, the producing party might be accused of spoliating data because the metadata may not be preserved if files are produced and then opened natively. Also, the producing party cannot redact documents for production and cannot brand the documents with a bates number or other similar overlay.

3.3 Working with an E-Evidence Expert

As shown in previous sections, dredging up voluminous electronic "skeletons" can be a daunting task. This section will address the considerations the litigation team should address when determining whether to handle the computer forensics investigation or electronic discovery production in-house or consult with an expert.

POTENTIAL LIMITATIONS OF CONDUCTING ELECTRONIC DISCOVERY IN-HOUSE

Not all e-discovery productions should be handled in the exact same manner. The amount of data requested, the type of hardware and software involved, the nature of the suit, and the amount in controversy all play into the complexity and cost that the producing party will face. On a case-by-case basis the litigation team will need to determine whether electronic discovery should be conducted by an in-house I.T. department, in-firm litigation support department, or an external e-evidence expert. What follows is a comprehensive discussion of factors to consider when faced with discovery of electronic documents.

Exposure to liability.

Even with the best intentions, conducting discovery internally exposes a company to liability. Electronic evidence, just like other types of evidence, is fragile. Failure to adhere to strict industry standards regarding data preservation and collection could not only result in the loss of critical data, but may impinge the credibility of any data that is recovered, potentially rendering it unreliable or even inadmissible in a court of law. Of all the necessary considerations, opening up the possibility for additional liability is probably the greatest factor in determining whether to consult an outside e-discovery expert.

Diversion of I.T. staff and resources allocated to existing projects.

The organizational and monetary opportunity costs of redirected workers must be considered in figuring the monetary expense of fulfilling the discovery requests in-house. Requesting an in-house I.T. team to collect, analyze, organize, and prepare electronic data for review in legal matters can acutely divert the focus of the whole IT department. Conducting e-discovery while maintaining business operations can prove to be a juggling act. The I.T. team must try to keep today's systems running while also attempting to restore and search yesterday's systems. Oftentimes, an e-evidence expert can complete data collection during nonbusiness hours so that company operations are interrupted only for a limited time (if affected at all). In determining whether to outsource the discovery duties, consider the disruption of day-to-day responsibilities in order to comply with the electronic document production.

Experience.

Asking someone with little or no e-discovery experience to comply with a comprehensive electronic data request can be a weighty demand. Data collection experts are specially trained to understand various topologies of I.T. systems and have experience with almost every hardware and software platform, as well as the expertise required to ensure that the evidentiary integrity of data is maintained throughout the gathering, sorting and production processes. E-evidence experts also offer consulting services designed to reduce costs, save time, and eliminate unnecessary efforts. In deciding whether to seek expert assistance, evaluate the experience of the internal I.T. team members or firm's litigation support staff.

Technology and Equipment.

In addition to considering the expertise of the I.T. staff, the available technology is also a factor in determining if an e-discovery request can be satisfied internally. Consider the following:

- E-evidence specialists typically maintain libraries of out-of-date software so that data created on antiquated systems is easily producible.
- E-discovery professionals maintain high-speed proprietary tools to ensure the fastest and most accurate collection and culling processes.
- Most experts use best practices security protocols to ensure that no damage occurs to the data or hardware.

- The majority of e-evidence specialists offer multiple output options for legal document review: printed documents, litigation support software, or online electronic repositories.

In evaluating the likelihood of using in-house resources for an e-data production, a company's I.T. or a firm's litigation support technology and equipment should be scrutinized.

Ability to meet deadlines.

E-discovery timelines are aggressive, and concern over the logistics of the data gathering and production is high. Satisfying the time limits required by the bench or opposing party may not be feasible for an in-house I.T. department while also continuing to attend to day-to-day company business. In-firm litigation support departments, however, are usually better staffed to handle the tight turnaround times, depending on the number of other matters they are managing at the time. The ability to meet deadlines must be a factor in deciding if a company's I.T. group or firm's litigation support team can manage the computer-based discovery.

Conflicts of interest for I.T. departments.

Searching a company's systems for responsive data creates potential conflicts of interest for the I.T. personnel. Asking an I.T. employee to infiltrate his or her colleagues' or supervisors' electronic-based communications opens up a variety of privacy and bias concerns. In addition, an internal e-discovery team could have difficultly forming objective searches when the future of the company is on the line. The impartiality of a third-party expert should be a factor in determining whether to perform e-discovery within the company.

Complexity of the request.

Lastly, as e-discovery technology evolves, e-discovery requests will become more elaborate. Even I.T. professionals or Litigation Support managers with electronic discovery experience might have difficulty handling e-discovery projects with complex aspects. The complexity of the discovery request should be taken into account when deciding whether to outsource electronic discovery needs.

As one author recently noted, "It is unrealistic to assume that I.T. professionals can pay attention to all the nuances of litigation, manage the lifecycle responsibilities associated with e-mail, and enforce an overall e-mail archive policy. Companies will be caught off guard by assuming that I.T. can shoulder this burden alone." *See* Kevin Craine,

"Here Come the Lawyers. Is Your I.T. Department Ready?" (<http://www.educomts.com/downloads/Herecomethelawyers.pdf>.) The best practice is to develop an e-discovery plan that balances the advantages of conducting in-house or in-firm e-discovery against the dangers of not consulting a specialist. In some cases, counsel has used their client's in-house I.T. staff or in-firm litigation support team with great success when complying with an electronic discovery request. Other companies have found outsourcing to be extremely cost-effective and are more comfortable handing the activity off to an e-evidence expert.

POTENTIAL LIMITATIONS OF CONDUCTING COMPUTER FORENSICS IN-HOUSE

Most of the e-discovery considerations discussed above apply when considering whether to consult an external computer forensics expert as well. In addition, there are a few supplementary considerations.

Best Practices Imaging Technology and Experience.

The first stage in a computer forensic investigation is to create a mirror image of the target hard drive. At a minimum, this requires imaging software and knowledge of its use. As discussed in previous chapters, both the client and its counsel can be at risk for sanction if best practices imaging protocols are not followed. The ability to image the media at issue is a factor to consider when weighing whether the investigation can proceed in-house or in-firm.

Ability to Track Chain of Custody.

Computer forensic investigators must be able to track chain of custody on all investigated media. As discussed previously, tracking a complete chain of custody is crucial in computer forensic matters. If the investigation is conducted internally, the company or law firm should be able to track the media's movement as well as every individual who had access to the media.

Data Recovery Experience.

In addition to computer forensic imaging software and general computer forensic analysis experience, most computer forensic investigators can recover inaccessible data from damaged media or systems. This is another factor to consider when establishing whether an investigation should be outsourced to a computer forensic expert.

Exposure to hostile information.

In some cases, computer forensic investigators are exposed to hostile content, such as pornography, contained on the computer being investigated. If the investigation is being conducted in-house or in-firm, employees should be warned of this risk and told how to appropriately handle the situation. Computer forensic investigators have experience handling this type of information and know how to avoid certain hostile files if irrelevant to the project. The potential for exposing in-house or in-firm employees to hostile information and the legal and human resources consequences should be considered when determining whether to conduct a computer forensics investigation in-house.

Possibility of Testifying in Court.

When an investigation is conducted internally, the employee conducting the investigation puts him or herself at risk for being called as a witness if the matter proceeds to trial. If this is the situation, the employee will likely be scrupulously questioned on his or her relevant experience and procedures used in the investigation. The potential for bias will also likely be strongly questioned. Most external computer forensic investigators have testimony experience. Companies facing a computer forensic investigation should consider this factor most heavily when determining whether to consult an expert.

Similar to the e-discovery considerations above, companies needing a computer forensic analysis should find an appropriate balance between handling a matter internally and consulting an expert. It has been our experience that given the extra considerations in the computer forensics area, counsel is quicker to consult an external expert in a computer forensic case than in an electronic discovery case.

FACTORS TO CONSIDER WHEN SELECTING AN EXPERT

Case law indicates that selecting the proper expert is of utmost importance. In *Gates Rubber Co. v. Bando Chem. Ind.*, 167 F.R.D. 90 (D. Colo. 1996), the court found that it was the lawyer's responsibility to use the best available technology to produce the most complete and accurate picture of the evidence. The court stated that a party's failure to select proper technology puts both the client and counsel at risk for sanction.

One case directly on point is *Residential Funding Corp. v. DeGeorge Fin. Corp.*, 306 F.3d 99 (2d. Cir. Sept. 26, 2002). At the trial court level, the defendant in the case requested e-mail from the time period relevant to the contract dispute. The plaintiff agreed to produce the e-mail and engaged an e-evidence vendor to do so. The plaintiff's selected vendor was unable to retrieve the e-mail for the relevant time periods from the plaintiff's backup tapes. Specifically, the plaintiff represented to the court, "the reason no e-mails were produced for [October–December 1998] from the backup tapes you received was either due to the fact that some of the tapes were physically damaged or corrupted or some tapes did not have e-mail on them at all." However, after receiving the tapes from the plaintiff, the defendant's e-evidence expert was able to retrieve the relevant e-mail in four days' time.

The trial court articulated that the reason the plaintiff was unable to produce the e-mails was its choice of hiring a vendor unable to retrieve them. On appeal, the Second Circuit reasoned that where a party breaches a discovery obligation by failing to produce evidence, the trial court has broad discretion in fashioning an appropriate sanction, including the discretion to delay the start of a trial, to declare a mistrial, or to issue an adverse inference instruction. Sanctions may be imposed where a party has not only acted in bad faith or grossly negligent, but also through ordinary negligence.

When selecting an e-evidence expert, it is important to take the following points into consideration.

- **Reputation and Experience.** Investigate several electronic evidence experts to gain a detailed understanding of their staff, capabilities, and processes. Seek recommendations from your colleagues. Conduct site visits for particularly large projects. Learn about standard project turnaround times.
- **Corporate Health, History & Integrity**. Consider the corporate health, history, and integrity of the expert's company. Is the company well-established and financially sound? Is the company a well-recognized thought leader in the industry with widespread credibility in its processes and staff? In the post-Enron era, is the expert's company operating with integrity and highest ethical standards?
- **Pricing Philosophy**. Learn about the expert's pricing philosophy. Take time to investigate each line item that your client will ultimately be charged for. Compare prices among experts. Try to ensure that there are no "hidden" charges by asking questions relating to each stage of an engagement, detailed in the respective e-discovery and computer forensic sections of this chapter.
- **Security, Confidentiality, and Chain of Custody Protocols.** Ask about the expert's commitment to protecting your data, includ-

ing an explanation of the physical building security and data security and confidentiality practices. Be certain that the expert maintains proper chain of custody protocols. Also, ask whether the expert uses a "need to know" policy with its employees, and how that policy is enforced.

- **Data Collection Options.** Look for an expert who allows data to be both shipped to the facility as well as collected onsite by trained data collection engineers. Consider the geographic locations from which data collection engineers can be dispatched. Ask about the expert's abilities to handle a variety of media sources. Inquire about the speed to which the data collection will occur.
- **Project Management.** Seek an e-evidence expert with a team of highly-qualified client services staff. All client services staff should have an understanding of both the legal and technical issues in a typical electronic evidence project. Also, ensure that you will be assigned a dedicated project manager and have access to that individual as necessary.
- **Flexibility & Adaptability.** E-evidence projects tend to grow in nature as the discovery or investigation progresses. Your e-evidence expert should be able to adapt to changes in the project scope or requirements quickly and professionally.

Electronic Discovery

- **Tool development.** Look for an expert who has developed proprietary technology that can grow and change as needs evolve, compared to an expert who has merely integrated "off-the-shelf" existing technology, confined by a third party tool's features and functionality.
- **Processing & Storage Capacity.** Your e-discovery expert should have considerable processing and storage capacity, being able to handle multiple projects at any point in time.
- **Multiple Review and Production Options.** The e-discovery expert should offer the full array of output options, including: native, paper, litigation support database, and online repository.

Computer Forensics

- **Advanced Imaging, Recovery, and Analysis Technology.** Request information about the expert's imaging, data recovery, and analysis tools. Are they using off-the-shelf tools or internally developed tools? Are they utilizing industry standard best practices data handling protocols?

- **Experienced & Recognized Experts**. Your computer forensic expert should provide a current curriculum vitae or resume, listing areas of expertise, representative projects, prior testimony, and memberships in industry related organizations. Being able to identify these areas will lend credibility to his or her analysis and findings if ever called to testify in court.

EXPERT LISTS

What follows below is our attempt to catalog current electronic evidence experts in today's marketplace. This list is merely a snapshot in time, as experts are continuously entering and exiting this evolving industry.

Electronic Discovery Service Providers

ACT Litigation Services
Bowne & Co.
CaseCentral Inc.
CaseData
Celerity Consulting
* Computer Forensics Inc.
Cricket Technologies
CompuLit Inc.
Daticon, Inc.
Discovery Mining Inc.
Discover-e Legal Inc.
* Doar Inc.
Dolphin Search Inc.
* Electronic Evidence Discovery, Inc.
Evidence Exchange
Fast Track Litigation Support
Fios, Inc.
Forensics Consulting Solutions
* FTI Consulting, Inc.
Ibis Consulting Inc.
IKON Office Solutions Inc.
Iron Mountain
* Kroll Ontrack Inc.
Lexis Nexis—Applied Discovery, Inc.

---

* Denotes a Provider of both E-Discovery and Computer Forensic Services

LitGroup.com
Litigation Solution Inc.
Merrill Corp.
On-site Sourcing, Inc.
Quorum Litigation Services
Spinelli Corp.
Steelpoint Technologies Inc.
TrueData Partners
Zantaz

Computer Forensics (only) Service Providers

Data Recovery Services Inc.
Deloitte & Touche
Ernst & Young
Guidance Software
KPMG
New Technologies Inc.
Online Security Inc.
PriceWaterhouse Coopers

E-Discovery and Computer Forensics Software Solutions

EnCase (Guidance Software)
Discovery Cracker (DocuLex)
HardCopy Pro Plus (Mobius Solutions, Inc.)
eDataMatrix (nMatrix Inc.)
Z-Print (Image Capture Engineering, Inc.)
dtSearch (dtSearch Corp.)

INDUSTRY SURVEYS

Several independent organizations have polled law firms and corporations regarding their choice of electronic discovery and computer forensic experts. These survey results provide guidance when navigating the sea of electronic evidence experts currently operating in this marketplace.

AmLaw Technology Survey

2002 (Seventh Annual Survey) was the first time that American Lawyer asked firms about their choice of electronic discovery vendors.

Figure 3.16 AmLaw Survey of Electronic Evidence Vendors Used by
Law Firms—2002

What electronic evidence vendors has the firm used in the past year?

	Firms	2002	2001
[Kroll] Ontrack	42	57%	n/a
Electronic Evidence	32	43%	n/a
Applied Discovery	24	32%	n/a
Fios	14	19%	n/a
Daticon	8	11%	n/a
Deloitte & Touche	4	5%	n/a
Other	22	30%	n/a

(74 firms answering)
Multiple answers allowed so total percentages exceed 100.
http://www.law.com/special/professionals/amlaw/2002/tech_survey/applications_
software.shtml

The same question was also asked in 2003 (Eighth Annual Survey).

Figure 3.17 AmLaw Survey of Electronic Evidence Vendors Used by
Law Firms—2003

What electronic evidence vendors has the firm used in the past year?

	FIRMS	2003	2002
Kroll Ontrack	36	31%	57%
Daticon	29	25%	11%
Applied Discovery	27	24%	32%
Electronic Evidence	26	23%	43%
Fios	19	17%	19%
Merrill	12	10%	—
Doar	8	7%	—
Deloitte & Touche	6	5%	5%
PricewaterhouseCoopers	6	5%	—
KPMG	4	4%	—
None	26	23%	—
Other	36	31%	30%

(115 firms answering; multiple responses allowed)
http://www.law.com/special/professionals/2003/basics.shtml

Corporate Counsel Survey

Corporate Counsel magazine conducts a yearly survey of in-house legal
departments, asking about technology and vendors used by America's
corporate legal departments. The 2003 results are listed below. The re-

sults are quite surprizing. However, they may be explained by the reality that most e-evidence matters are managed by outside counsel.

Figure 3.18 Knowledge Management and Electronic Data Discovery

In the past two years has the legal department used any electronic data discovery vendors?

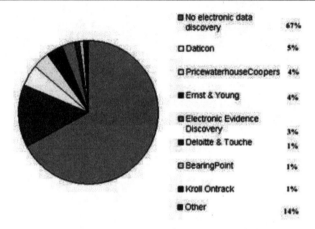

▣ No electronic data discovery	67%
▢ Daticon	5%
▢ PricewaterhouseCoopers	4%
■ Ernst & Young	4%
▣ Electronic Evidence Discovery	3%
■ Deloitte & Touche	1%
▢ BearingPoint	1%
■ Kroll Ontrack	1%
■ Other	14%

CHAPTER ❖ 4

Putting all of the pieces together

4.1 Practical Considerations

In this text, we have tried to shed light on what we deemed to be the most important and impactful topics relating to electronic evidence. While we feel that this text is comprehensive, it is by no means the final word. If one thing is true, it is that the legal and technical realities of electronic evidence continue to evolve at a breakneck pace. It will be the responsibilities of the authors and every reader to keep pace with these inevitable changes and continue to truly integrate the realities of the digital age into the practice of law.

After completing this text, it may seem as though there is an impossible amount of information to be absorbed and integrated into your already hectic practice. But, as we pointed out, it is really the same game with just some slightly new rules. The best advice we can give is to remember that all of the principles and realities of discovery and of litigation still apply in the electronic world. It is just a matter of learning a few new twists. To that end, we have compiled some key points to remember and focus on moving forward. They are as follows:

- **Remember marginal utility.** The issues at stake in your litigation and the amount in controversy in the case should govern the scope to which e-evidence issues are explored, just as they govern the degree to which aspects of all cases are pursued. Evaluate how much it will cost to collect, review, and produce the electronic evidence and look for cost-shifting arguments. The challenge is to engage in electronic discovery appropriately without spending undue time or money on this aspect of your case.

- **Remember Rule 26.** Whether you are working on a case involving hundreds of backup tapes or just a single hard drive, do not forget basic discovery principles. You are looking for relevant documents—this does not mean you need to review every piece of paper your client ever created. Remember also that most e-evidence case law centers on the realities of Federal Rule of Civil Procedure 26(b)(2)(i), (ii), (iii), which can be a litigator's best friend. Take the time to review them and employ them in your arguments.

- **Be careful what you wish for and remember the goose and gander lesson.** Be careful what you wish for....you just might get it. Sometimes, a producing party's strategy is to dump a mound of electronic documents on the receiving party. Then, you are faced with the burden of reviewing it all. While your opposing party might hand over the smoking gun, the fact that it is extremely buried will make it challenging for you to find. Worse yet, beware of the "goose and gander" phenomenon. Whatever you request your opponent to produce, they will ask the same of you. Consider scope limitations in your pre-trial conferences with the opposing party.

- **Do not be intimidated by the technology.** Computer forensics and electronic discovery are not as hard as they seem. Grasp the overarching themes and make the technology conform to your case strategy, the rest will fall into place. Also, consider cultivating a relationship with an expert resource that you can trust. You will find that your understanding of both the technology and legal issues consistently improve.

4.2 Where do we go from here? What is on the horizon?

We are standing on the brink of cutting-edge technological and legal developments with regards to computer forensics and electronic discovery. What are our predictions as to where this industry will go?

- **Rule developments.** The Federal Rules of Civil Procedure Advisory Committee has held several meetings and requested input from leaders in the field. Based on committee members' indications, the committee is likely to propose changes to the Federal Rules of Civil Procedure (specifically Rule 26 and 34). The breadth and depth of the changes is unknown; however, they will likely address the role of metadata and acceptable formats for disclosure and production of electronic evidence. It is likely that any changes promulgated by the committee will not come into effect until 2008 or beyond, given the very nature of the rule-making process and the current pace of the committee. (*See* remarks by Judge Shira Ann Scheindlin at the "Electronic Evidence Thought Leadership Luncheon" in New York City on September 23, 2003, www.krollontrack.com.)

- **New common law rules**. Litigators practicing in this area will see continued electronic discovery and computer forensics common law development, specifically case law outlining "reasonableness" and "fairness" tests and factors. Also, look for development on topics previously untouched by courts, such as voicemail, instant messaging, etc. As judges become more savvy on these topics, they will not shy away from tackling issues where there is currently little direction. The continued evolution of case decisions and any diverging viewpoints based upon geography or case type will be interesting to track. It is likely that this evolution will continue to provide opportunities for advocacy well into the future.

- **Continued development of "best practices" standards by legal think tanks and other influencing groups**. Law and policy think tanks, like The Sedona Conference and other influencing bodies, such as the American Bar Association, have issued "best practices" guides for dealing with electronic evidence. Similar to Restatements, these guidelines are not law. Yet groups of lawyers, scholars, and judges from across the country have honed these documents to make them as useful as possible to practitioners. Look for further refinement of these guidelines and issuance of standards in other areas, such as electronic document retention and preservation. (*See The Sedona Principles: Best Practices Recommendations and Principles for Addressing Electronic Document Production,* http://www.thesedonaconference.org/publications_html. *See also* the American Bar Association's Civil Discovery Standards pertaining to electronic discovery, http://www.abanet.org/litigation/taskforces/electronic/home.html.)

- **New technological developments.** Just as quickly as the legal world is catching up to speed on these issues, technological developments continue to occur. Software engineers in this area are working on tackling foreign character data, e-mail chain tracking, message retrieval from uncommon e-mail packages, and production of documents in an online repository format.

The final lesson from all of this is simple: stay tuned.

APPENDIX ❖ A

Electronic Discovery and Computer Forensics Case Law (Organized by Topic)

Discoverability

- *Bethea v. Comcast*, 218 F.R.D. 328 (D.D.C. 2003). Former employee sought to compel the defendant to allow her to inspect their computer systems to determine whether the defendant possessed any additional documents that had not yet been produced in discovery. The defendant argued that the plaintiff should not be allowed to inspect its computers because the defendant had already produced all unprivileged documents in response to the plaintiff's discovery requests. Additionally, the defendant claimed that the plaintiff did not show that relevant material existed on the computer systems or that the defendant was unlawfully withholding documents. Ruling in favor of the defendant, the court noted that the plaintiff did not show that the documents she sought actually existed or that the defendant unlawfully failed to produce them. The court further declared that mere suspicion that another party failed to respond to document requests was not enough to justify court-ordered inspection of the defendant's computer systems.
- *Farmers Ins. Co. v. Peterson*, 81 P.3d 659 (Okla. 2003). In a discovery dispute, the district court ordered the defendant to search insurance claim files for the years 2000, 2001, and 2002 and to pro-

duce documents containing complaints from Oklahoma insureds on medical payment claims. The defendant insurer claimed the request was unduly burdensome because to comply, it would have to manually examine 600,000 closed paper files and 3,300-3,400 electronic files. The defendant estimated the average examination time per file at 30 minutes. On appeal from the district court order, the Oklahoma Supreme Court noted that the expenditure of time and money to conduct the search in accordance with the plaintiff's request would be unduly burdensome on the defendant. However, the court was hesitant to excuse the defendant from meeting the plaintiff's discovery demands noting that the defendants "unilateral decision on how it stores information cannot, by itself, be a sufficient reason for placing discoverable matter outside the scope of discovery." The court ordered the defendant to use a statistical sampling technique to meet the trial court's "muster for integrity of the process and protect both litigants from distortive effects" to produce discovery.

- *In re Ford Motor Company*, 345 F.3d 1315 (11th Cir. 2003). The plaintiff brought claims against Ford Motor Company alleging that the seatbelt buckle of her automobile, which unlatched during an accident, was defectively designed. After serving several document requests, the plaintiff filed a motion to compel seeking direct access to Ford's electronic databases to conduct searches for claims related to unlatching seatbelt buckles. These databases recorded all customer contacts with Ford, as well as all records of dealers and personnel, among other things. The trial court granted the plaintiff's motion to compel. Ford appealed, filing petition for a writ of mandamus. The appellate court held that the plaintiff was not entitled to direct, unlimited access to Ford's computer databases, stating that without constraints, the lower court's order granted the plaintiff access to information that would not be discoverable without Ford first having had an opportunity to object.

- *Theofel v. Farey Jones*, 341 F.3d 978 (9th Cir. 2003), *amended by*, 359 F.3d 1066 (9th Cir. 2004). Seeking email discovery, a party in a commercial litigation issued a third party subpoena on the opposing party's Internet Service Provider (ISP). Instead of limiting the scope of the subpoena to particular subject matters, custodians, or time periods, the subpoena sought all email to or from the opposing party. The ISP substantially complied, but when the opposing party learned of the subpoena, it moved to quash. The court severely criticized the subpoenaing party for its overbroad subpoena and issued $9,000 in sanctions. The employees of the subpoenaed party then brought a new civil suit against the subpoenaing party and its attorney under the Stored Communications Act, the Wiretap Act and the Computer Fraud and Abuse Act. The trial court granted a motion to dismiss the new suit, finding that no claim was stated. The Ninth Circuit reversed and reinstated the civil suit, holding that an overbroad subpoena is not valid especially when directed against a third party that may not have the resources to oppose the subpoena. The ISP's consent by complying with the email production was invalid since the subpoenaing party had at least constructive knowledge of the subpoena's invalidity and thus any consent was obtained deceptively and through mistake.

- *First USA Bank v. PayPal, Inc.*, 76 Fed.Appx. 935 (Fed.Cir. 2003). In a patent infringement action, the plaintiff subpoenaed the defendant's former chief executive officer, specifically requesting the court to compel his deposition and to require him to produce his laptop computer for forensic inspection. The former-CEO had used the computer while employed by the defendant and subsequently purchased it from the defendant when he left its employ. Despite objection, the magistrate judge ordered the former-CEO to be available for deposition and approved a search protocol. The search protocol allowed electronic evidence consultants to create a forensic copy of the computer's hard drive, identify any potentially relevant documents, and, if such documents were found and identified, allow the former-CEO to create a privilege log. The district court affirmed the magistrate's order and former-CEO appealed. The appellate court dismissed the former-CEO's appeal of the lower court's non-final interlocutory discovery order.

- *United States v. Bailey*, 272 F.Supp.2d 822 (D.Neb. 2003). The FBI suspected that an employee within American Family Insurance was distributing child pornography using his company email account. Pursuant to a subpoena, American Family Insurance accessed the contents of the defendant's email account and reported to the FBI that pornographic images were found. Based on this information, the FBI was issued a warrant to search the defendant's office space and computer. The defendant moved to suppress evidence of child pornography located during the search of his work computer. The court held that the defendant did not have an expectation of privacy in the information stored

on his work computer given his employer's practices, procedures, and regulation over the use of the computer property.
Specifically, the company had a log-in notice that warned of possible monitoring or searching and required users to click "OK"
to proceed. The employer also posted company computer-use
policies on its intranet site and sent email notification to all users
reminding them to read the policy.

- *Wright v. AmSouth Bancorp*, 320 F.3d 1198 (11th Cir. 2003). In an
age discrimination suit, the plaintiff sought discovery of computer disks and tapes containing "all word processing files created, modified and/or accessed" by five of the defendant's employees spanning a two and a half year period. The court denied
the plaintiff's motion to compel because his request was overly
broad and unduly burdensome and made no reasonable showing of relevance.

- *Bryant v. Aventis Pharmaceuticals, Inc.*, 2002 WL 31427434 (S.D.
Ind. Oct. 21, 2002). The Indiana court mentioned without further
comment that emails were recovered from the plaintiff's computer after her termination, confirming the general discoverability of email evidence. The court considered the content of these
emails in granting summary judgment in favor of the defendant.

- *In re CI Host, Inc.*, 92 S.W.3d 514 (Tex. 2002). Customers brought
a breach of contract class action against the company hosting
their web services. During discovery, the trial court ordered the
defendant to preserve and produce computer backup tapes containing potentially relevant evidence. The defendant objected
that the request was overbroad, demanded confidential information, and was in violation of the federal Electronic Communications Privacy Act. The appellate court held that in light of
the defendant's failure to produce evidence supporting its objections as required by Texas Rule of Civil Procedure 193.4(a),
the trial court did not abuse its discretion in ordering the contents of the tapes to be produced.

- *Southern Diagnostic Assoc. v. Bencosme*, 833 So. 2d 801 (Fla. Dist.
Ct. App. 2002). The appellate court quashed an order against
Southern Diagnostic, a non-party in an insurance suit brought
by Bencosme, compelling discovery of certain contents of its
computer system. The appellate court held that that trial court's
order was overly broad, setting no parameters or limitations on
the inspection of Southern Diagnostic's computer system and
make no account that the computer system contained confidential and privileged information. The appellate court directed the

trial court to craft a narrowly tailored order that accomplishes the purposes of the discovery requests and provides for confidentiality.

- *Collette v. St. Luke's Roosevelt Hospital*, 2002 WL 31159103 (S.D.N.Y. Sept. 26, 2002). The New York court mentioned without further comment that emails were made available during discovery, confirming the general discoverability of email evidence.
- *MHC Investment Comp. v. Racom Corp.*, 209 F.R.D. 431 (S.D. Iowa 2002). The Iowa court mentioned without further comment that emails were made available during discovery confirming the general discoverability of email evidence.
- *Rowe Entertainment, Inc. v. The William Morris Agency*, 2002 WL 975713 (S.D.N.Y. May 9,2002). "Rules 26(b) and 34 for the Federal Rules of Civil Procedure instruct that computer-stored information is discoverable under the same rules that pertain to tangible, written materials."
- *Stallings-Daniel v. Northern Trust Co.*, 2002 WL 385566 (N.D. 111. Mar. 12, 2002). In an employment discrimination action, the plaintiff moved for reconsideration of the court's denial of electronic discovery of the defendant's email system. The court, in denying the plaintiff's motion for reconsideration, determined that the plaintiff presented no new information that justified an intrusive electronic investigation.
- *Dikeman v. Stearns*, 560 S.E.2d 115 (Ga. Ct. App. 2002). In a suit brought by a law firm regarding its client's unpaid legal invoices, the defendant requested, among other things, a full and complete copy of the law firm's computer hard drive that was used to generate documents pertaining to the defendant's case. Refusing to order the discovery, the court found the defendant's requests to be overbroad, oppressive, annoying.
- *McPeek v. Ashcroft*, 202 F.R.D. 31 (D.D.C. 2001). ". . . [E]conomic considerations have to be pertinent if the court is to remain faithful to its responsibility to prevent 'undue burden or expense' . . . If the likelihood of finding something was the only criterion, there is a risk that someone will have to spend hundreds of thousands of dollars to produce a single email. That is an awfully expensive needle to justify searching a haystack."
- *Ex Parte Wal-mart, Inc.*, 809 So. 2d 818 (Ala. 2001). In a personal injury case, the plaintiff sought discovery of Wal-mart's electronic database containing customer incident reports and employee accident review forms. The appellate court held that dis-

covery order should have been restricted to falling-merchandise incidents with geographic and temporal limits set forth by the trial court.

- *White v. White*, 781 A.2d 85 (N.J. Super. Ct. Ch. Div. 2001). In a divorce action, the husband filed a motion to suppress his email that had been stored on the hard drive of the family computer. The court held that the wife did not unlawfully access stored electronic communications in violation of the New Jersey Wiretap Act and did not intrude on his seclusion by accessing those emails. "Having a legitimate reason for being in the files, plaintiff had a right to seize evidence she believed indicated her husband was being unfaithful. . . . Is rummaging through files in a computer hard drive any different than rummaging through files in an unlocked file cabinet . . . Not really."

- *Demelash v. Ross Stores, Inc.*, 20 P.3d 447 (Wash. Ct. App. 2001). In an action for a false shoplifting arrest, the court stated, "A trial court must manage the discovery process in a fashion that promotes full disclosure of relevant information while at the same time protecting against harmful side effects. Consequently, a court may appropriately limit discovery to protect against requests that are unduly burdensome or expensive." The court limited the scope of to a computerized summary of the store's files.

- *Milwaukee Police Assoc. v. Jones*, 615 N.W.2d 190 (Wis. Ct. App. 2000). In considering the provisions of the state's open records laws, the court concluded that the city's production of an analog tape was insufficient when a digital version existed. The court stated, "A potent open records law must remain open to technological advances so that its statutory terms remain true to the law's intent."

- *Itzenson v. Hartford Life and Accident Ins. Co.*, 2000 WL 1507422 (E.D. Pa. Oct. 10, 2000). "It is difficult to believe that in the computer era" that the defendant could not identify files and filter out information based on specific categories.

- *In re Dow Corning Corp.*, 250 B.R. 298 (Bankr. E.D. Mich. 2000). Federal Government did not satisfy its obligation to make medical records stored in computer databases available to Debtor, where Government directed Debtor to warehouses around the world where the information was stored.

- *Van Westrienen v. Americontinental Collection Corp.*, 189 F.R.D. 440 (D. Or. 1999). The court held that "plaintiffs are not entitled to unbridled access [of] defendant's computer system . . . plaintiffs should pursue other less burdensome alternatives, such as identifying the number of letters and their content."

■ *Caldera, Inc. v. Microsoft Corp.*, 72 F.Supp.2d 1295 (D. Utah 1999). A federal district court found that a series of intra-company emails offered "direct evidence" that the corporation was actively trying to destroy a competitor.

■ *Playboy Enters., Inc. v. Welles*, 60 F.Supp.2d 1050 (S.D. Cal. 1999). The court held that the defendant's hard drive was discoverable because it was likely that relevant information was stored on it. Production of such electronic information would not be unduly burdensome upon the defendant.

■ *Linnen v. A.H. Robins Co.*, 1999 WL 462015 (Mass. Super. June 16, 1999). "A discovery request aimed at the production of records retained in some electronic form is no different in principle, from a request for documents contained in any office file cabinet." The court continued, "To permit a corporation such as Wyeth to reap the business benefits of such [computer] technology and simultaneously use that technology as a shield in litigation would lead to incongruous and unfair results."

■ *Symantec Corp. v. McAfee Assoc., Inc.*, 1998 WL 740807 (N.D. Cal. Aug. 14, 1998). The plaintiff sought to obtain the entire source code for all of the defendant's products dating back to 1995, as well as copies of all hard drives which had access to the server from which the information was copied. The court found that production of this magnitude would be unduly burdensome to the defendant, both in terms of volume and in terms of the proprietary nature of the information sought.

■ *Storch v. IPCO Safety Prods. Co.*, 1997 WL 401589 (E.D. Pa. July 16, 1997). "This Court finds that in this age of high-technology where much of our information is transmitted by computer and computer disks, it is not unreasonable for the defendant to produce the information on computer disk for the plaintiff."

■ *Strasser v. Yalamanchi*, 669 So. 2d 1142 (Fla. Dist. Ct. App. 1996). The court ruled that the trial court's discovery order should be quashed because (1) unrestricted access to defendant's entire computer system was overly broad and would pose a threat to confidential records and (2) there was little evidence that the purged documents could be retrieved.

■ *Fennell v. First Step Designs, Ltd.*, 83 F.3d 526 (1st Cir. 1996). The court denied the plaintiff's broad request for discovery of defendant's entire hard drive. The court explained that the costs, burdens, delays, and likelihood of discovering the evidence must be weighed against the importance of the requested evidence. The court held requesting party must show a "particularized likelihood of discovering appropriate material."

- *Anti-Monopoly, Inc. v. Hasbro, Inc.*, 1995 WL 649934 (S.D.N.Y. Nov. 3, 1995). "The law is clear that data in computerized form is discoverable even if paper 'hard copies' of the information have been produced. . . [T]oday it is black letter law that computerized data is discoverable if relevant."

- *Murlas Living Trust v. Mobil Oil Corp.*, 1995 WL 124186 (N.D. 111. Mar. 20, 1995). The court refused to require the defendant to undergo intrusive or burdensome discovery for its electronic files where the burden is not justified by the relevance of the evidence likely to be discovered.

- *Crown Life Ins. Co. v. Craig*, 995 F.2d 1376 (7th Cir. 1993). Computer data is discoverable under Federal Rule of Procedure 34.

- *Aviles v. McKenzie*, 1992 WL 715248 (N.D. Cal. Mar. 17, 1992). In an action involving claims of wrongful termination and employment discrimination, the plaintiff presented email messages that demonstrated he was fired for whistle blowing about unsafe and illegal company practices.

- *Lawyers Title Ins. Co. v. United States Fidelity & Guar. Co.*, 122 F.R.D. 567 (N.D. Cal. 1988). The court rejected, as broadly framed and intrusive, a request to inspect the responding party's entire computer system where it was a mere possibility that responding party might produce applicable documents. The court required a showing that this inspection would lead to evidence that had not already been produced.

- *Santiago v. Miles*, 121 F.R.D. 636 (W.D.N.Y. 1988). The court noted that "[a] request for raw information in computer banks is proper and the information is obtainable under the discovery rules."

- *Daewoo Elecs. Co. v. United States*, 650 F. Supp. 1003 (Ct. Int'l Trade 1986), *rev'd on other grounds* 6 F.3d 1511 (Fed. Cir. 1993). The court rejected the government's narrow discovery position, stating that disclosure orders should be construed liberally and should not be impeded by technical objections. The court further explained, "[I]t would be a dangerous development in the law if new techniques for easing the use of information become a hindrance to discovery of disclosure in litigation."

- *Bills v. Kennecott Corp.*, 108 F.R.D. 459 (C.D. Utah 1985). "[C]ertain propositions will be applicable in virtually all cases, namely, that information stored in computers should be as freely discoverable as information not stored in computers, so parties requesting discovery should not be prejudiced thereby; and the party responding is usually in the best and most economical position to call up its own computer stored data."

Procedure

- *In re Merrill Lynch & Co., Inc. Research Reports Sec. Litig.*, 2004 WL 305601 (S.D.N.Y Feb. 18, 2004). Pursuant to a section of the Securities Exchange Act of 1934, the plaintiff sought an order lifting the automatic stay of discovery during the pendency of a motion to dismiss. The plaintiff contended that discovery was necessary to preserve and restore emails deleted by the defendant. The court cited U.S. Code provisions permitting discovery when the legal sufficiency of the complaint has not been decided "only if exceptional circumstances, such as the necessity 'to preserve evidence or to prevent undue prejudice to [a] party,' exist." The defendant declared that it was aware of the preservation obligations and was taking all necessary steps to preserve all potentially relevant electronic documents. Therefore, the court denied the plaintiff's motion because the plaintiff failed to establish an "imminent risk" of data being deleted and rendered irretrievable.

- *Fraser v. Nationwide Mutual Ins. Co.*, 352 F.3d 107 (3rd Cir. 2003). In an employment termination suit, the plaintiff alleged that the defendant violated the Electronic Communications Privacy Act (ECPA) by searching, without the plaintiff's express permission, the plaintiff's email stored on the defendant's central file server. The ECPA prohibits "intentionally access[ing] without authorization a facility through which an electronic communication service is provided." The court held that because the plaintiff's email was stored on the defendant's system, the defendant's search of the plaintiff's email fell within the exception to protection of the ECPA, which allows seizures of email authorized "by the person or entity providing a wire or electronic communication service."

- *Go2Net, Inc. v. CI Host, Inc.*, 60 P.3d 1245 (Wash. Ct. App. 2003). After discovery commenced in a suit to collect payment due under a services contract, the parties exchanged document requests. In responding to the defendant's requests, the plaintiff provided some documents, but advised that one of its servers had crashed and was in the process of being rebuilt. The plaintiff stated that it would supplement its production at a later date.

A day prior to the summary judgment hearing in the case, the plaintiff produced the additional emails from the rebuilt server. The trial court issued summary judgment in favor of the plaintiff. On appeal, the defendant argued that the trial court abused its discretion in refusing to vacate the summary judgment order in light of "newly discovered evidence," namely the internal email messages produced just prior to the summary judgment hearing. The appellate court found that the email messages were not "newly discovered evidence" where there was nothing to suggest that the plaintiff deliberately tried to hide these documents.

- *Dodge, Warren, & Peters Ins. Servs. v. Riley,* 130 Cal.Rptr.2d 385 (Cal. Ct. App. 2003). Prior to termination of their employment, the defendants copied and took with them volumes of computerized data maintained in the plaintiff's files and storage media. The plaintiff sued the defendants alleging claims of misappropriation of trade secrets, unfair business practices, breach of fiduciary duty and breach of contract. The appellate court affirmed the trial court's order issuing a preliminary injunction against the defendants, requiring the preservation of electronic evidence and ordering them to allow a court-appointed expert to copy the data, recover lost or deleted files, and perform automated searches of the evidence under guidelines agreed to by the parties or established by the court.

- *United States v. Moussaoui,* 2003 WL 548699 (E.D.Va. Jan. 7, 2003). The defendant claims that the government failed to provide him with information retrieved from various computers used by the defendant. The court held that the government provided the defendant with sufficient information, including: information about the authentication of the computer hard drives, confirmation that the computer evidence had not been contaminated, the timing of the forensic examinations, and the software used to restore a hard drive image. The court further stated that the defense possessed the computer hard drives at issue and had expert resources and subpoena power to conduct any further investigation it deemed necessary.

- *In re Livent, Inc. Noteholders Sec. Litig.,* 2003 WL 23254 (S.D.N.Y. Jan. 2, 2003). In a securities litigation, the defendant accounting firm produced approximately 25 email pages from the files of a particular individual at issue, in addition to 14 emails from other employees. The plaintiffs suspected this production was incomplete, and moved the court for: (1) an order "directing Deloitte to make a thorough search of all its computer systems, servers and other storage devices, back-up tapes, and the individual hard drives of employees who worked on the Livent audits" and (2) an order directing the defendant "to produce all responsive materials found within 30 days, along with a written explanation of all the steps it has taken to find responsive materials." The court denied the plaintiffs request and directed the defendant to produce a written explanation of all steps taken to find responsive email. The court directed the parties to consult the *Rowe* decision and, if unable to reach resolution, to inform the court.

- *In re Amsted Indus.*, 2002 WL 31844956 (N.D.Ill. Dec. 17, 2002). In a suit by the plaintiff employees against their employer for breach of fiduciary duty and other wrongs stemming from a hostile takeover with use of employee stock assets, the court considered the plaintiffs' various discovery motions, including a motion compelling the defendants to retrieve email and documents generated on or after January 1, 1997. In response to the plaintiffs' discovery requests, the defendants limited its investigation to word searches of its backup tapes and only produced relevant documents generated after January 1, 1999. The production did not include email. The plaintiffs argued that the defendants' search of electronic documents was inadequate, and that the defendants should have actually searched the hard drive of each individual defendant and each person having access to relevant information. The court ordered the defendants to re-search their backup tapes under a broader subject matter and time period. The court also indicated they should search the in-box, saved, and sent folders of any relevant individual's email in the same manner. The court determined the additional searches were not so burdensome or expensive as to require a limiting of the requests.

- *Gambale v. Deutsche Bank*, 2002 WL 31655326 (S.D.N.Y. Nov. 21, 2002). As a step toward resolving several discovery disputes, the Magistrate Judge ordered the defendants to serve an affidavit explaining the steps they have taken to search their paper and electronic files for documents responsive to the plaintiffs discovery requests and outlining the feasibility and cost of retrieving such electronic documents. The Magistrate then stated that the plaintiff must choose between two options for producing the electronic data: (1) follow the protocol set forth in *Rowe Entertainment v. William Morris Agency*, 205 F.R.D. 421 (S.D.N.Y. 2002), with the slight modification set forth in *Murphy Oil USA, Inc. v. Fluor Daniel, Inc.*, 2002 WL 246439 (E.D.La. Feb. 19, 2002), or (2) confer with the defendant and propose a joint protocol.

- *Kormendi v. Computer Associates Int'l, Inc.*, 2002 WL 31385832 (S.D.N.Y. Oct. 21, 2002). The parties in this employment case jointly wrote the Magistrate, requesting reconsideration and clarification of a prior order. The court previously had ordered the defendant to produce all email messages mentioning the plaintiff over a one-year time period, with the plaintiff to pay for the cost of the search. In the letter to the Magistrate, the defendant stated that it had already produced the emails from persons involved in the suit and had no method to locate and reconstruct emails mentioning the plaintiff for the listed period because its document retention policy called for employees to retain emails for a period of only thirty days. The Magistrate noted that the plaintiff should seek other means of attaining the sought after emails, such as searching the computers of other employees who might have saved the emails. The plaintiff must still bear the cost of searching for these emails.

- *Advanced Micro Devices, Inc. v. Intel Corp.*, 292 F.3d 664 (9th Cir. 2002). In a dispute relating to the market conduct of Intel Corp, Advanced filed a complaint with the European Commission, and sought discovery according to practices and rules in the United States under federal law. Adopting a broad interpretation of the scope of discovery rights in cases involving foreign tribunals, the court permitted domestic-style discovery under 28 U.S.C. § 1782 in an investigation conducted by the European Community Directorate.

- *Thompson v. Thompson*, 2002 WL 1072342 (D.N.H. May 30, 2002). The copying of email messages from the hard drive of a personal computer does not constitute interception of electronic communications for the purposes of the Electronic Communications Privacy Act of 1986. The court reasoned that an interception can only occur "during transmission" of electronic communication transfers; thus, the acquisition of stored email does not qualify as an interception under the ECPA.

- *The Gorgen Co. v. Brecht*, 2002 WL 977467 (Minn. Ct. App. May 14, 2002). The plaintiff brought suit against former employees for misappropriation of trade secrets. Prior to serving the complaint, the plaintiff obtained a TRO, which prohibited the defendants from destroying or altering electronic documents and provided for expedited discovery of relevant electronic data.

The appellate court found that the district court abused its discretion by issuing the TRO and by denying the defendants' motion to dissolve it. The appellate court stated, "Although the TRO seems reasonable on its face . . . this issue cannot be resolved at this early stage of the litigation without a showing of irreparable harm or without complying with the rules of procedure."

- *Tulip Computers Int'l v. Dell Computer Corp.*, 2002 WL 818061 (D.Del. Apr. 30, 2002). On the plaintiff's motion to compel in a patent infringement case, the court stated that "[T]he procedure that Tulip has suggested for the discovery of email documents seems fair, efficient, and reasonable." The court ordered the defendant to produce the hard disks of certain company executives to the plaintiff's electronic discovery expert for key word searching. After the expert completes the key word search, the plaintiff will give the defendant a list of the emails that contain those search terms. The defendant will then produce the emails to the plaintiff, subject to its own review for privilege and confidentiality.
- *Murphy Oil USA, Inc. v. Fluor Daniel, Inc.*, 2002 WL 246439 (E.D. La. Feb. 19, 2002). The court used the eight-factor balancing test set forth in *Rowe* to determine operating protocols and the cost shifting formula. It placed the burden on the producing party to elect one of two proposed protocols.
- *Rowe Entertainment, Inc. v. The William Morris Agency*, 205 F.R.D. 421 (S.D.N.Y. 2002). Denying defendants' motion for a protective order insofar as it sought to preclude the discovery of email altogether, the court set forth an eight factor balancing test for identifying responsive emails while protecting privileged documents. *See also Rowe Entertainment, Inc. v. The William Morris Agency*, 2002 WL 975713 (S.D.N.Y. May 9, 2002). After reanalyzing and reaffirming Judge Francis' eight factor balancing test, the court upheld the January 15, 2002 Order that granted defendants' motion to shift the costs of production of their email communications to the plaintiffs.
- *Columbia Communications v. Echostar*, 2 Fed.Appx. 360 (4th Cir. 2001). In a contract dispute, the court held that failure of the lessor to turn over certain computer databases during discovery did not justify a judgment for the distributor or a new trial.
- *Perez v. Volvo Car Corp.*, 247 F.3d 303 (1st Cir. 2001). In a suit under the Racketeer Influenced and Corrupt Organizations Act, internal Volvo emails, which could have made a dispositive dif-

ference on the issue of Volvo's knowledge of the fraud involved in the suit, were not called to the district court's attention until after the court had issued summary judgment. Volvo claimed these emails offered too little, too late. However, the First Circuit disagreed, "After all, Volvo did not produce the emails to the plaintiffs until January 2000 (the same month that Volvo filed its summary judgment motion)—and then only in Swedish. Given the timing, the sheer volume of documents involved in the case, and the need for translation, fundamental fairness counsels in favor of treating the emails as newly-discovered evidence within the purview of Federal Rule of Civil Procedure 59(e)."

- *Benton v. Allstate Ins. Co.*, 2001 WL 210685 (C.D. Cal. Feb. 26, 2001). The court refused to grant a continuance on the defendant's summary judgment motion where the plaintiff claimed that he had not had an adequate opportunity to conduct discovery of defendant's computer system. The court concluded that the plaintiff did not show that a further continuance was necessary to prevent irreparable harm or that further discovery will enable him to obtain evidence essential to his opposition to the motion.

- *America Online, Inc. v. Anonymous*, 542 S.E.2d 377 (Va. 2001). In a case of first impression, the court refused to allow a corporation to seek information from AOL without revealing its identity.

- *Superior Consultant Co. v. Bailey*, 2000 WL 1279161 (E.D. Mich. Aug. 22, 2000). The court ordered the defendant to create and produce for the plaintiff a backup file of the defendant's laptop computer, and a backup file of any personal computer harddrive to which the defendant had access.

- *United States v. VISA*, 1999 WL 476437 (S.D.N.Y. July 7, 1999). In a suit against VISA and MasterCard, the parties agreed to narrow the scope of the archived email search, both in terms of the number of employees whose email is to be produced and the number of days per month for which email is to be produced. The court reserved decision about which party will ultimately bear the cost of producing email.

- *Concord Boat v. Brunswick Corp.*, 1996 WL 33347247 (E.D.Ark. Dec. 23, 1996). The plaintiffs contend that the defendant's search for and production of relevant information was insufficient because it failed to review all computer documents and email. The plaintiffs filed motions to compel discovery of electronic information and to prevent further destruction of documents. The defendant asserted that the search was reasonable and submitted that the plaintiffs' demands were overly broad and unduly burdensome. The court ordered the parties to have a meeting with counsel and computer experts for both sides, conducting a good faith discussion to see whether agreement can be reached on a procedure to further search the defendant's email, the choice of an expert, the procedure for specifying the expert's responsibilities, and allocation of the costs. The court also ordered the defendant to produce a detailed description of the defendant's electronically stored information.

- *Carbon Dioxide Indus. Antitrust Litig.*, 155 F.R.D. 209 (M.D. Fla. 1993). "[D]epositions to identify how data is maintained and to determine what hardware and software is necessary to access the information are preliminary depositions necessary to proceed with merits discovery."

Production of Data

- *Ranta v. Ranta*, 2004 WL 504588 (Conn. Super. Feb. 25, 2004). In a recent divorce proceeding, a superior court judge ordered the plaintiff "to stop using, accessing, turning on, powering, copying, deleting, removing or uninstalling any programs, files and or folders, or booting up her lap top computer. . ." The order also directed the plaintiff to hand over all floppy disks, CDs, zip files or other similar types of computer storage devices. The judge further required the plaintiff to turn in her laptop to the court clerk's office. Both the plaintiff and the defendant were instructed to share equally all costs associated with hiring a computer forensics expert to inspect the laptop. Additionally, the defendant was required to buy a new laptop for the plaintiff.
- *Super Film of Am., Inc. v. UCB Films, Inc.*, 219 F.R.D. 649 (D. Kan. 2004). In a collection action, the defendant moved to compel the plaintiff to produce electronic data including email, spreadsheets, and databases. The plaintiff argued that it could not be compelled to produce the documents because it did not have control of the documents as required by FRCP Rule 34(a). The court determined that under Rule 34(a), the plaintiff possessed the requisite control because the plaintiff had "the right, authority, or ability to obtain the requested document." The plaintiff further contended that it had produced all electronic documents off of its two computer systems that were within its "knowledge and expertise" and offered to allow the defendant's technicians to inspect the computers. The defendant rejected this offer stat-

ing that it would unreasonably shift the discovery burden and expense to the defendant. The court agreed with the defendant, noting that "the court cannot relieve a party of its discovery obligations based simply on that party's unsupported assertion that such obligations are unduly burdensome." The court further found that the plaintiff did not make the required showing that complying with the defendant's request would unduly burden the plaintiff in terms of time, money, and procedure. Thus, the court ordered the plaintiff to produce the electronic documents within 30 days.

■ *Marcin Eng'g, L.L.C. v. Founders at Grizzly Ranch*, L.L.C., 2003 WL 23190385 (D.Colo. Dec. 18, 2003). The plaintiff brought suit for payment of civil engineering services provided to the defendant and moved for summary judgment. The defendant moved to deny summary judgment based on the need to reopen discovery, claiming that the plaintiff "intentionally withheld" computer data that was relevant and material to defendant's claims. The "withheld" data included the computerized versions of the plaintiff's work product, of which the defendant had already obtained hard copies. The court did not allow the defendant to reopen discovery because the defendant did not allege that the plaintiff's production was deficient (because it omitted the computerized versions) until nearly five months after the discovery cut-off. The court stated that the defendant "was dilatory both in failing to review Marcin's hard copy work product when it was timely produced and also in failing to inform Marcin and the court that it believed the production was incomplete." The plaintiff counterclaimed for sanctions against the defendant, stating that the defendant failed to produce certain documents responsive to the plaintiff's discovery requests, including an email that terminated the plaintiff from the project. The defendant asserted that it diligently searched for the email but could not find it. Based on defendant's diligent attempt to locate the documents, the court did not impose sanctions for failure to produce the documents.

■ *In re Honeywell Int'l Sec. Litig.*, 2003 WL 22722961 (S.D.N.Y. Nov. 18, 2003). In response to a subpoena, the defendant's financial auditor, a non-party to the securities suit, produced several thousand documents in hardcopy. The plaintiffs complained that they were unable to review the documents and sought an electronic version of these documents, or alternatively a complete hardcopy set produced in the order they are kept in the ordinary course of business, specifically claiming that the documents were produced in a way that makes it impossible to determine which attachment belongs with a particular document. The auditor claimed that it had provided a complete index for the documents and attachments and that electronic copies were only accessible with the aid of its proprietary software. The court found that the auditor's production was insufficient because it was not produced as kept in the usual course of business and ordered the auditor to produce its documents in electronic form.

- *Renda Marine v. United States*, 58 Fed.Cl. 57 (Fed. Cl. 2003). In a government contract suit, a dispute arose regarding both parties' duties to preserve evidence. Specifically, the plaintiff moved the court to compel access to the defendant's hard drives, backup tapes, and email systems, alleging that the defendant did not search any hard drives or backup tapes in preparing its response to the plaintiff's document production requests. The defendant denied these allegations. The plaintiff further alleged that the defendant routinely deleted email even after commencement of the suit and moved the court to sanction the defendant for such spoliation of evidence. The court held that, upon notice that litigation might occur, the defendant had a legal obligation to preserve evidence related to the plaintiff's claim. The court directed the defendant to produce, at its expense, backup tapes created after such notice and to provide the plaintiff with access to the requested hard drive. The court further ordered the defendant to produce backup tapes pre-dating notice of the suit at the plaintiff's expense.
- *Giardina v. Lockheed Martin Corp.*, 2003 WL 1338826 (E.D.La. Mar. 14, 2003). In an employment discrimination suit, the plaintiff's discovery requests sought a list of all "non-work related Internet sites" accessed with sixteen different company computers. The defendant objected to this request as overly broad and unduly burdensome as it would require creation of detailed and lengthy reports that would take many hours to compile. The magistrate judge granted plaintiff's motion to compel and awarded attorney fees and the District court affirmed.
- *Lakewood Eng'g v. Lasko Prod.*, 2003 WL 1220254 (N.D.Ill. Mar. 14, 2003). In a patent infringement suit, the plaintiff produced email and other electronic documents after the close of the discovery period. The court found that while the plaintiff did not engage in a good faith effort to produce all requested discovery in a

timely manner, the cost to the defendant was minimal and therefore refused to issue sanctions. To the extent that it had not already done so, the plaintiff was ordered to produce all emails generated or received by the inventor relating to the patent at issue.

- *Zhou v. Pittsburgh State University,* 2003 WL 1905988 (D.Kan. Feb. 5, 2003). In an employment discrimination suit, the plaintiff sought to compel the defendant to produce computer generated documents (instead of typewritten documents compiled by hand already produced) reflecting the salaries of defendant's faculty. Relying on the Advisory Committee Notes to F.R.C.P. 34, the court stated, "[T]he disclosing party must take reasonable steps to ensure that it discloses any back-up copies of files or archival tapes that will provide information about any 'deleted' electronic data." The court granted the plaintiff's motion to compel and ordered the defendant to disclose all data compilations, computerized data and other electronically-recorded information reflecting the salaries of defendant's faculty. The court further ordered the parties to preserve evidence that they know, or should know, is relevant to the ongoing litigation, including preservation of all data compilations, computerized data and other electronically-recorded information.

- *McPeek v. Ashcroft,* 212 F.R.D. 33 (D.D.C. 2003). In its August 1, 2001 Order, the court ordered the defendant to search certain backup tapes to assist in ascertaining whether additional searches were justified. After completing this backup tape sample, the parties could not agree whether the search results produced relevant information such that a second search was justified. The magistrate stated, "[t]he frustration of electronic discovery as it relates to backup tapes is that backup tapes collect information indiscriminately, regardless of topic. One, therefore, cannot reasonably predict that information is likely to be on a particular tape. This is unlike the more traditional type of discovery in which one can predict that certain information would be in a particular folder because the folders in a particular file drawer are arranged alphabetically by subject matter or by author." After examining the likelihood of relevant data being contained on each of the backup tapes, the magistrate ordered additional searches of selected backup tapes likely to contain relevant evidence.

- *York v. Hartford Underwriters Ins. Co.,* 2002 WL 31465306 (N.D.Okla. Nov. 4, 2002). In a case alleging bad faith in processing an insurance claim, the defendant opposed the plaintiff's 30(b)(6) deposition request on the subject of defendant's use of a claims adjusting software program called "Colossus." The court found that the defendant failed to demonstrate that the "Colossus" program was proprietary or confidential and ordered that the plaintiff should be given the opportunity to discover what data was inputted into "Colossus" concerning her claim. The court also ordered the defendant to provide a Rule 30(b)(6) witness to testify to the use of the "Colossus" program. Granting part of the defendant's motion for a protective order, the court held that the nature and extent of the defendant's use of "Colossus" may be confidential and entitled to protection from third parties.

■ *Eolas Technologies Inc. v. Microsoft Corp.*, 2002 WL 31375531 (N.D.Ill. Oct. 18,2002). In a patent infringement suit against Microsoft, the parties engaged in extensive motion practice, both on dispositive summary judgment issues and on various discovery issues. With regard to one discovery motion aimed at obtaining information which the defendant alleged was outside the scope of the issues in the case, the court restricted discovery to spreadsheet data regarding licenses, revenue and profitability of "accused server versions of Windows 2000 and Windows NT 4.0 operating system software with Internet Explorer." With regard to another discovery motion, addressing whether certain email messages in a chain of messages must be produced, the court ordered the defendant to produce certain emails to and from one key individual so that the court could analyze the documents *in camera* and then make a determination as to whether the plaintiff is entitled to receive them in an unredacted form.

■ *Jones v. Goord*, 2002 WL 1007614 (S.D.N.Y. May 16,2002). The plaintiffs, prison inmates bringing suit against the New York State Corrections Commission for prison overcrowding, requested the production of six different electronic databases maintained by the New York state prison system. The plaintiffs claimed that the electronic information would be more valuable than the already produced hard copies because the information would be more manipulable. The court refused to compel discovery of the databases because the burden of the proposed discovery outweighed its likely benefit, particularly in light of the plaintiff's failure to seek discovery in a timelier manner and the vast amount of material that had already been produced in hard copy. The court stated, "As electronic mechanisms for storing and retrieving data have become more common, it has increasingly behooved courts and counsel to become familiar with such methods, and to develop expertise and procedures for incorporating 'electronic discovery' into the familiar rituals of litigation."

- *Kaufman v. Kinko's Inc.*, 2002 WL 32123851 (Del. Ch. Apr. 16, 2002). The court granted the plaintiffs' motion to compel the defendants' production of certain email messages retrievable from the defendant backup system. The defendants' argument that the burdens of the retrieval process outweighed any evidentiary benefit that the plaintiffs would obtain from the documents was unpersuasive. Instead, the court stated, "Upon installing a data storage system, it must be assumed that at some point in the future one may need to retrieve the information previously stored. That there may be deficiencies in the retrieval system . . . cannot be sufficient to defeat an otherwise good faith request to examine the relevant information."

- *United States Fidelity & Guaranty Co. v. Braspetro Oil Servs. Co.*, 2002 WL 15652 (S.D.N.Y. Jan. 7, 2002). In a discovery dispute concerning the potential waiver of privilege with respect to materials provided to defendants' expert witnesses, the court ordered the defendants to produce all materials provided to their experts—privileged or unprivileged, whether in paper or electronic form.

- *Braxton v. Farmer's Ins. Group*, 209 F.R.D. 651 (N.D.Ala. 2002). In a class action brought under the Fair Credit Reporting Act, the plaintiffs sought emails from non-party individual insurance agents of the defendant's insurance company. The defendant objected, claiming that enforcement of the subpoena would subject the agents to an undue burden. The court refused to require the non-party insurance agents to engage in the task of "combing through their email files and other records in search of the documents sought by the plaintiff." The court ordered the defendant to locate and produce relevant emails, newsletters, and other correspondence that it sent to its agents.

- *McNally Tunneling v. City of Evanston*, 2001 WL 1568879 (N.D. 111. Dec. 10, 2001). In a dispute between a construction contractor and the City of Evanston, the court denied Evanston widescale access to both hard-copy and electronic versions of McNally's computer files where Evanston's need for both sets of documents was not fully briefed to the court. However, where McNally's hard-copy productions were incomplete, the court ordered McNally to supplement the hard-copy versions with its computer files to ensure that it has produced all of the relevant information.

- *Unnamed Physician v. Board of Trustees of St. Agnes Medical Center,* 113 Cal.Rptr.2d 309 (Cal. Ct. App. 2001). In a physician review hearing, the hospital was ordered to provide the physician with all existing documents related to the hospital's computer programs, except those of a proprietary nature.
- *Hayes v. Compass Group USA, Inc.,* 202 F.R.D. 363 (D. Conn 2001). The plaintiff in an age discrimination action requested information on similar claims filed against the defendant. The defendant advised the court of the burden and expense involved with such a request given that some of the data was stored in a non-searchable computer format. The court ordered the defendant to manually search the unsearchable computer data and to produce all information for which it had computer search capabilities.
- *In re the Matter of the Application of Lees,* 121 N.Y.S.2d 254 (N.Y. Sup. Ct. 2001). A rape defendant submitted an *ex parte* motion asking that the victim and a third party be ordered to turn over their computers for inspection. The defendant sought to uncover an email in which the victim falsely claimed to have been raped on a prior occasion. The application of the defendant was granted to the extent that he could show cause to the court.
- *McPeek v. Ashcroft,* 202 F.R.D. 31 (D.D.C. 2001). In a sexual harassment action against plaintiff's employer, the plaintiff sought to force the defendant to search its backup systems for data that was deleted by the user but was stored on backup tape. The defendant rebutted that the remote possibility of yielding relevant evidence could not justify the costs involved. Instead of ordering recovery and production of relevant documents from all of the existing backup tapes, the magistrate ordered the defendant to restore and produce responsive emails from one person's computer over a one year period. After this sample data was produced and accessed, the magistrate would then determine if a broader recovery and search was warranted given the burden and expense.
- *Kleiner v. Burns,* 2000 WL 1909470 (D. Kan. Dec. 15, 2000). The court ordered the defendant Yahoo! to disclose all electronic data compilations in its possession, custody, and control that are relevant to disputed facts. The court also ordered parties to preserve evidence that they know, or should know, is relevant to the ongoing litigation, including preservation of all data compila-

tions, computerized data and other electronically-recorded information.

- *Illinois Tool Works, Inc. v. Metro Mark Prod. Ltd.*, 43 F.Supp.2d 951 (N.D. 111. 1999). In an unfair competition case, the court ordered the defendant to produce for inspection its computer after the plaintiff showed that the defendant had been less than forthcoming in producing hard copies of requested documents. The court further issued sanctions, in the form reasonable attorney's fees and costs, for the failure to comply with the discovery orders.

- *Alexander v. FBI*, 186 F.R.D. 78 (D. D.C. 1998). The court concluded that it was appropriate to order an examination of employee's computer hard drive and server to determine whether responsive documents that had not been already produced actually existed. *See also Alexander v. FBI*, 188 F.R.D. 111 (D.C. Cir. 1998). The court refused to require the defendants to completely restore all deleted files and email where the plaintiff did not propose "targeted and appropriately worded searches of backed-up and archived email and deleted hard drives for a limited number of individuals."

- *Sattar v. Motorola, Inc.*, 138 F.3d 1164 (7th Cir. 1997). The plaintiff sought hard copies of over 200,000 emails, since its system was unable to read defendant's electronic files. The appellate court affirmed the district court's ruling that a more reasonable accommodation was (1) some combination of downloading the data from the tapes to conventional computer disks or a computer hard-drive, (2) loaning the plaintiff a copy of the necessary software, or (3) offering the plaintiff on-site access to its own system. If all of those options failed, the court ordered that the parties would each bear half the cost of the copying the 200,000 emails.

- *Smith v. Texaco, Inc.*, 951 F. Supp. 109, (E.D. Tex 1997), *rev'd on other grounds* 263 F.3d 394 (5th Cir. 2001). Modifying the original state court TRO in a race discrimination case, the court permitted the moving of certain documents in the ordinary and usual course of business and the deletion of electronic records in the ordinary and usual course of business, provided that hard copy records be made and kept.

- *Strauss v. Microsoft Corp.*, 1995 WL 326492 (S.D.N.Y. June 1, 1995). The court denied Microsoft's motion to exclude evidence of offensive emails in a hostile work environment lawsuit.

- *Easley, McCaleb & Assoc., Inc. v. Perry,* No. E-2663 (Ga. Super. Ct. July 13, 1994). The court ordered that deleted files on defendant's computer hard drive are discoverable, and plaintiff's expert must be allowed to retrieve all recoverable files. The court issued an order detailing the protocol for reviewing the electronic data.
- *Torrington Co., v. United States,* 786 F. Supp. 1027 (Ct, Int'l Trade 1992). The plaintiff requested access to confidential materials contained on a computer tape, the plaintiff also requested hard copies of the data. The court refused to order the defendant to create the computer tapes from scratch where the plaintiff had already received the documents in paper form. In reaching its decision, the court stated, "Where the burden, cost and time required to produce the tapes is virtually equal on both parties, then the burden of producing the tapes falls on the party requesting the information."
- *PHE, Inc. v. Department of Justice,* 139 F.R.D. 249 (D.D.C. 1991). The court ordered the plaintiff to produce computerized tax records even though the plaintiff possessed no computer program to retrieve or display the records. "Although no program may presently exist to obtain the information requested, the court is satisfied that with little effort the plaintiffs can retrieve the necessary and appropriate information. . . It would not be unreasonable to require the plaintiffs to incur modest additional expenditures so as to provide the defendants with the discovery necessary to establish that they are not acting in bad faith and vindictively."
- *In re Air Crash Disaster at Detroit Metro,* 130 F.R.D. 634 (E.D. Mich. 1989). In litigation brought after a passenger jet crash, the court ordered the aircraft manufacturer to provide relevant flight simulation data on computer-readable nine-track magnetic tape even though the aircraft manufacturer had already provided the data in hard copy print-outs. Because material did not currently exist on magnetic tape, the requesting party (the airline) was required to pay all reasonable and necessary costs associated with manufacture of tape.
- *Timken Co. v. United States,* 659 F. Supp 239 (Ct. Int'l Trade 1987). The court ordered production of data stored on computer tape even though it had been previously produced in a paper format.
- *Williams v. Owens-Illinois, Inc.,* 665 F.2d 918 (9th Cir. 1982). In an employment discrimination suit, the court refused to order pro-

duction of the electronic information on computer tape where all the data was previously produced in hard copy. Therefore, the court determined that the Appellants were not deprived of any data.

- *City of Cleveland v. Cleveland Electric Illuminating Co.*, 538 F. Supp. 1257 (N.D. Ohio 1980). In an antitrust suit brought by a city against an electric utility, the court ordered the electric utility was entitled to pretrial production by the city of computer data and calculations underlying conclusions contained in reports of certain experts the city intended to call as witnesses.

- *National Union Elec. Corp. v. Matsushita Elec. Ind. Co.*, 494 F. Supp. 1257 (E.D. Pa. 1980). The defendant filed a motion to compel production of a computer tape containing the information that the plaintiff previously produced in a hard copy. The court required the plaintiff to have computer experts create a computer-readable tape containing data previously supplied to the defendant in printed form.

- *Pearl Brewing Co. v. Joseph Schiltz Brewing Co.*, 415 F. Supp. 1122 (S.D. Tex. 1976). In an antitrust action, the court allowed the defendant to inspect and copy the computer programs and systems documentation at issue and to depose the plaintiff's computer experts as to the creation of the systems.

- *Adams v. Dan River Mills, Inc.*, 54 F.R.D. 220 (W.D. Va. 1972). In an employment discrimination case, the court required the defendant to provide an electronic version of the printouts already submitted to the plaintiff. "Because of the accuracy and inexpensiveness of producing the requested documents in the case at bar, this court sees no reason why the defendant should not be required to produce the computer cards or tapes and the W-2 print-outs to the plaintiffs."

Costs

- *Open TV v. Libertate Technologies*, 219 F.R.D. 474 (N.D.C.A. 2003). The plaintiff requested that the defendant produce copies of its source code for various products at issue in the litigation. The defendant objected to the request, claiming that producing this data would be overly burdensome, but offered to make the source code data available for review at its facilities. The plaintiff rejected this offer, claiming that it inappropriately shifted the costs of production to the requesting party as the code must be extracted at its expense. Relying on the analysis set forth in

Zubulake cases, the court found that the source code data was stored in an inaccessible format for purposes of discovery. The court used the *Zubulake* seven factor balancing test to determine that the parties should split the costs of extracting the data equally, with the defendant bearing the copying costs once the data has been extracted.

- *Xpedior Credit Trust v. Credit Suisse First Boston,* 2003 WL 22283835 (S.D. N.Y. Oct. 2, 2003). The plaintiff moved for an order to compel the defendant to produce certain electronic documents in connection with the breach of contract action. The defendant countered with a motion for a protective order requiring the plaintiff to bear half the costs of producing the electronic documents. The documents at issue reside on optical disks and DLT tapes. Applying the *Zubulake* seven factor cost shifting test, the court found that cost shifting was not appropriate and ordered the defendant to bear its own costs in producing the electronic data.

- *Zubulake v. UBS Warburg,* 217 F.R.D. 309 (S.D.N.Y. 2003). In a gender discrimination suit against her former employer, the plaintiff requested that the defendant produce "[a]ll documents concerning any communication by or between UBS employees concerning plaintiff." The defendant produced 350 pages of documents, including approximately 100 pages of email. The plaintiff knew that additional responsive email existed that the defendant had failed to produce because she, in fact, had produced approximately 450 pages of email correspondence. She requested that the defendants produce the email from archival media. Claiming undue burden and expense, the defendant urged the court to shift the cost of production to the plaintiff, citing the *Rowe* decision. Stating that a court should consider cost-shifting only when electronic data is relatively inaccessible (such as in this case), the court considered the *Rowe* 8-factor cost shifting test. The court noted that the application of the Rowe factors may result in disproportionate cost shifting away from large defendants, and the court modified the test to 7 factors: (1) the extent to which the request is specifically tailored to discover relevant information; (2) the availability of such information from other sources; (3) the total cost of production compared to the amount in controversy; (4) the total cost of production compared to the resources available to each party; (5) the relative ability of each party to control costs and its incentive to do so; (6) the importance of the issue at stake in the litigation and; (7) the relative benefits to the parties of obtaining the information. The court ordered the defendant to produce, at its own expense, all responsive email existing on its optical disks, active servers, and five backup tapes as selected by the plaintiff. The court determined that only after the contents of the backup tapes are reviewed and the defendant's costs are quantified, the court will conduct the appropriate cost-shifting analysis. *See also Zubulake v. UBS Warburg*, 216 F.R.D. 280 (S.D.N.Y. 2003).

- *Computer Assocs. Int'l, Inc. v. Quest Software, Inc.*, 2003 WL 21277129 (N.D.Ill. June 3, 2002). The plaintiff brought a copyright infringement and trade secret misappropriation suit against six of defendant's employees arising from improper use of some of plaintiff's software source code. The plaintiff asked the defendants to make specific work and home computer hard drives available for electronic imaging so that the plaintiff could search for and reconstruct deleted files that would be otherwise undiscoverable. The defendants argued that the drives contained privileged information relating directly to this litigation and worked with a computer consultant to remove the privileged information from the images and indicate where the removed information was located. The defendants filed a motion to require the plaintiff to pay for the computer consultation that was necessary to prepare the drives for disclosure. After seeking advice from the *Rowe* 8-factor cost shifting test, the court determined that the defendants' costs were analogous to the review of documents for privileged information and should not be shifted to the requesting party.

- *Medtronic v. Michelson*, 2003 WL 21212601 (W.D. Tenn. May 13, 2003). In a trade secret violation suit, the defendant sought to compel the plaintiff to respond fully to discovery requests by producing data contained on a large number of computer network backup tapes. The plaintiff timely responded, claiming that the discovery requests were unduly burdensome because of the costs associated with extracting backup tape data and reviewing it for relevance and privilege. The parties did not dispute the relevance of the electronic data at issue. Agreeing that producing the backup data as a whole would be burdensome on the plaintiff, the court applied the *Rowe* 8 factor cost-shifting test to determine burden and cost. Finding that the majority of the factors favored shifting a portion of discovery costs to the defendant, the court outlined a detailed discovery protocol.

- *Byers v. Illinois State Police,* 2002 WL 1264004 (N.D. Ill. June 3, 2002). In an employment discrimination suit, the plaintiffs sought an order compelling the defendants to produce archived emails. The court stated, "Based on the cost of the proposed search and the plaintiffs' failure to establish that the search will likely uncover relevant information, the court concludes that the plaintiffs are entitled to the archived emails only if they are willing to pay for part of the cost of production. . . . Requiring the plaintiffs to pay part of the cost of producing the emails will provide them with an incentive to focus their requests." The court granted the motion to the extent that the plaintiffs bear the cost of licensing the archived email software while the defendants continue to bear the expense of review for responsive, privileged, and confidential documents.
- *In re Bristol-Myers Squibb Securities Litigation,* 2002 WL 169201 (D.N.J. Feb. 4, 2002). The court modified the plaintiff's original discovery cost commitment where the defendants "dumped" an extraordinary number of paper documents resulting in a prohibitive copying charge. The court also denied the defendant's motion for the plaintiff's one-half cost contribution for document scanning costs, but instead required the plaintiff to pay only for the nominal cost of copying compact discs. The court reiterated the importance of a Rule 26(f) conference to discuss electronic discovery issues, including the fair and economical allocation of costs.
- *Rowe Entertainment, Inc. v. The William Morris Agency,* 2002 WL 63190 (S.D.N.Y. Jan. 16,2002). Denying defendants' motion for a protective order insofar as it sought to preclude the discovery of email altogether, the court adopted a balancing approach, consisting of eight factors, to determine whether discovery costs should be shifted. *See also Rowe Entertainment, Inc. v. The William Morris Agency,* 2002 WL 975713 (S.D.N.Y. May 9, 2002). After reanalyzing and reaffirming Judge Francis' eight factor balancing test, the court upheld the January 15, 2002 Order that granted the defendants motion to shift the costs of production of their email communications to the plaintiff.
- *GTFM, Inc., v. Wal-Mart Stores,* 2000 WL 1693615 (S.D.N.Y. Nov. 9, 2000). The court allowed the plaintiff to recover fees for the inspection of Wal-Mart's computer records and facilities by plaintiff's expert and also upheld fees and expenses caused by Wal-Mart's failure to provide accurate discovery information in

response to valid discovery requests. The court found the award of expenses "reasonable in view of the prior repeated misinformation provided by Wal-Mart concerning the availability of information. . ."

- *Zonaras v. General Motors Corp.*, 1996 WL 1671236 (S.D. Ohio Oct. 17, 1996). In this case, the plaintiff sought to compel discovery of data compiled concerning different crash test dummy tests. In response, the defendant GMC asserted that it produced data tracings and backup materials for all but eleven of these tests, and objects to production of the remaining tests "as unduly burdensome and expensive." After balancing the elements outlined in Rule 26(b)(2)(iii), the court ordered the defendant GMC to produce data tracings and backup materials of the eleven tests where the benefits of the discovery outweighed the expense of production. Because admissibility of the electronic evidence was still undecided, the court ordered the plaintiffs to pay half the production costs.

- *Toledo Fair Hous. Ctr. v. Nationwide Mut. Ins. Co.*, 703 N.E.2d 340 (Ohio C.P. 1996). The court ordered discovery of certain documents from defendant's database. Judge stated that the defendant cannot avoid discovery simply because their own record keeping scheme makes discovery burdensome. The court ordered the defendant to pay costs of the discovery.

- *Anti-Monopoly, Inc. v. Hasbro, Inc.*, 1995 WL 649934 (S.D.N.Y. Nov. 3, 1995). The court found that the law is clear that data in computerized form is discoverable even if paper copies of the information have been produced. The producing party can be required to design a computer program to extract the data from its computerized business records. But such an order is subject to the court's discretion as to the allocation of the costs of designing such a computer program.

- *In re Brand Name Prescription Drugs Antitrust Litig.*, 1995 WL 360526 (N.D. HI. June 15, 1995). The court found that expense of retrieving electronic data was mainly due to defendant's own record-keeping scheme. As such, the court required the defendant to produce its responsive, computer-stored email at its own expense, subject to some limitations. The court also instructed the plaintiffs to narrow the scope of their request. Parties were also encouraged by the court to confer regarding scope of requests for emails.

- *Rhone-Poulenc Rarer, Inc. v. Home Indemnity Co.*, 1991 WL 111040 (E.D. Pa. June 17, 1991). An unwieldy computerized record-keeping system, which requires heavy expenditures in money and time to produce relevant records, is simply not an adequate excuse to frustrate discovery. The plaintiff was required to pay for copies of any documents on microfilm/microfiche which the plaintiff requests, while defendants bear the burden of searching and producing the documents.

- *Williams v. Du Pont*, 119 F.R.D. 648 (W.D. Ky. 1987). The discovering party must bear costs of data production and reimburse responding party for a portion of its expense in assembling the database.
- *Delozier v. First Nat'l Bank of Gatlinburg*, 109 F.R.D. 161 (E.D. Tenn. 1986). "A court will not shift the burden of discovery onto the discovering party where the costliness of the discovery procedure involved is entirely a product of the defendant's recordkeeping scheme over which the plaintiff has no control."
- *Bills v. Kennecott Corp.*, 108 F.R.D. 459 (C.D. Utah 1985). The court denied defendant's motion requiring the plaintiff to pay the cost the defendant incurred in producing a printout of computer data that the plaintiff sought through discovery. The court based its holding on that the amount of money involved was not excessive or inordinate, that the relative expense and burden in obtaining the data would have been substantially greater for the plaintiffs as compared with the defendant, that the amount of money required to obtain the data as set forth by the defendant would have been a substantial burden to the plaintiffs, and that the defendant was benefited to some degree by producing the data.
- *Oppenheimer Fund, Inc. v. Sanders*, 437 U.S. 340 (1982). "[W]e do not think a defendant should be penalized for not maintaining his records in the form most convenient to some potential future litigants whose identity and perceived needs could not have been anticipated." Where the expense of creating computer programs that would locate the desired data was the same for both parties, the court ordered that the party seeking the information must bear the cost of production.

Preservation & Spoliation

- *Rambus, Inc. v. Infineon Techs. AG*, 2004 WL 383590 (E.D.Va. Feb. 26, 2004), *amended by*, 2004 WL 547536 (E.D.Va. Mar. 17, 2004). The defendant moved to compel the production of documents including those documents relating to the plaintiff's document retention policy. The defendant alleged that the plaintiff instituted a document-purging program despite being on notice of impending litigation for the patents at issue. In support of its allegations, the defendant pointed to internal emails that reflected the plaintiff's "Shred Day," an event in which the plaintiff's employees shredded about two million documents as part of its document retention and destruction policy. At trial, the plaintiff did not dispute that it "destroyed some documents because of their 'discoverability'." Additionally, the trial court found that the plaintiff's creation of its document retention policy clearly demonstrated that the plaintiff was on notice that the defendant might be bringing patent infringement lawsuits. The plaintiff argued that its true motive was not to destroy potentially discoverable information and that the plaintiff was legitimately trying to reduce search and review costs. The court concluded that even if the plaintiff "did not institute its document retention policy in bad faith, if it reasonably anticipated litigation when it did so, it is guilty of spoliation." The court further noted that "even if it was merely instituting a valid purging program, even valid purging programs need to be put on hold when litigation is 'reasonably foreseeable'." As such, the court granted the defendant's motion and ordered the plaintiff to immediately produce documents about its document containing information about or relating to the creation, preparation, or scope of the plaintiff's document retention policy.

- *Anderson v. Crossroads Capital Partners, L.L.C.*, 2004 WL 256512 (D.Minn. Feb. 10, 2004). In a sexual harassment and whistleblower lawsuit, the defendants sought to recover the hard drive of plaintiff's personal computer because it allegedly contained an October 2001 document outlining the harassment. After a protracted discovery battle, the defendants sought a Motion to Compel and the judge ordered the plaintiff to furnish the defendant with a "copy of all documents/files relevant to this litigation that exist on Ms. Anderson's personal computer as well as those that have been deleted or otherwise adulterated." Pursuant to the judge's Order, the defendants' computer forensic expert examined the plaintiff's hard drive and discovered that a data wiping software application had been installed after the plaintiff had agreed not to "delete any existing documents" in a deposition. The computer forensic expert also found that the hard drive installed in the machine was manufactured in August 2002. The plaintiff claimed that she did not use the software program to destroy evidence, but that she used it routinely to protect her computer files. She also stated that in her view she owned the same computer throughout the litigation despite changing the hard drive in 2002. The defendants then moved to dismiss the complaint due to plaintiff's alleged discovery violations and destruction of evidence. The court noted that the plaintiff's "exceedingly tedious and disingenuous claim of naiveté regarding her failure to produce the requested discovery . . . defies the bounds of reason" but was not sufficiently egregious to warrant dismissal of the case. Instead, the court issued an adverse inference jury instruction because the plaintiff intentionally destroyed evidence and attempted to suppress the truth.

- *Wiginton v. Ellis*, 2003 WL 22439865 (N.D.Ill. Oct. 27, 2003). Two days after filing a sexual harassment class action suit, plaintiff's counsel sent the defendant a preservation letter requesting that all electronic materials and records relevant to the lawsuit be retained. Upon receipt of this letter, the defendant sent one email to its employees requiring preservation of all documents relating to the plaintiff. The defendant continued to follow its normal document retention and destruction policies until several months later when the court entered a preservation order. Email system backup tapes were destroyed and former employees' hard drives (including the plaintiff's former supervisor) were not saved. The plaintiff sought a motion for spoliation sanctions. The court found that the defendant had the duty to preserve relevant electronic documents that were likely to be the subject of discovery requests, had knowledge of this duty, and willfully and intentionally did not fulfill this duty. Despite this, the court denied the plaintiff's motion for sanctions, stating that the extent of the lost electronic documents was not known. The court stated that the backup data that was preserved and produced by the defendant may perhaps give some insight into what was destroyed. If the plaintiff's expert is able to discover relevant documents on the backup tapes, then the plaintiff will be allowed to renew its motion for sanctions.

- *Kucala Enters. Ltd. v. Auto Wax Co.*, 2003 WL 22433095 (N.D.Ill. Oct. 27, 2003). After conducting an evidentiary hearing, the magistrate judge in the patent infringement suit *Kucala Enters. Ltd. v. Auto Wax Co.*, 2003 WL 21230605 (N.D.Ill. May 27, 2003), recommended that the plaintiff's claims be dismissed and that attorneys' fees and expenses attributable to the motion for sanctions be granted against the plaintiff for destroying computer evidence. The federal district judge rejected the magistrate's recommendation that the plaintiff's claims be dismissed with prejudice. The magistrate did so despite the fact that the plaintiff used computer software called "Evidence Eliminator" to delete files the night before a scheduled discovery inspection. The district judge stated that the interest of justice would be best served by adjudicating the claim and counterclaim at issue. The court upheld the magistrate's recommendation that the plaintiff bear the expenses flowing from the discovery misconduct.

- *Keir v. UnumProvident*, 2003 WL 21997747 (S.D.N.Y. Aug. 22, 2003). In an ERISA class action suit, the plaintiffs sought an order from the court directing the defendant to preserve all electronic evidence relevant to the matter. After noting that the defendant "already had a duty to preserve any tapes containing emails as of the date litigation commenced," the court ordered the defendant to preserve all relevant electronic data and to specifically preserve six days of email records which were contained on backup tapes and hard drives. Instead of preserving all existing backups, or conducting a full tape email backup, the defendant's technical staff decided to implement a special snapshot backup which would only preserve emails on the system as of the day or days the snapshot was taken. In evaluating defendant's conduct with respect to the preservation order, the court stated that "UnumProvident had ample time in the weeks before the December 27 [preservation] Order was signed to consult with its IT Department and with IBM to inform itself about the technological issues relevant to the preservation of electronic data so that it could bring accurate information to the negotiations of the preservation order and the conferences with the court in which the December 27 Order was shaped, and comply promptly with the Order after it was issued." The court found the defendant's failure to preserve was unintentional and criticized the defendant's poor compliance with the preservation order. The court recommended that further action be taken to determine the feasibility of retrieving the lost data and the extent of prejudice to the plaintiffs in order for the court to fashion a remedy for the plaintiffs.

- *Positive Software Solutions v. New Century Mortgage Corp.*, 259 F.Supp.2d 561 (N.D.Tex. 2003). To ensure no other potentially relevant information was deleted, the court ordered the defendants to preserve all backups and images of servers and personal computers that contain or contained files at issue. The court further ordered the defendant to refrain from deleting any such files still resident on any servers or personal computers and to preserve all backups or images. Finding the scope substantially overbroad, the court denied the plaintiff's motion to compel imaging "of all of defendants' media potentially containing any of the software and electronic evidence relevant to the claims in this suit" and "all images of [defendants'] computer storage facilities, drives, and servers taken to date."

- *Liafail, Inc. v. Learning 2000, Inc.,* 2002 WL 31954396 (D.Del. Dec. 23, 2002). The defendant alleges that upon issuing its document requests, the plaintiff engaged in electronic data spoliation including intentionally deleting computer files and damaging hardware. The court stated that the plaintiff's position on the whereabouts of the requested documents indicated questionable discovery tactics. Nevertheless, because the court record was unclear as to what had been produced, and what must still be produced, the court decided not to immediately sanction the plaintiff. Rather, the court gave the plaintiff time to correct or clarify the record by producing the requested documents which it has claimed as available. The court stated that should the plaintiff choose not to heed the court's order, the court would order sanctions in the form of an adverse inference jury instruction.

- *Antioch v. Scrapbook Borders, Inc.,* 210 F.R.D. 645 (D.Minn. 2002). In a copyright infringement action, the plaintiff moved for issuance of an order directing the defendant to: preserve records, expedite discovery, compel discovery, and appoint a neutral computer forensics expert. Emphasizing the potential for spoliation of the computer data, the court stated "we conclude that the defendants may have relevant information, on their computer equipment, which is being lost through normal use of the computer, and which might be relevant to the plaintiff's claims, or the defendants' defenses."

- *Lombardo v. Broadway Stores, Inc.,* 2002 WL 86810 (Cal. Ct. App. Jan. 22, 2002). The court upheld sanctions where the defendant destroyed computerized payroll data that was the subject of the plaintiff's discovery request.

- *RKI, Inc. v. Grimes,* 177 F.Supp.2d 859 (N.D. 111. 2001). In a trade secret misappropriation action against plaintiff's former employee, the court found that the defendant defragmented his home computer in an effort to prevent the plaintiff from learning that he had deleted confidential information and software. The court ordered the defendant to pay $100,000 in compensatory damages, $150,000 in punitive damages, attorneys' fees, and court costs.

- *Heveafil Sdn. Bhd. v. United States*, 2001 WL 194986 (Ct. Int'l Trade Feb 27, 2001). In an action challenging a U.S. Department of Commerce administrative review of an "antidumping order," the court determined that the plaintiff failed to act to the best of its ability where six months after receiving notice about maintaining its source documents, it deleted relevant data from its computer system. The court found that the plaintiff "did not cooperate to the best of its ability because after receiving notice from [the Department of Commerce], it knew or should have known to maintain th[is] source document."

- *Trigon Ins. Co. v. United States*, 204 F.R.D. 277 (E.D.Va. 2001). Based on computer forensic expert analysis, the court found that the defendant willfully and intentionally destroyed documents that should have been produced during discovery. The court issued adverse inferences and reimbursement of plaintiff's attorneys fees as damages for the spoliation. *Trigon Ins. Co. v. United States*, 2002 WL 31864265 (E.D.Va. Dec. 17, 2002.). Despite objection by the defendant, the court found plaintiff's fees and expenses (in the amount of $179,725.70) for hiring and deposing computer forensics experts and briefing and adjudicating the issues related to the spoliation warranted and reasonable.

- *Pennar Software Corp. v. Fortune 500 Sys. Ltd.*, 2001 WL 1319162 (N.D.Cal. Oct. 25, 2001). In a breach of contract suit, the court imposed sanctions upon the defendant in the form of attorney's fees for committing spoliation of evidence and prolonging the discovery process. The court based its findings on the defendant's failure to present a maintenance policy, log files, or backup tapes that would track the website maintenance and deletion procedures. When the evidence was produced, the court found that the defendant tampered with and deleted evidence in order to evade personal jurisdiction.

- *In re Pacific Gateway Exchange, Inc.*, 2001 WL 1334747 (N.D.Cal. Oct. 17, 2001). In a securities violation case, the court lifted the discovery stay, stating "The court finds that there is a significant risk that relevant documents, both paper and electronic, could be irretrievably lost, which could result in prejudice to the plaintiff."

- *Minnesota Mining & Mfg. v. Pribyl*, 259 F.3d 587 (7th Cir. 2001). The plaintiff brought suit against three former employees for misappropriation of trade secrets. The appellate court affirmed the trial court's negative inference instruction to the jury where the one defendant committed spoliation of evidence by downloading six gigabytes of music onto his laptop, which destroyed many files sought by the plaintiff, the night before the defendant was to turn over his computer pursuant to the discovery request. However, the fact that hard drive space was destroyed on one defendant's computer did not relieve the plaintiff from proving the elements of its claims.

- *Long Island Diagnostic Imaging v. Stony Brook Diagnostic Assocs.*, 286 A.D.2d 320 (N.Y. App. Div. 2001). Where the defendants purged their computer databases against court order and produced compromised and unusable backup tapes, the court dismissed the parties' counterclaims and third-party complaint as spoliation sanctions. The court stated: "The striking of a party's pleading is a proper sanction for a party who spoliates evidence."

- *Danis v. USN Communications*, 2000 WL 1694325 (N.D. Dl. Oct. 23, 2000). The court found that the defendant failed to properly preserve information on the computer database. The court allowed the trial judge to inform jury that some of the gaps in the case were caused by defendant's failure to turn over computer tapes and documents. The court fined the CEO of the defendant company $10,000 for failing to properly preserve such electronic information, but denied plaintiff's motion for default judgment.

- *Mathias v. Jacobs*, 197 F.R.D. 29 (S.D.N.Y. 2000), *vacated* 2001 WL 1149017 (S.D.N.Y. Sept. 27, 2001). The court found the plaintiff had a duty to preserve information contained on a Palm Pilot. Since plaintiff's conduct did not destroy evidence, but rather just made it more difficult to discover, the court imposed monetary sanctions as a consequence of the spoliation.

- *Illinois Tool Works, Inc. v. Metro Mark Prod., Ltd.*, 43 F.Supp.2d. 951 (N.D. 111. 1999). The court held that sanctions, in the form of attorney's fees and additional discovery costs, against the defendant were warranted as a remedy for spoliation.

- *Linnen v. A.H. Robins Co.*, 1999 WL 462015 (Mass. Super. June 16, 1999). The defendant Wyeth failed to preserve emails and neglected turning over database information ordered by the court. The court sanctioned Wyeth for such "inexcusable conduct" and allowed spoliation inference to be given to jury.

- *Telecom Int'l Amer., Ltd. v. AT & T Corp.*, 189 F.R.D. 76 (S.D.N.Y. 1999). "Even without a specific discovery order, a district court may impose sanctions for spoliation of evidence, exercising its inherent power to supervise the litigation before it."

- *United States v. Koch Ind.*, 197 F.R.D. 463 (N.D. Okla. 1998). The plaintiff claimed that the defendant thwarted discovery attempts by destroying backup computer tapes and files. The court found that the defendant failed in its duty to preserve evidence that it should have known was relevant. The court allowed the plaintiff to inform jury that computer tapes and files were destroyed but did not allow negative inference.
- *Lauren Corp. v. Century Geophysical Corp.*, 953 P.2d 200 (Colo. Ct. App. 1998). The court held, as a matter of first impression, that a trial court may impose attorney fees and costs as sanction for bad faith and willful destruction of evidence, even absent a specific discovery order.
- *In re Cheyenne Software, Inc. v. Securities Litig.*, 1997 WL 714891 (E.D.N.Y. Aug. 18, 1997). In a securities proceeding, the court imposed $15,000 in attorney's fees and sanctions for failing to heed the court's discovery order. The court also compelled the defendant to bear the cost of downloading and printing up to 10,000 pages of additional documents responsive to appropriate keyword searches requested by the plaintiff.
- *Chidichimo v. University of Chicago Press*, 681 N.E.2d 107 (111. App. Ct. 1997). Some jurisdictions recognize a tort action for negligent spoliation of evidence.
- *ABC Home Health Servs. v. IBM Corp.*, 158 F.R.D. 180 (S.D. Ga. 1994). In action for breach of contract, the court sanctioned IBM for destroying computer files in anticipation of litigation.
- *First Tech. Safety Sys., Inc. v. Depinet*, 11 F.3d 641 (6th Cir. 1993). "In order to justify proceeding *ex parte* . . . the applicant must do more than assert that the adverse party would dispose of evidence if given notice." Instead, the party must demonstrate that the adverse party has a "history of disposing of evidence or violating court orders. . ."
- *Cabinetware Inc., v. Sullivan*, 1991 WL 327959 (E.D. Cal. July 15, 1991). The court issued a default judgment as a sanction for spoliation of electronic evidence. "Destruction of evidence cannot be countenanced in a justice system whose goal is to find the truth through honest and orderly production of evidence under established discovery rules."
- *Computer Assocs. Int'l, Inc. v. American Fundware, Inc.*, 133 F.R.D. 166 (D. Colo. 1990). The court issued a default judgment where the defendant revised portions of the source code after being

served in the action, and thus put on notice that the source code was irreplaceable evidence. Revised code was a central piece of evidence to the litigation.

- *William T. Thompson Co. v. General Nutrition Corp.*, 593 F. Supp. 1443 (C.D. Cal. 1984). GNC was ordered to preserve all records that were maintained in the ordinary course of its business; despite this, company employees were instructed that these judicial orders "should not require us to change our standard document retention or destruction policies or practices." The court ordered a default judgment and over $450,000 in monetary sanctions, where GNC deleted electronic documents that were not otherwise available.

Sanctions

- *Attorney Grievance Comm 'n of Maryland v. Potter*, 2004 WL 422548 (Md. Mar. 9, 2004). The court considered a Petition for a Disciplinary Action filed by the Attorney Grievance Commission against the defendant, an attorney, for violating the Maryland Rules of Professional Conduct. Upon resigning from a law firm, the defendant took paper files pertaining to two clients of the firm stating that he believed that the clients would choose to have the defendant continue to represent them. Additionally, the defendant deleted the client files from the firm's computer without authorization from the firm. The computer records included all documents prepared by the defendant and the firm's secretaries relating to matters involving the clients. The Commission sought suspension of the attorney's license alleging that the defendant committed "a criminal act that reflects adversely on the lawyer's honesty, trustworthiness or fitness as a lawyer in other respects." The judge appointed to hear the initial action held that the defendant did not violate the Code. However, the court of appeals reversed, finding by "clear and convincing evidence" that the defendant's conduct in deleting the files violated the Rules of Professional Conduct. The court further noted, "[n]otwithstanding the attorney's motive, lawyers in this State may not delete computer records or take client files . . . without authorization." The court concluded that the defendant's misconduct warranted a 90 day suspension from the practice of law.
- *Invision Media Communications, Inc. v. Federal Ins. Co.*, 2004 WL 396037 (S.D.N.Y. Mar. 2, 2004). In an action for breach of an insurance contract, the defendant moved to compel production of

documents and requested monetary sanctions, contending that the plaintiff made false statements regarding the location and existence of its documents and destroyed evidence relevant to the lawsuit. Among the documents requested by the defendant were email communications sent by the plaintiff. Specifically, the defendant sought "All electronic mail communications sent or received by the plaintiffs during August 2001, September 2001 and October 2001." The plaintiff represented to the defendant that the emails could not be produced because the plaintiff archived email on its servers for only a two week period. The court found these statements false because the plaintiff eventually disclosed the requested emails after further investigation. Accordingly, the court awarded the defendant costs and attorneys fees, noting that "[a] reasonable inquiry by the plaintiffs counsel . . . would have alerted counsel that the plaintiff possessed electronic mail that fell within the scope of Federal's document request . . . the plaintiff has disregarded its discovery obligations, made misleading statements regarding the existence and location of relevant evidence, and/or failed to make reasonable inquiries into matters pertinent to the pretrial discovery phase of this litigation."

- *Thompson v. United States*, 219 F.R.D. 93 (D.Md. 2003). The plaintiff served upon the defendants a series of Rule 34 document production requests seeking electronic records and email. When the defendants failed fully to produce these records, the plaintiffs filed a motion seeking sanctions. The court issued Rule 37(b)(2) relief to the plaintiffs by ruling that the defendants could not call certain witnesses unless they were able to demonstrate that there were no responsive email records generated or received by the witness or, if such records did exist, that they had been produced to the plaintiffs by a certain date. Long after the discovery cutoff deadline and the court's sanction order, the defendant announced that it had discovered 80,000 email records, after having repeatedly told the plaintiff and the court that email records either did not exist or already had been produced. The court revised its previous sanction order, (1) precluding the defendants from introducing into evidence any of the 80,000 emails that were "discovered" at the last minute; (2) ordering that counsel for the defendants were forbidden to use any of these emails to prepare any of their witnesses for testimony at trial, and that at trial counsel for the defendants were forbidden from attempting to refresh the recollection of any of their witnesses by using any of the undisclosed emails; (3) ordering that the plaintiffs were permitted to use any of the 80,000 emails during their case and in cross-examining any of the defendants witnesses; (4) ordering that, if the plaintiffs incurred any additional expense and attorney's fees in connection with reviewing the 80,000 records and analyzing them for possible use at trial, this could be recovered from the defendants upon further motion to the court; and (5) ordering that if, at trial, the evidence revealed additional information regarding the non-production of email, the plaintiffs were free to make a motion to the court that the failure to produce email records as ordered by this court constituted a contempt of court.

- *Zubulake v. UBS Warburg,* 2003 WL 22410619 (S.D.N.Y. Oct. 22, 2003). In the restoration effort that occurred according to previous e-discovery decisions in the matter, the parties discovered that certain backup tapes were missing and that emails had been deleted. The plaintiff moved for evidentiary and monetary sanctions against the defendant for its failure to preserve the missing tapes and emails. The court found that the defendant had a duty to preserve the missing evidence, since it should have known that the emails may be relevant to future litigation. Although the plaintiff did not file her charges until August 2001, by April of that year, "almost everyone associated with Zubulake recognized the possibility that she might sue," the court wrote. The court also found that the defendant failed to comply with its own retention policy, which would have preserved the missing evidence. The judge found that although the defendant had a duty to preserve all of the backup tapes at issue, and destroyed them with the requisite culpability, the plaintiff could not demonstrate that the lost evidence would have supported her claims. Therefore, it was inappropriate to give an adverse inference instruction to the jury. Even though an adverse inference instruction was not warranted, the court ordered the defendant to bear the plaintiff's costs for re-deposing certain witnesses for the limited purpose of inquiring into the destruction of electronic evidence and any newly discovered emails.

- *Landmark Legal Foundation v. Environmental Protection Agency,* 272 F.Supp.2d 70 (D.D.C. 2003). Concerned that documents responsive to its Freedom of Information Act request would not survive the transition between governmental administrations, the plaintiff requested the court to enter a preliminary injunction prohibiting the EPA from destroying, removing, or tampering with potentially responsive documents. The court granted the motion and issued an injunction. Despite the court's order, the hard drives of several EPA officials were reformatted, email backup tapes were erased and reused, and individuals deleted received emails. The court found the EPA in contempt and concluded that the appropriate sanction was to impose sanctions in the form of the plaintiff's attorney's fees and costs incurred as a result of the EPA's conduct.

■ *Commissioner v. Ward*, 580 S.E.2d 432 (N.C. App. 2003). In this matter, the plaintiffs and the defendants engaged in a long and complex discovery battle relating to the protocols for discovery of both paper and electronic documents stored off-site by the defendants. Upon plaintiffs' first motion to compel, the court ordered the defendants to permit the plaintiffs to examine, review and copy stored documents and make a good faith search for other documents, including all electronic data on DAT tapes, for inspection and review by the plaintiffs. When the defendants failed to cooperate, the plaintiffs sought a second motion to compel. Prior to the hearing on this second motion, the parties entered into a consent order which included provisions allowing the plaintiffs to examine, inspect and copy "all information stored in computers, computer hard drives, removable electronic data storage media, diskettes, magnetic tapes, CD ROMs, zip discs and jazz discs" and requiring the defendants to produce all backup data and describe in writing the process used to access the data. Again the defendants failed to comply with the consent order in providing the required electronic information. The plaintiffs then made its third motion to compel and sought sanctions. Finding that the defendants had intentionally and willfully refused to comply with discovery, the trial court sanctioned the defendants by ordering them to produce, at their cost, copies of the backup tape data. The appellate court affirmed the sanctions.

■ *Hildreth Mfg. v. Semco, Inc.*, 785 N.E.2d 774 (Ohio Ct. App. 2003). The appellate court found no basis for defendant's motion for contempt for spoliation of computer evidence. The court found that even though the plaintiff failed to preserve data contained on the computer hard drives at issue, there was not a reasonable possibility that the hard drives contained evidence that would have been favorable to the defendant's claims.

■ *Metropolitan Opera Assoc., Inc. v. Local 100*, 212 F.R.D. 178 (S.D.N.Y. 2003). In a labor dispute, the defendants failed to comply with discovery rules, specifically failing to search for, preserve, or produce electronic documents. The court stated "[C]ounsel (1) never gave adequate instructions to their clients about the clients' overall discovery obligations, what constitutes a 'document' . . .; (2) knew the Union to have no document retention or filing systems and yet never implemented a systematic procedure for document production or for retention of documents, including electronic documents; (3) delegated document production to a layperson who (at least until July 2001) did not even understand himself (and was not instructed by counsel) that a document included a draft or other non-identical copy, a computer file and an e-mail; (4) never went back to the layperson designated to assure that he had 'establish[ed] a coherent and effective system to faithfully and effectively respond to discovery requests,' . . . and (5) in the face of the Met's persistent questioning and showings that the production was faulty and incomplete, ridiculed the inquiries, failed to take any action to remedy the situation or supplement the demonstrably false responses, failed to ask important witnesses for documents until the night before their depositions and, instead, made repeated, baseless representations that all documents had been produced." The court granted severe sanctions, finding liability on the part of the defendants and ordering the defendants to pay plaintiff's attorneys' fees necessitated by the discovery abuse by defendants and their counsel. The court found that lesser sanctions, such as an adverse inference or preclusion, would not be effective in this case "because it is impossible to know what the Met would have found if the Union and its counsel had complied with their discovery obligations from the commencement of the action."

- *Residential Funding Corp. v. DeGeorge Fin. Corp.*, 306 F.3d 99 (2d. Cir. 2002). The defendants appeal the trial court's denial of defendants' motion for sanctions, specifically in the form of an adverse jury instruction, for the plaintiff's failure to produce email in time for trial. The Second Circuit held that where a party breaches a discovery obligation by failing to produce evidence, the trial court has broad discretion in fashioning an appropriate sanction, including the discretion to delay the start of a trial, to declare a mistrial, or to issue an adverse inference instruction. Sanctions may be imposed where a party has not only acted in bad faith or grossly negligent, but also through ordinary negligence. Vacating the trial court's sanctions order, the circuit court reversed and remanded with instructions for a renewed hearing on discovery sanctions.

- *Williams v. Saint-Gobain Corp.*, 2002 WL 1477618 (W.D.N.Y. June 28, 2002). In an employment discrimination suit, the court refused to issue sanctions or attorney's fees stemming from myriad discovery disputes. Despite an earlier assertion that no further responsive documents could be located, the defendant produced emails obtained from an executive's computer five days before trial. The court found no evidence of any bad faith as to the withholding or destruction of the emails and issued the parties an extended time period to complete discovery. The court ordered each party to bear its own discovery costs.
- *DeLoach v. Philip Morris Co.*, 206 F.R.D. 568 (M.D.N.C. 2002). The plaintiffs sought discovery sanctions alleging that the defendant's expert report relied on computerized transaction data that was deliberately withheld from the plaintiffs during discovery. The discovery request at issue sought "[a]ll summary documents (including electronic data) relating to your leaf tobacco bids, purchases, or price paid, including but not limited to the entire Tobinet database in electronic form, but excluding individual transaction documents such as purchase orders and invoices." The plaintiffs were only provided the database data after the defendant's expert report was issued (in which the defendant's expert relied heavily on this other computerized data). The court held that the withholding of the data resulted in unfairness to the plaintiffs and allowed the plaintiffs to respond to the report and provided no opportunity for the defendant to reply.
- *Cobell v. Norton*, 206 F.R.D. 324 (D.D.C. 2002). The court issued sanctions, including attorneys fees and expenses, under Rule 37 based upon the defendants' request for a protective order clarifying that it "may produce email in response to discovery requests by producing from paper records of email messages rather than from backup tapes and may overwrite backup tapes." The defendants had previously been ordered to produce the email messages from the back-up tapes. The court held that the defendants' motion for protective order clarifying their duty to produce the email was not appropriate.
- *Sheppard v. River Valley Fitness One*, 203 F.R.D. 56 (D.N.H. 2001). The plaintiffs served several requests for discovery upon the defendant which defined the term "documents" broadly, encom-

passing both paper documents and electronic communications. However, defendant's attorney (Whittington) failed to turn over the requested documents in a timely fashion and some of the documents were lost or destroyed. The court held, "Notwithstanding Whittington's habit of trying to obstruct discovery in this case, I find that in this instance Whittington's failure to produce computer records and to retain all drafts or other documents relating to the Aubin settlement reflects a lack of diligence rather than an intentional effort to abuse the discovery process. Nevertheless, Whittington's failure to fully comply with this court's March 22 order has unfairly prejudiced the plaintiffs by depriving them of the opportunity to question Aubin about the contents of the documents." The court ordered the defendant's attorney to pay $500 to the plaintiff.

- *Lexis-Nexis v. Beer*, 41 F.Supp.2d 950 (D. Minn. 1999). Employer sued former employee for misappropriation of trade secrets. The court issued monetary sanctions against former employee where former employee failed to produce a specific copy of an electronic database he made at the time of his resignation.

- *New York State Nat'l Org. for Women v. Cuomo*, 1998 WL 395320 (S.D.N.Y. July 14, 1998). The court refused to impose sanctions on the defendant for destroying computer databases where there was no showing that the defendant deleted computer databases or destroyed monthly summary reports in order to impede litigation and the plaintiffs failed to demonstrate that they were prejudiced by the loss of the records.

- *Procter & Gamble Co. v. Haugen*, 179 F.R.D. 622 (D.Utah 1998), *rev'd on other grounds*, 222 F.3d 1262 (10th Cir. 2000). In an unfair competition case, the defendant moved for sanctions against the plaintiff, alleging that the plaintiff violated its duty to preserve relevant email communications of five key employees identified by the plaintiff as containing relevant information. Finding a sanctionable breach of the plaintiff's discovery duties, the court sanctioned the plaintiff $10,000–$2,000 for each of the five custodians. In addition, the plaintiff objected to an order limiting the scope of a keyword search that the plaintiff desired to conduct on the defendant's electronic databases. The court held that the keyword searching limitation prevented discovery of information relevant to the plaintiff's claims. The plaintiff was allowed to submit a list of 25 keywords given that the proposed terms were not so extensive as to render general commercial or competitive information. *See also Procter & Gamble Co. v. Haugen*, 2003 WL 22080734 (D.Utah Aug. 19, 2003). The defendant then moved to dismiss the case with prejudice. The court granted the defendant's motion where the plaintiff failed to preserve relevant electronic data that it knew was critical to the case, violating four separate discovery orders requiring production of the data. The court found that it was "basically impossible" for the defendant to defend the case without the electronic data that was apparently no longer available.

- *In re Prudential Ins. Co. Sale Practices Litig.*, 169 F.R.D. 598 (D.N.J. 1997). Life insurer's consistent pattern of failing to prevent unauthorized document destruction in violation of a court order, in a suit alleging deceptive sales practices, warranted sanctions requiring payment of $1 million to court and payment of some plaintiff's attorney fees and costs.

- *Gates Rubber Co. v. Bando Chem. Ind.*, 167 F.R.D. 90 (D. Colo. 1996). The court awarded sanctions (ten percent of the plaintiff company's total attorney fees and costs) where defendant's employees continuously destroyed (by overwriting) electronic evidence. The court criticized defendant's expert for not making an image copy of the drive at issue for production.

- *Crown Life Ins. Co. v. Craig*, 995 F.2d 1376, 1382-83 (7th Cir. 1993). Affirmed trial court's decision to sanction insurer and enter default judgment (counterclaim) against insurer when it failed to comply with discovery order requesting raw data from database. Data from a computer said to be "documents" within the meaning of FRCP 34.

- *American Banker Ins. Co. v. Caruth*, 786 S.W.2d 427 (Tex. Ct. App. 1990). Courts can impose sanctions on parties that fail to comply with electronic discovery requests.

- *Capellupo v. FMC Corp.*, 126 F.R.D. 545 (D. Minn. 1989). In gender-based employment discrimination action, court held that employer's knowing and intentional destruction of documents warranted an order requiring employer to reimburse employees for twice resulting expenditures.

- *Leeson v. State Farm Mut. Ins. Co.*, 546 N.E.2d 782 (Ill. App. Ct. 1989). Appellate Court held that defendant's claims were justified on grounds of oppressiveness, and therefore, the trial court abused its discretion in entering default sanctions for defendant's failure to comply with the discovery order. Such production would have been overly burdensome where compliance would have required the defendant to create a computer program to find the records and at least 15 minutes for an analyst to look through each of the 2,100 claims.

- *National Assoc. of Radiation Survivors v. Turnage*, 115 F.R.D. 543 (N.D. Cal. 1987). The court imposed sanctions on party that altered and destroyed computer documents in the regular course of business. The court appointed special master to oversee the discovery process.

Work Product Doctrine & Privilege

- *Baptiste v. Cushman & Wakefield, Inc.*, 2004 WL 330235 (S.D.N.Y. Feb. 20, 2004). In an employment discrimination lawsuit, the court addressed the issue of whether an email was protected by the attorney-client privilege. The email contained advice from the defendant's counsel regarding legal matters concerning the plaintiff, one of the defendant's employees at the time. The plaintiff, who claimed that a printed copy of the email was left anonymously on her desk, argued that the email was not protected by the attorney-client privilege because it was not labeled as protected, was not authored or circulated to attorneys, and did not refer to or contain legal advice. The plaintiff further argued that in the event the email was privileged, it was inadvertently produced, thus waiving any of the defendant's attorney-client privilege claims. The court determined that the first four paragraphs of the email were protected by the attorney-client privilege because "the email was clearly conveying information and advice given . . . by . . . outside counsel." However, the court concluded that the final paragraph of the email was not protected because it contained the defendant's own impressions and frustrations about the plaintiff's job performance. Finally, the court decided that the defendant did not waive the attorney-client privilege with respect to the first four paragraphs of the email. In response to the plaintiff's requests, the defendant did not produce the email and the defendant further identified the email as privileged attorney-client information in the privilege log submitted to the plaintiff's counsel. As such, the court ordered that the original email should be returned to the defendant and reproduced in a redacted form to the plaintiff.
- *United States v. Stewart*, 287 F. Supp. 2d 461 (S.D.N.Y. 2003). The defendant prepared an email in response to her attorneys' requests for factual information in the furtherance of their legal representation. A day later, the defendant accessed the email and

forwarded it to her daughter. The court held that the email was protected work product and that the defendant did not waive its immunity by forwarding the document to her daughter.

- *United States v. Rigas*, 281 F. Supp. 2d 733 (S.D.N.Y. 2003). The government in a bank fraud, wire fraud, and securities fraud case issued grand jury subpoenas to several executives and top-employees in the company, Adelphia Communications Corporation, being investigated. Adelphia produced copies of 26 computer hard drives in response to the subpoenas. The Assistant United States Attorneys assigned to the matter directed their staff to install the hard drives in certain computer terminals belonging to the United States Attorney's Office ("USAO") so that the data could be reviewed. The staff was informed that the hard drives "were evidence" and should be installed in such a way as to prevent additions to or deletions from those drives. Shortly thereafter, the computer consultant hired by defense counsel was permitted to make copies of the hard drives in question at the main USAO office. In the course of reviewing the images, defense counsel's computer expert determined that several USAO confidential files associated with the case at issue as well as other pending cases were produced during the imaging. The defendants argued that the Government waived its work product privilege when it voluntarily permitted defense counsel to copy the hard drives. The Government contended that disclosure of USAO files was inadvertent and therefore did not constitute waiver of the privilege. The court used a four part balancing test to determine that no waiver of privilege had occurred.

- *RLS v. United Bank of Kuwait*, 2003 WL 1563330 (S.D.N.Y. Mar. 26, 2003). In a contract dispute arising from the defendant's alleged failure to pay the plaintiff commissions due under the terms of written consulting agreements, the court concluded that the defendant did not meet its burden of demonstrating that two emails were subject to privilege protection under the common interest rule.

- *Murphy Oil USA v. Fluor Daniel*, No. 2:99-cv-03564 (E.D. La. Dec. 3, 2002). This Order follows the court's decision *in Murphy Oil USA, Inc. v. Fluor Daniel, Inc.*, 2002 WL 246439 (E.D. La. Feb. 19, 2002) ordering the defendant to produce relevant email communications archived on backup tapes. In this motion to compel before the court, the plaintiff sought production of a particular email and argued that the defendant waived the attorney-client privilege by voluntarily producing the contents of an email. Two copies of the email in question existed on the defendant's backup tapes: (1) the email attached to a message from the mail system administrator stating that the attached email was not deliverable due to an error in the mail address and (2) a copy of the same email sent to the correct email address. The defendant produced a privilege log identifying the subject email as an attorney-client communication, but at the same time inadvertently produced the administrator email and attachment. The court held that this inadvertent disclosure waived the attorney-client privilege and granted the plaintiff's motion to compel.

- *eSpeed, Inc. v. Chicago Board of Trade*, 2002 WL 827099 (S.D.N.Y. May 1, 2002). Cantor Fitzgerald, a third party and partial owner of the plaintiff, asserted the attorney-client privilege with respect to a series of emails and attachments addressing a patent purchase negotiation. These emails and attachments were sent by an outside attorney to an employee of Cantor Fitzgerald. The court examined the emails and attachments *in camera* and ordered production finding that the messages and documents did not contain client confidences and were not privileged.

- *Harris v. WHMC, Inc.*, 2002 WL 1821989 (Tx. Ct. App. Aug. 8, 2002). In a medical malpractice suit, the plaintiff appealed the trial court's exclusion from evidence certain email correspondence based on privilege. The trial court ruled that the plaintiff could use the emails at trial for impeachment purposes, but the emails themselves would not be admitted. The appellate court concluded that even if the trial court erred in excluding the emails, it was harmless error and did not cause an improper judgment.

- *Hambarian v. C.I.R.*, 118 T.C. 35 (U.S. Tax Ct. June 13, 2002). For use in connection with a criminal tax proceeding, the defendants' attorney created searchable, electronic databases containing documents turned over by the Prosecutor during discovery. The Respondent, in the civil tax proceeding at bar, sought a motion to compel discovery of these electronic document databases from the Petitioners/defendants. The court stated that "As the Petitioner failed to make the requisite showing of how the disclosure of the documents selected would reveal the defense attorney's mental impressions of the case, the requested documents and computerized electronic media are not protected by the work product doctrine."

- *City of Reno v. Reno Police Protective Assoc.*, 59 P.3d 1212 (Nev. 2002). The court overturned the Employee Relations Board's decision that documents sent by email cannot be considered privileged. The court stated that "[C]ourts have generally looked to the content and recipients of the email to determine if the email is protected" and held that documents transmitted by email are protected by the attorney-client privilege.

- *Koen v. Powell,* 212 F.R.D. 283 (E.D. Pa. 2002). In a legal malpractice suit, the court held that the attorney-client privilege and work product doctrine did not shield the defendants from turning over emails relating to the threatened malpractice suit.
- *Bertsch v. Duemeland,* 639 N.W.2d 455 (N.D. 2002). In an action alleging tortious interference with a business relationship, the appellate court affirmed a lower court's denial of the plaintiff's motion to compel discovery of data from some of the defendant's computers. Specifically, the court denied the plaintiff access to computers purchased by the defendant after the transaction that gave rise to the litigation. The court reasoned that the resulting data could not be relevant to the case, and that granting access "would not lead to relevant information" and "could result in disclosure of privileged and confidential information." The court had previously permitted e-discovery of the defendant's computer that was owned at the time of the alleged torts.
- *United States v. Sungard Data Systems,* 173 F.Supp.2d 20 (D.D.C. 2001). In an antitrust action, the court set forth specific confidentiality requirements, including a precise method for designating confidential electronic documents.
- *Long v. Anderson University,* 204 F.R.D. 129 (S.D.Ind. Oct. 30, 2001). The court found that the attorney-client privilege applied to electronic mail sent from a University human resources director to the dean of students regarding a conversation with counsel and his legal advice in a Civil Rights action against the University.
- *Wesley College v. Pitts,* 1997 WL 557554 (D. Del. Aug. 11, 1997). The court found that the defendant waived its work-product privilege when the email was distributed to several third parties.
- *State of Minnesota v. Phillip Morris,* 1995 WL 862582 (Minn. Ct. App. Dec. 26, 1995). Petitioners seek relief from a trial court's discovery order claiming that the material is attorney work product. The trial court made specific findings that (a) the computerized databases include fields containing objective information, (b) release of the specified information will not reveal the

impressions, opinions, or theories of counsel, and (c) respondents have met the standards for disclosure. Both the trial court and the court of appeals found unpersuasive the Petitioners' argument that the mere selection of documents for inclusion in the database would reveal attorney strategies.

- *Scovish v. Upjohn Co.*, 1995 WL 731755 (Conn. Super. Ct. Nov. 22, 1995). The court found that database was within attorney work-product, but that the plaintiff had substantial need of the information in the database and undue hardship would result if it was not produced. The court ordered the defendant to produce the database after removing any portions that contain subjective thoughts and opinions.
- *Ciba-Geigy Corp. v. Sandoz, Ltd.*, 916 F. Supp. 404 (D.N.J. 1995). The defendants produced all documents from database without conducting a privilege review. The court held that privilege is waived where the disclosure is a result of "gross negligence."
- *United States v. Keystone Sanitation Co.*, 885 F. Supp. 672 (M.D. Pa. 1994). In complying with the court's discovery order, the defendant inadvertently disclosed email messages that contained potentially confidential communications. This inadvertent disclosure waived any attorney-client privilege that may have protected portions of the email.
- *IBM v. Comdisco, Inc.*, 1992 WL 52143 (Del. Super. Ct. Mar. 11, 1992). The court allowed production of a portion of an email message claimed to be privileged because a portion of the email message was intended to be disclosed to persons outside the attorney/client privilege. Because it relayed legal advice from IBM's counsel, the other portion of the email was found to be privileged.
- *Burroughs v. Barr Lab., Inc.*, 143 F.R.D.611 (E.D.N.C. 1992), *vacated in part on other grounds* 40 F.3d 1223 (Fed. Cir. 1994). The court held that the attorney work product privilege applied to printed results of computerized database searches.
- *Indiana Coal Council v. Nat'l Trust for Historic Preservation*, 118 F.R.D. 264 (D. D.C. 1988). The court held that the work product doctrine prevented the plaintiff from gaining access to the defendant's legal research resources and findings conducted through a computer assisted legal research system.
- *Hoffman v. United Telecomms., Inc.*, 117 F.R.D. 436 (D. Kan. 1987). In an interrogatory, the plaintiff requested specific information concerning a computer file containing information regarding

possible employment discrimination. The court denied requesting parry's motion to compel finding that since the data would reveal defendant's discovery plan, the information was protected by the work-product doctrine.

- *Transamerican Computer Co. v. IBM*, 573 F.2d 646 (9th Cir. 1978). The court was more lenient regarding waiver of privilege where the party was required to produce larger amounts of data and where they actually performed some degree of privilege review.

Experts

- *In re Lorazepam and Clorazepate Antitrust Litig. v. Mylan Lab., Inc.*, 300 F. Supp. 2d 43 (D.D.C. 2004). In a class action antitrust lawsuit, the plaintiff sought to compel discovery of electronic documents. The defendant objected to the request arguing that the documents had already been produced. The plaintiff responded, claiming that the unindexed document "dump" produced on CD-ROM did not meet defendant's obligation to match documents with discovery requests as closely as possible. The court required the plaintiff to take the CD-ROM's to a computer forensic or electronic discovery expert before the court would require the defendant to index the information. The e-evidence expert was to ascertain whether the electronic information could be read and searched by commercially available software or converted to a format in which it could be done.
- *Physicians Interactive v. Lathian Sys., Inc.*, 2003 WL 23018270 (E.D.Va. Dec. 5, 2003). The plaintiff, the host of a medical website, contends that the defendant's employee secretly hacked into the plaintiff's website and stole confidential customer lists and computer software code. The plaintiff moved for a temporary restraining order, preliminary injunction, and limited expedited discovery order. Specifically, the plaintiff requested permission to enter defendant's computer server, work and home desktop and notebook computers, and any sites where the computers used in the alleged attacks were located to secure a mirror image of the computer equipment containing electronic data concerning defendant's alleged attack on plaintiff's website. The court found that the plaintiff made a preliminary showing of an invasion of its computer system, unauthorized copying of its customer list, and theft of its trade secrets. The court granted the plaintiff's request and directed that discovery must be done with the assistance of a computer forensic expert.

- *Premier Homes and Land Corp. v. Cheswell, Inc.*, 240 F. Supp. 2d 97 (D.Mass. 2002). In a property dispute, the plaintiff used an email purportedly sent from one of defendant's stockholders to the plaintiff's president to form the core of its claim that the defendant was not complying with the terms of a lease. The defendant filed an ex parte motion to preserve certain electronic evidence and expedite the production of electronic records. The court, stating that it was necessary to determine the origin of the disputed email, ordered defendant's experts to create mirror images of plaintiff's computer hard drives, backup tapes, and other data storage devices. Soon thereafter, the plaintiff confessed to his attorney that he had fabricated the email by pasting most of a heading from an earlier, legitimate message and altering the subject matter line. The defendant's motion to dismiss was granted and the court ordered the plaintiff to pay the defendant's attorney and expert fees and court costs for committing a fraud on the court.

- *Taylor v. State*, 93 S.W.Sd 487 (Tex. App. 2002). On appeal, the defendant argued that the trial court's refusal to order the State to provide him with a complete copy of the hard drive in question as "material physical evidence" for inspection requires reversal. Likening the situation to a drug case in which the defendant has the right to have the contraband reviewed by an independent expert, the appellate court stated, "mere inspection of the images . . . is not the same as an inspection of the drive itself (or an exact copy thereof). It is certainly not the same as an independent forensic examination of the contents of the hard drive by an expert."

- *In re Pharmatrak, Inc. Privacy Litigation*, 220 F.Supp.2d 4 (D. Mass. 2002), *rev'd on other grounds, In re Pharmatrak, Inc.*, 329 F.3d 9 (1st Cir. 2003). In a class action Privacy matter, the plaintiffs alleged that the defendants had secretly intercepted and accessed plaintiffs' personal information and Web browsing habits through the use of "cookies" and other devices, in violation of state and federal law. The plaintiffs raised claims under The Wiretap Act, The Stored Communications Act, and The Computer Fraud and Abuse Act. Using computer forensic tools, plaintiffs' expert was able to analyze the defendant's Website tracking logs and determine that the defendants had captured and possessed detailed private information about the plaintiffs, including their: names, addresses, telephone numbers, dates of birth, sex, insurance status, medical conditions, education levels, occupations, and email content. Finding that the plaintiffs failed to establish necessary elements of each of the above listed statutes, the court issued Summary Judgment in favor of the defendants.

- *United States v. Lloyd*, 269 F.3d 228 (3rd Cir. 2001). The Third Circuit has ruled that a man convicted of planting a computer "time bomb" that crippled operations at New Jersey-based Omega Engineering Corp. is not entitled to a new trial on the basis of a juror prejudice. The ruling reinstates the verdict in which the defendant was convicted on one count of computer sabotage. Computer experts were essential in recovering the evidence of the "time bomb."
- *Munshani v. Signal Lake Venture Fund II*, 13 Mass.L.Rptr. 732 (Mass.Super. 2001). In a dispute over authentication of an email message, the court appointed a neutral computer forensics expert. Based on the expert's analysis and report, the court found that the plaintiff intentionally fabricated the disputed email and then attempted to hide that fabrication. The court dismissed the plaintiff's suit and ordered him to pay the defendant's expert and attorney fees.
- *Northwest Airlines v. Local 2000*, C.A. No. 00-08DWF/AJB (D. Minn. Feb. 2, 2000) (Order on defendants' Motion for Protective Order and plaintiff's Motion to Compel Discovery); *Northwest Airlines v. Local 2000*, C.A. No. 00-08DWF/AJB (D. Minn. Feb. 29, 2000) (Memorandum Opinion and Order). The court ordered plaintiff's expert to act as a neutral 3rd party expert; on behalf of the court, the expert collected and imaged the defendants' personal hard drives and provided the parties with a complete report of all data "deemed responsive." The court issued detailed protocol for conducting the electronic discovery.
- *Simon Property Group v. mySimon, Inc.*, 194 F.R.D. 639 (S.D. Ind. 2000). On plaintiff's motion to compel in a trademark case, the court held that the plaintiff was entitled to attempt to recover deleted computer files from computers used by defendant's employees. The court required that protective measures be taken, including plaintiff's appointment of an expert who would serve as an officer of the court and turn over the recovered information to defendant's counsel for appropriate review.
- *Playboy Enters., Inc. v. Welles*, 60 F. Supp.2d 1050 (S.D. Cal. 1999). The court appointed a computer expert who specialized in the field of electronic discovery to create a "mirror image" of defendant's hard drive. The court reserved Respondent's right to object to production after data capture by expert and review of materials.

- *National Assoc. of Radiation Survivors v. Turnage,* 115 F.R.D. 543 (N.D. Cal. 1987). The court imposed sanctions on party that altered and destroyed computer documents in the regular course of business. The court appointed special master to oversee the discovery process.
- *United States v. IBM,* 76 F.R.D. 97 (S.D.N.Y. 1977) Where the defendant was to produce information to the plaintiff pursuant to prior court orders, but production did not comport with spirit and intent of those orders and was highly technical and complex in nature, the court determined that "exceptional conditions" existed, warranting appointment of examiner. The examiner's duties included reporting to court as to information that the defendant possessed and produced and supervising discovery.

Computer Forensic Protocols

- *State v. Voorheis,* 2004 WL 258178 (Vt. Feb. 13, 2004). The appellate court affirmed the trial court's finding that "instant messaging" text was sufficient evidence to support the defendant's conviction of incitement and attempt of use of a child in a sexual performance. The State introduced evidence recovered from a computer forensic examination of the computer system and floppy disks taken from the child's home. The computer forensic expert recovered text from "instant messaging" conversations in which the defendant discussed with the child's mother a plan to have a lewd photo shoot. At trial, the expert noted that instant messaging is not usually saved on a computer and that saving it to floppy disks required "concentrated effort." Based on the instant messaging evidence, the jury found the defendant guilty. The defendant argued that the instant messaging text was "meager evidence" of guilt, since the text had allegedly been altered and edited. The court rejected this claim finding that the retrieved electronic conversations, together with witness testimony, offered ample evidence to support the jury's findings.
- *Kupper v. State,* 2004 WL 60768 (Tex. App. Jan. 14,2004). The defendant appealed his sexual assault conviction, challenging the admissibility of email messages retrieved from the defendant's deleted files on his work computer and an email message and a photograph retrieved from the temporary internet files on his work computer. At trial, a police detective trained in computer forensics testified that she imaged the defendant's home and work computers and engaged in a computer forensic investigation to locate the evidence in question against the defendant.

The appellate court rejected the defendant's arguments and concluded that the police detective's testimony established that the appearance, contents, substance, internal patterns, or other distinctive characteristics, taken in conjunction with the circumstances, authenticated the computer evidence. The court further determined that there was no evidence raising chain of custody issues.

- *Commonwealth v. Simone*, 2003 WL 22994245 (Va. Cir. Ct. Nov. 12, 2003). The court determined that the defendant knowingly possessed three sexually explicit images of juveniles found in the cache of his computer even though the images could have appeared on the defendant's computer screen as "pop-ups" for websites other than ones intentionally accessed or manually downloaded by the defendant. The computer forensic investigator recovered the sexually explicit images from the computer's directory cache, also known as temporary internet files. The investigator testified that when accessing a website, a computer operator normally cannot stop these images from being placed in the cache; however, images must actually appear on the computer screen before they are automatically placed in the cache. The court rejected the defense's argument and determined that the defendant exhibited knowing possession of the three child pornography images contained in his computer's cache/temporary Internet files.

- *The Carlton Group v. Tobin*, 2003 WL 21782650 (S.D.N.Y. July 31, 2003). The plaintiff, a financial services company, brought suit against several defendants claiming that the defendants deleted files from the plaintiff's computers, conspired to steal confidential and proprietary information from its computer network, and used that information to compete unlawfully with the plaintiff. One group of defendants, Mission Capital, is a company that competes directly with the plaintiff's company, and the individual Mission Capital defendants were formerly employed by the plaintiff. The other group of defendants, PDP Capital, is an investment advisor and fund management company and does not compete with the plaintiff or Mission Capital. All parties in the suit maintain offices in the same business suite, and all tenants of this office suite share a communication switch and data transmission line which connect the tenants' computers to the Internet. As such, all the computers in the suite constitute a network, although the tenants do not have access to each other's computers. PDP defendants sought Rule 11 sanctions against the plaintiff and plaintiff's counsel for filing suit against them lacking in evidentiary support. The plaintiff maintains that its allegations against PDP were objectively reasonable based upon information from computer forensic experts that PDP had deliberately established a link between computer systems to move data back and forth between the plaintiff's computer network and the PDP computer. Denying the PDP defendants' motion for Rule 11 sanctions, the court held that the plaintiff made a substantial pre-filing inquiry that gave them a reasonable basis for believing that PDP defendants conspired with the Mission defendants.

- *Four Seasons Hotels and Resorts v. Consorcio Barr*, 267 F.Supp.2d 1268 (S.D.Fla. 2003). The plaintiff brought an action against the defendant licensee alleging, among other things, violations of the Computer Fraud and Abuse Act, Electronic Communications Privacy Act, and Uniform Trade Secrets Act. A computer forensic investigation revealed that the defendant accessed the plaintiff's computer network, downloaded confidential data onto backup tapes, fabricated electronic evidence, and deleted files and overwrote data prior to his computer being turned over for inspection to the plaintiff. The court held that the defendant acquired the plaintiff's confidential customer information through improper means, namely, by theft and by espionage through electronic means. The court issued a judgment for the plaintiff and ordered monetary damages, among other relief.
- *People v. Carratu*, 755 N.Y.S.2d 800 (N.Y. Sup. Ct. 2003). The defendant moved to suppress computer evidence seized from his home and subsequently searched by the police department's computer forensic examiners. The defendant claimed that the search warrants and supporting affidavits limited the search to documentary evidence relating to his illegal cable box operation and thus, the forensic examiner violated the defendant's Fourth Amendment rights upon inspection of non-textual files with folder names clearly relating to other illegal activity. Granting the suppression motion, in part, the court stated, "In view of the Fourth Amendment's 'particularity requirement,' a warrant authorizing a search of the text files of a computer for documentary evidence pertaining to a specific crime will not authorize a search of image files containing evidence of other criminal activity."
- *United States v. Sanchez*, 59 M.J. 566 (A.F. Ct. Crim. App. 2003). A federal appellate military judge determined that the govern-

ment produced sufficient evidence to prove that the defendant knowingly possessed child pornography images stored in his computer's temporary Internet files. After making a mirror image of the computer's hard drive, investigators used a software program called "Carve This" to uncover remnants of files that were overwritten or deleted from the hard drive. The program found that the presence of the images on the hard drive was consistent with someone viewing them on the Internet and the images then being automatically saved to the hard drive by the web browser. Combining this with evidence of the defendant's subscriptions to nude teen websites, the court determined that the evidence supported the allegation that the defendant knowingly possessed the pornographic images.

- *United States v. Triumph Capital Group*, 211 F.R.D. 31 (D.Conn. 2002). In order to prevent spoliation of evidence in a public corporation case, the government sought and obtained a search warrant to search and seize a laptop computer at issue. The warrant did not limit the search to any particular area of the hard drive. However, it did limit the government to search for and seize only certain evidence relating specifically to the charges and to follow detailed protocols to avoid revealing any privileged information. So that the data would not be altered, the government made mirror images of the hard drive and then proceeded with the computer forensic investigation. The defendants argued that this mirroring amounted to a search and seizure of the entire hard drive and moved to suppress all evidence from the laptop. The court determined that although the search warrant limited the scope of the information that investigators could search for, technical realities required the government to make complete mirror images of the hard drive. Furthermore, the court ruled that copying a file does not necessarily constitute seizure of that file and that examining a file more than once does not constitute multiple searches under the Fourth Amendment.
- *United States v. Al-Marri*, 230 F.Supp.2d 535 (S.D.N.Y. 2002). In the wake of the September 11th attacks, the FBI visited the defendant's home persuing tips of the defendant's allegedly suspicious activity. The FBI agents obtained the defendant's consent to search his home and, with his affirmative consent and cooperation, seized his laptop computer, disks, and CDs for further investigation. Investigation of the computer hardware revealed evidence of credit card fraud. The defendant moved to suppress

the computer evidence, arguing that even if he validly consented to a search of his home, that consent did not encompass the contents of his computer. The court denied the motion to suppress and ruled that the FBI's lawful search of the defendant's home encompassed the right to search the computer as a closed container.

- *State v. Townsend*, 57 P.3d 255 (Wash. 2002) (Bridge, J. concurring). The principal issue the court resolved was whether a police officer violated a provision in Washington's privacy act when he saved and printed email and real time client-to-client ICQ messages between the defendant and a fictitious child. The court upheld the conviction and held that the act was not violated. In a concurring opinion, one judge further addressed the unique aspects of electronically created and stored email. "Technically, email messages are permanently recorded since 'most email programs keep copies of every message a user ever wrote, every message the user ever received, and every message the user deleted.' . . . Although some email services may offer the possibility of 'shredding' an email message, arguably the equivalent of actually deleting it, the email file may still be retrievable using certain software. 'A deleted file is really not a deleted file, it is merely organized differently.' "

- *Moench v. Red River Basin Board*, 2002 WL 31109803 (Minn. Ct. App. Sept. 24,2002). The plaintiff was forced to resign from his executive director position after being confronted with allegations that pornographic images were found on his computer. The plaintiff's employer used a computer forensic expert to investigate the pornographic material stored in the cache file of the plaintiff's computer. Given that the plaintiff's employment was terminated for cause, the Commissioner of Economic Security refused to issue unemployment benefits. The appellate court reversed the denial of benefits stating that the evidence in the record did not support the finding that the plaintiff intentionally downloaded or stored any pornographic material on his computer.

- *United States v. Bach*, 310 F.3d 1063 (8th Cir. 2002). In a criminal prosecution for possession of child pornography, Yahoo! technicians retrieved, pursuant to a search warrant, all information from the defendant's email account. The lower court ruled that the seizure of the emails by Yahoo! was unlawful because police were not present when the defendant's email account was searched. Reversing the lower court's opinion, the appellate court held that Yahoo!'s search of the defendant's emails without a police officer present was reasonable under the Fourth Amendment and did not violate the defendant's privacy rights.

- *United States v. Tucker*, 150 F.Supp.2d 1263 (D. Utah 2001). The defendant was found guilty of knowing possession of child pornography. The conviction was largely supported by computer forensic evidence found in the form of deleted Internet cache files that were saved to the defendant's hard drive when he viewed the various websites. (*See also United States v. Tucker*, 305 F.3d 1193 10th Cir. 2002).

- *State v. Guthrie*, 627 N.W.2d 401 (S.D. 2001). In a criminal prosecution for murder, a computer specialist conducted several forensic searches on a computer used by the defendant, finding that the computer had been used to conduct numerous Internet searches on subjects related to the incidents surrounding the murder. In addition, the forensic analysis was able to reveal that a computer printed suicide note, offered to exculpate the defendant, was created several months after the victim's death. *State v. Guthrie*, 2002 WL 31618440 (S.D. Nov. 20, 2002). Anticipating that the State would not have time to thoroughly examine the evidence against the defendant for murdering his wife, Defense counsel failed to disclose the victim's purported computerized suicide note during the discovery period. The appellate court affirmed the trial court's finding that defense counsel acted in bad faith by holding this evidence back from discovery. The appellate court also held that the fees of the State's computer forensic expert were reasonable because the expert was highly qualified in computer forensics.

- *Adobe Sys., Inc. v. Sun South Prod, Inc.*, 187 F.R.D. 636 (S.D. Cal. 1999). In a computer piracy suit, the court denied plaintiff's *ex parte* application for a temporary restraining order. The court based its decision on the fact that it is more difficult to erase evidence that is magnetically encoded on a computer hard disk than it is to physically destroy floppy disks, compact discs, invoices, and other tangible forms of evidence. "Manual or automated deletion of that software may remove superficial indicia, such as its icons or presence in the user's application menu. However, telltale traces of a previous installation remain, such as abandoned subdirectories, libraries, information in system files, and registry keys. . . Even if an infringer managed to delete every file associated with plaintiffs' software, the plaintiff could still recover many of those files since the operating system does not actually *erase* the files, but merely marks the space consumed by the files as free for use by other files."

- *Byrne v. Byrne,* 650 N.Y.S.2d 499 (N.Y. Sup. Ct. 1996). In a divorce proceeding, the wife sought access to her husband's computer, which husband used for both business and personal purposes even though computer was provided by husband's employer. The wife was awarded such access to search the computer for information about the couple's finances and marital assets.

Admissibility

- *J.P. Morgan Chase Bank v. Liberty Mutual Ins.,* 2002 WL 31867731 (S.D.N.Y. Dec. 23, 2002). In a suit against insurance companies that had guaranteed payment in the event of Enron's bankruptcy, the court weighed the admissibility of several emails. The court determined that emails authored by senior bank officials would be allowed into evidence and that a reasonable juror could find these emails probative of the defendants' central proposition that the transactions were actually uninsurable "off-the-books" loans.
- *Kearley v. Mississippi,* 843 So. 2d 66 (Miss. Ct. App. 2002). A criminal defendant was convicted of sexual battery and appealed on several issues including proper authentication of emails which he allegedly sent to the victim. The appellate court held that the victim's testimony that she had received and printed the emails on her computer was sufficient authentication under the rules of evidence, and the court upheld the conviction.
- *State v. Cook,* 2002 WL 31045293 (Ohio Ct. App. Sept. 13, 2002). The defendant appealed his conviction for possessing nude images of minors, claiming in part that the trial court erred in admitting materials, over the defendant's objection, that were generated from a "mirror image" of the defendant's hard drive. After a detailed discussion of the mirror imaging process, the authenticity of the data taken from the image, and the possibility for tampering, the appellate court found that the trial court properly admitted the evidence.
- *Perfect 10, Inc. v. Cybernet Ventures, Inc.,* 213 F.Supp.2d 1146 (C.D. Cal. 2002). In a copyright and trademark infringement action, the court refused to find that all evidence printed from websites is inauthentic and inadmissible. Instead, the court found that the printouts were properly authenticated under Fed.R.Evid. 901 (a) where the plaintiffs CEO adequately established that the ex-

hibits attached to his declaration were "true and correct copies of pages printed from the Internet that were printed by [him] or under his direction."

- *New York v. Microsoft Corp.*, 2002 WL 649951 (D.D.C. Apr. 12, 2002). Microsoft challenged several emails appended to the written testimony of one of the plaintiff's witnesses, claiming that the statements contained therein were inadmissible hearsay. The court excluded multiple email messages using the following reasoning: (1) they were offered for the truth of the matters they asserted, (2) had not been shown to be business records as required under Rule 803(6), and (3) contained multiple levels of hearsay for which no exception had been established.

- *Sea-Land Service, Inc. v. Lozen Int'l*, 285 F.3d 808 (9th Cir. 2002). The court ruled that the trial court should have admitted an internal company email, which an employee of the plaintiff had forwarded to the defendant. The defense persuasively argued on appeal that the email was not excludable hearsay because her remarks in forwarding the email manifested an adoption or belief in truth of the information contained in the original email. The court ruled that this satisfied the requirements for an adoptive admission under Fed.R.Evid. 801(d)(2)(B).

- *Harveston v. State*, 798 So. 2d 638 (Miss. Ct. App. 2001). In a criminal burglary prosecution, the court refused to allow in computer database print-outs under the State's business records exception to the hearsay rule. The court held that the State failed to meet its burden because "[T]here was no evidence offered as to the means by which the information . . . was compiled. The only testimony came from an investigating officer who limited his testimony to the fact that law enforcement officers routinely make use of such information. [However, t]he reliability of the information in 'business records' is determined by the competence of the *compiler* of the information and not the extent of the *consumer's* reliance on information received from another source."

- *V Cable Inc. v. Budnick*, 23 Fed.Appx. 64 (2nd Cir. 2001). In an investigation of illegal sales and distribution of cable equipment, the police seized computers believed to contain relevant evidence of the crime. After holding the computers in question, the police sent them to an independent software company for analysis. Appellant's argument implies that, once they left police custody, the computers and any records obtained there from became corrupted and, therefore, inadmissible under Rule 803(6) of the Federal Rules of Evidence. The court found the documents to be sufficiently trustworthy to be admitted under Rule 803(6).

- *United States v. Meienberg*, 263 F.3d 1177 (10th Cir. 2001). The government introduced print-outs of computerized records and the defendant objected to these print-outs based on lack of authentification. The court held that the government met its burden by presenting a witness who testified that the print-outs were a record of all transactions. The court held that this was in accordance with Federal Rule of Evidence 901(b)(7).
- *Bowe v. State*, 785 So. 2d 531 (Fla. Dist. Ct. App. 2001). "An email 'statement' sent to another is always subject to the limitations of the hearsay rule."
- *People v. Markowitz*, 721 N.Y.S.2d 758 (N.Y. Sup. Ct. 2001). In a larceny and possession of stolen property suit, the court admitted computer databases that indicated how much money should have been collected by the defendant toll-booth worker. The testimony of an employee of the company that prepared the databases was sufficient foundation for admission of the electronic records.
- *Hardison v. Balboa Ins. Co.*, 4 Fed. Appx. 663 (10th Cir. 2001). To prove that an insurance company had followed notice of cancellation requirements, the court admitted computer files and print-outs regarding how the cancelled policy was processed and maintained. The court stated that computer business records are admissible under Rule 803(6) "if the offeror establishes a sufficient foundation in the record for [their] introduction."
- *Broderick v. State*, 35 S.W.3d 67 (Tex. App. 2000). In child sex abuse prosecution, the court affirmed the trial court's admission of a duplicate of defendant's hard drive, in place of the original. The court concluded that the state's best evidence rule did not preclude admission because the computer expert testified that the copy of the hard drive exactly duplicated the contents of the hard drive.
- *St. Clair v. Johnny's Oyster & Shrimp*, 76 F.Supp.2d 773 (S.D. Tex. 1999). "[A]ny evidence procured off the Internet is adequate for almost nothing, even under the most liberal interpretation of the hearsay exception."
- *SKW Real Estate Ltd. v. Gallicchio*, 716 A.2d 903 (Conn. App. Ct. 1998). A computer-generated document is admissible in a foreclosure action, pursuant to the business records exception to the hearsay rule.

- *Monotype Corp. v. Int'l Typeface Corp.*, 43 F.3d 443 (9th Cir. 1994). The court declined admission of a detrimental email in a license infringement action, due to the prejudicial nature of the message and fact that the email was not admissible under the business record exception.
- *United States v. Bowers*, 920 F.2d 220 (4th Cir. 1990). Computer data consisting of IRS taxpayer data compilations is admissible as official records.
- *United States v. Catabran*, 836 F.2d 453 (9th Cir. 1988). Computer printouts are admissible as business records under the Federal Rules of Evidence 803{6), provided that proper foundational requirements are first established.
- *State of Wash. v. Ben-Neth*, 663 P.2d 156 (Wash. Ct. App. 1983). Computer-generated evidence is hearsay but may be admitted as a business record provided a proper foundation is laid.
- *United Stales v. Vela*, 673 F.2d 86 (5th Cir. 1982). The court admitted computerized telephone bills under the Business Records exception where a telephone company employee laid the proper foundation for the reliability of the telephone bills record-keeping process. In describing the reliability of the computer generated documents, the court stated that the computerized reports "would be even more reliable than . . . average business record(s) because they are not even touched by the hand of man."

APPENDIX ❖ B

Rules and Statutes Impacting Electronic Evidence

Local Rules & State Statutes

Eastern and Western Districts of Arkansas Local Rule 26.1
http://www.are.uscourts.gov/local_rules.html

The Fed.R.Civ.P. 26(f) report filed with the court must contain the parties' views and proposals regarding the following:

(4) Whether any party will likely be requested to disclose or produce information from electronic or computer-based media. If so:

    (a) whether disclosure or production will be limited to data reasonably available to the parties in the ordinary course of business;

    (b) the anticipated scope, cost and time required for disclosure or production of data beyond what is reasonably available to the parties in the ordinary course of business;

    (c) the format and media agreed to by the parties for the production of such Data as well as agreed procedures for such production;

    (d) whether reasonable measures have been taken to preserve potentially discoverable data from alteration or destruction in the ordinary course of business or otherwise;

    (e) other problems which the parties anticipate may arise in connection with electronic or computer-based discovery.

California Code of Civil Procedure §2017
http://www.leginfo.ca.gov/cgi-bin/displaycode?section=ccp&
group=02001-03000&file=2016-2036

(e) (1) Pursuant to noticed motion, a court may enter orders for the use of technology in conducting discovery in cases designated as complex pursuant to Section 19 of the Judicial Administration Standards, cases ordered to be coordinated pursuant to Chapter 3 (commencing with Section 404) of Title 4 of Part 2, or exceptional cases exempt from case disposition time goals pursuant to Article 5 (commencing with Section 68600) of Chapter 2 of Title 8 of the Government Code, or cases assigned to Plan 3 pursuant to paragraph (3) of subdivision (b) of Section 2105 of the California Rules of Court. In other cases, the parties may stipulate to the entry of orders for the use of technology in conducting discovery.

(2) An order authorizing that discovery may be made only upon the express findings of the court or stipulation of the parties that the procedures adopted in the order meet all of the following criteria: (A) They promote cost-effective and efficient discovery or motions relating thereto. (B) They do not impose or require undue expenditures of time or money. (C) They do not create an undue economic burden or hardship on any person. (D) They promote open competition among vendors and providers of services in order to facilitate the highest quality service at the lowest reasonable cost to the litigants. (E) They do not require parties or counsel to purchase exceptional or unnecessary services, hardware, or software.

(3) Pursuant to these orders, discovery may be conducted and maintained in electronic media and by electronic communication. The court may enter orders prescribing procedures relating to the use of electronic technology in conducting discovery, including orders for the service of requests for discovery and responses, service and presentation of motions, production, storage, and access to information in electronic form, and the conduct of discovery in electronic media. The Judicial Council may promulgate rules, standards, and guidelines relating to electronic discovery and the use of such discovery data and documents in court proceedings.

(4) Nothing in this subdivision shall diminish the rights and duties of the parties regarding discovery, privileges, procedural rights, or substantive law.

(5) If a service provider is to be used and compensated by the parties, the court shall appoint the person or organization agreed upon by the

parties and approve the contract agreed upon by the parties and the service provider. If the parties do not agree on the selection, each party shall submit to the court up to three nominees for appointment together with a contract acceptable to the nominee and the court shall appoint a service provider from among the nominees. The court may condition this appointment on the acceptance of modifications in the terms of the contract. If no nominations are received from any of the parties, the court shall appoint one or more service providers. Pursuant to noticed motion at any time and upon a showing of good cause, the court may order the removal of the service provider or vacate any agreement between the parties and the service provider, or both, effective as of the date of the order. The continued service of the service provider shall be subject to review periodically, as agreed by the parties and the service provider, or annually if they do not agree. Any disputes involving the contract or the duties, rights, and obligations of the parties or service providers may be determined on noticed motion in the action.

(6) Subject to these findings and the purpose of permitting and encouraging cost-effective and efficient discovery, "technology," as used in this section, includes, but is not limited to, telephone, e-mail, CD-ROM, Internet web sites, electronic documents, electronic document depositories, Internet depositions and storage, videoconferencing, and other electronic technology that may be used to improve communication and the discovery process.

(7) Nothing in this subdivision shall be construed to modify the requirement for use of a stenographic court reporter as provided in paragraph (1) of subdivision (l) of Section 2025. The rules, standards, and guidelines adopted pursuant to this subdivision shall be consistent with the requirement of paragraph (1) of subdivision (l) of Section 2025 that deposition testimony be taken stenographically unless the parties agree or the court orders otherwise.

(8) Nothing in this subdivision shall be construed to modify or affect in any way the process used for the selection of a stenographic court reporter.

Middle District of Florida Local Court Rule 3.03(f)
http://www.flmd.uscourts.gov

Litigants' counsel should utilize computer technology to the maximum extent possible in all phases of litigation *i.e.*, to serve interrogatories on opposing counsel with a copy of the questions on computer disk in addition to the required printed copy.

Illinois Supreme Court Rules 201(b)(1) & 214

http://www.state.il.us/court/SupremeCourt/Rules/Art_II/ArtII.
htm#201

http://www.state.il.us/court/SupremeCourt/Rules/Art_II/ArtII.
htm#214

201(b)(1)—*Full Disclosure Required.* Except as provided in these rules, a party may obtain by discovery full disclosure regarding any matter relevant to the subject matter involved in the pending action, whether it relates to the claim or defense of the party seeking disclosure or of any other party, including the existence, description, nature, custody, condition, and location of any documents or tangible things, and the identity and location of persons having knowledge of relevant facts. The word "documents," as used in these rules, includes, but is not limited to, papers, photographs, films, recordings, memoranda, books, records, accounts, communications and all retrievable information in computer storage.

214—Any party may by written request direct any other party to produce for inspection, copying, reproduction photographing, testing or sampling specified documents, objects or tangible things, or to permit access to real estate for the purpose of making surface or subsurface inspections or surveys or photographs, or tests or taking samples, or to disclose information calculated to lead to the discovery of the whereabouts of any of these items, whenever the nature, contents, or condition of such documents, objects, tangible things, or real estate is relevant to the subject matter of the action. The request shall specify a reasonable time, which shall not be less than 28 days except by agreement or by order of court, and the place and manner of making the inspection and performing the related acts. One copy of the request shall be served on all other parties entitled to notice. A party served with the written request shall (1) produce the requested documents as they are kept in the usual course of business or organized and labeled to correspond with the categories in the request, and all retrievable information in computer storage in printed form or (2) serve upon the party so requesting written objections on the ground that the request is improper in whole or in part. If written objections to a part of the request are made, the remainder of the request shall be complied with. Any objection to the request or the refusal to respond shall be heard by the court upon prompt notice and motion of the party submitting the request. If the party claims that the item is not in his or her possession or control or that he or she does not have information calculated to lead to the discovery of its whereabouts, the party may be ordered to submit to examination in open court or by deposition regarding such claim. The party producing documents shall furnish an affidavit stating whether the production is complete in accordance with the request.

A party has a duty to seasonably supplement any prior response to the extent of documents, objects or tangible things which subsequently come into that party's possession or control or become known to that party.

This rule does not preclude an independent action against a person not a party for production of documents and things and permission to enter upon real estate.

Maryland Rule of Civil Procedure 2-504.3
http://198.187.128.12/maryland/lpext.dll?f=templates&fn=fs-main.htm&2.0

(a) *Definition—computer-generated evidence.*—"Computer-generated evidence" means (1) a computer-generated aural, visual, or other sensory depiction of an event or thing and (2) a conclusion in aural, visual, or other sensory form formulated by a computer program or model. The term does not encompass photographs merely because they were taken by a camera that contains a computer; documents merely because they were generated on a word or text processor; business, personal, or other records or documents admissible under Rule 5-803 (b) merely because they were generated by computer; or summary evidence admissible under Rule 5-1006, spread sheets, or other documents merely presenting or graphically depicting data taken directly from business, public, or other records admissible under Rules 5-802.1 through 5-804.

(b) *Notice—*
   (1) Except as provided in subsection (b) (2) of this Rule, any party who intends to use computer-generated evidence at trial for any purpose shall file a written notice within the time provided in the scheduling order or no later than 90 days before trial if there is no scheduling order that:
      (A) contains a descriptive summary of the computer-generated evidence the party intends to use, including (i) a statement as to whether the computer-generated evidence intended to be used is in the category described in subsection (a) (1) or subsection (a) (2) of this Rule, (ii) a description of the subject matter of the computer-generated evidence, and (iii) a statement of what the computer-generated evidence purports to prove or illustrate; and
      (B) is accompanied by a written undertaking that the party will take all steps necessary to (i) make available any equipment or other facility needed to present the evidence

in court, (ii) preserve the computer-generated evidence and furnish it to the clerk in a manner suitable for transmittal as a part of the record on appeal, and (iii) comply with any request by an appellate court for presentation of the computer-generated evidence to that court.

(2) Any party who intends to use computer-generated evidence at trial for purposes of impeachment or rebuttal shall file, as soon as practicable, the notice required by subsection (b) (1) of this Rule, except that the notice is not required if computer-generated evidence prepared by or on behalf of a party-opponent will be used by a party only for impeachment of other evidence introduced by that party-opponent. In addition, the notice is not required if computer-generated evidence prepared by or on behalf of a party-opponent will be used only as a statement by a party-opponent admissible under Rule 5-803 (a).

(c) *Required disclosure; additional discovery.* Within five days after service of a notice under section (b) of this Rule, the proponent shall make the computer-generated evidence available to any party. Notwithstanding any provision of the scheduling order to the contrary, the filing of a notice of intention to use computer-generated evidence entitles any other party to a reasonable period of time to discover any relevant information needed to oppose the use of the computer-generated evidence before the court holds the hearing provided for in section (e) of this Rule.

(d) *Objection.* Not later than 60 days after service of a notice under section (b) of this Rule, a party may file any then-available objection that the party has to the use at trial of the computer-generated evidence and shall file any objection that is based upon an assertion that the computer-generated evidence does not meet the requirements of Rule 5-901 (b) (9). An objection based on the alleged failure to meet the requirements of Rule 5-901 (b) (9) is waived if not so filed, unless the court for good cause orders otherwise.

(e) *Hearing and order.* If an objection is filed under section (d) of this Rule, the court shall hold a pretrial hearing on the objection. If the hearing is an evidentiary hearing, the court may appoint an expert to assist the court in ruling on the objection and may assess against one or more parties the reasonable fees and expenses of the expert. In ruling on the objection, the court may require modification of the computer-generated evidence and may impose conditions relating to its use at trial. The court's ruling on the objection shall control the subsequent course of the action. If the court rules that the computer-generated evidence may be used at trial, when it is used, (1) any party may, but need not, present any admissible evidence that was presented at the hearing on the objection, and (2) the party objecting to the evidence is not required to re-state an objection made in writing or at the hearing in order to preserve that objection for appeal. If the court excludes or restricts the use of computer-generated evidence, the proponent need not make a subsequent offer of proof in order to preserve that ruling for appeal.

(f) *Preservation of computer-generated evidence.* The party offering computer-generated evidence at any proceeding shall preserve the computer-generated evidence, furnish it to the clerk in a manner suitable for transmittal as a part of the record on appeal, and present the computer-generated evidence to an appellate court if the court so requests.

Supreme Court of Mississippi Rule 26(b)(5)
http://www.mssc.state.ms.us/rules/default.asp

Rule 26(b)(5) *Electronic Data.* To obtain discovery of data or information that exists in electronic or magnetic form, the requesting party must specifically request production of electronic or magnetic data and specify the form in which the requesting party wants it produced. The responding party must produce the electronic or magnetic data that is responsive to the request and is reasonably available to the responding party in its ordinary course of business. If the responding party cannot-through reasonable efforts-retrieve the data or information requested or produce it in the form requested, the responding party must state an objection complying with these rules. If the court orders the responding party to comply with the request, the court may also order that the requesting party pay the reasonable expenses of any extraordinary steps required to retrieve and produce the information.

District of New Jersey Local Civil Rule 26.1(d)
http://pacer.njd.uscourts.gov/

(1) *Duty to Investigate and Disclose.* Prior to a Fed. R. Civ. P. 26(f) conference, counsel shall review with the client the client's information management systems including computer-based and other digital systems, in order to understand how information is stored and how it can be retrieved. To determine what must be disclosed pursuant to Fed. R. Civ. P. 26(a) (1), counsel shall further review with the client the client's information files, including currently maintained computer files as well as historical, archival, back-up, and legacy computer files, whether in current or historic media or formats, such as digital evidence which may be used to support claims or defenses. Counsel shall also identify a person or persons with knowledge about the client's information management systems, including computer-based and other

digital systems, with the ability to facilitate, through counsel, reasonably anticipated discovery.

(2) *Duty to Notify.* A party seeking discovery of computer-based or other digital information shall notify the opposing party as soon as possible, but no later than the Fed. R. Civ. P. 26(f) conference, and identify as clearly as possible the categories of information which may be sought. A party may supplement its request for computer-based and other digital information as soon as possible upon receipt of new information relating to digital evidence.

(3) *Duty to Meet and Confer.* During the Fed. R. Civ. P. 26(f) conference, the parties shall confer and attempt to agree on computer-based and other digital discovery matters, including the following: (a) Preservation and production of digital information; procedures to deal with inadvertent production of privileged information; whether restoration of deleted digital information may be necessary; whether back up or historic legacy data is within the scope of discovery; and the media, format, and procedures for producing digital information; (b) Who will bear the costs of preservation, production, and restoration (if necessary) of any digital discovery.

Texas Rule of Civil Procedure 196.4

To obtain discovery of data or information that exists in electronic or magnetic form, the requesting party must specifically request production of electronic or magnetic data and specify the form in which the requesting party wants it produced. The responding party must produce the electronic or magnetic data that is responsive to the request and is reasonably available to the responding party in its ordinary course of business. If the responding party cannot—through reasonable efforts—retrieve the data or information requested or produce it in the form requested, the responding party must state an objection complying with these rules. If the court orders the responding party to comply with the request, the court must also order that the requesting party pay the reasonable expenses of any extraordinary steps required to retrieve and produce the information.

District of Wyoming Local Civil Rule 26.1(d)
http://www.ck10.uscourts.gov/wyoming/district/pdfforms/local rules-cv.pdf

(3) Prior to a Fed.R.Civ.P. 26(f) conference, counsel should carefully investigate their client's information management system so that they are

knowledgeable as to its operation, including how information is stored and how it can be retrieved. Likewise, counsel shall reasonably review the client's computer files to ascertain the contents thereof, including archival and legacy data (outdated formats or media), and disclose in initial discovery (self-executing routine discovery) the computer based evidence which may be used to support claims or defenses.

(A) Duty to Notify. A party seeking discovery of computer-based information shall notify the opposing party immediately, but no later than the Fed.R.Civ.P. 26(f) conference of that fact and identify as clearly as possible the categories of information which may be sought.

(B) Duty to Meet and Confer. The parties shall meet and confer regarding the following matters during the Fed.R.Civ.P.26(f) conference:

  (i) Computer-based information (in general). Counsel shall attempt to agree on steps the parties will take to segregate and preserve computer-based information in order to avoid accusations of spoliation;

  (ii) E-mail information. Counsel shall attempt to agree as to the scope of e-mail discovery and attempt to agree upon an e-mail search protocol. This should include an agreement regarding inadvertent production of privileged e-mail messages.

  (iii) Deleted information. Counsel shall confer and attempt to agree whether or not restoration of deleted information may be necessary, the extent to which restoration of deleted information is needed, and who will bear the costs of restoration; and

  (iv) Back-up data. Counsel shall attempt to agree whether or not back-up data may be necessary, the extent to which back-up data is needed and who will bear the cost of obtaining back-up data.

FEDERAL STATUTES

Computer Fraud and Abuse Act—Regulates fraud and related activity in connection with computers.
http://caselaw.lp.findlaw.com/scripts/ts_search.pl?title=18&sec=1030

Note: Portions of the CFAA were amended by the USA Patriot Act of 2001. For a discussion of the Patriot Act's impact on the CFAA, visit: http://www.usdoj.gov/criminal/cybercrime/PatriotAct.htm.

Title 18 Part I Chapter 47 Section 1030(a) (as of 01/23/2000)
(a) Whoever—

(1) knowingly accesses a computer without authorization or exceeds authorized access, and by means of such conduct obtains information that has been determined by the United States Government pursuant to an Executive order or statute to require protection against unauthorized disclosure for reasons of national defense or foreign relations, or any restricted data, as defined in paragraph r. of section 11 of the Atomic Energy Act of 1954, with the intent or reason to believe that such information so obtained is to be used to the injury of the United States, or to the advantage of any foreign nation;

(2) intentionally accesses a computer without authorization or exceeds authorized access, and thereby obtains information contained in a financial record of a financial institution, or of a card issuer as defined in section 1602(n) of title 15, or contained in a file of a consumer reporting agency on a consumer, as such terms are defined in the Fair Credit Reporting Act (15 U.S.C. 1681 et seq.);

(3) intentionally, without authorization to access any computer of a department or agency of the United States, accesses such a computer of that department or agency that is exclusively for the use of the Government of the United States or, in the case of a computer not exclusively for such use, is used by or for the Government of the United States and such conduct affects the use of the Government's operation of such computer;

(4) knowingly and with intent to defraud, accesses a Federal interest computer without authorization, or exceeds authorized access, and by means of such conduct furthers the intended fraud and obtains anything of value, unless the object of the fraud and the thing obtained consists only of the use of the computer;

(5) intentionally accesses a Federal interest computer without authorization and by means of one or more instances of such conduct alters, damages, or destroys information in any such Federal interest computer, or prevents authorized use of any such computer or information, and thereby—

   (A) causes loss to one or more others of a value aggregating $1,000 or more during any one year period; or
   (B) modifies or impairs, or potentially modifies or impairs the medical examination, medical diagnosis, medical treatment, or medical care of one or more individuals; or

(6) knowingly and with intent to defraud traffics (as defined in section 1029) in any password or similar information through which a computer may be accessed without authorization, if—

(A) such trafficking affects interstate or foreign commerce; or

(B) such computer is used by or for the Government of the United States;

shall be punished as provided in subsection (c) of this section.

(b) Whoever attempts to commit an offense under subsection (a) of this section shall be punished as provided in subsection (c) of this section. (c) The punishment for an offense under subsection (a) or (b) of this section is—

(1)(A) a fine under this title or imprisonment for not more than ten years or both, in the case of an offense under subsection (a)(1) of this section which does not occur after a conviction for another offense under such subsection, or an attempt to commit an offense punishable under this subparagraph; and

(B) a fine under this title or imprisonment for not more than twenty years, or both, in the case of an offense under subsection (a)(1) of this section which occurs after a conviction for another offense under such subsection, or an attempt to commit an offense punishable under this subparagraph; and

(2)(A) a fine under this title or imprisonment for not more than one year, or both, in the case of an offense under subsection (a)(2), (a)(3) or (a)(6) of this section which does not occur after a conviction for another offense under such subsection, or an attempt to commit an offense punishable under this subparagraph; and

(B) a fine under this title or imprisonment for not more than ten years, or both, in the case of an offense under subsection (a)(2), (a)(3) or(a)(6) of this section which occurs after a conviction for another offense under such subsection, or an attempt to commit an offense punishable under this subparagraph; and

(3)(A) a fine under this title or imprisonment for not more than five years or both, in the case of an offense under subsection (a)(4) or (a)(5) of this section which does not occur after a conviction for another offense under such subsection, or an attempt to commit an offense punishable under this subparagraph; and

(B) a fine under this title or imprisonment for not more than ten years, or both, in the case of an offense under subsection (a)(4) or (a)(5)

of this section which occurs after a conviction for another offense under such subsection, or an attempt to commit an offense punishable under this subparagraph.

(d) The United States Secret Service shall, in addition to any other agency having such authority, have the authority to investigate offenses under this section. Such authority of the United States Secret Service shall be exercised in accordance with an agreement which shall be entered into by the Secretary of the Treasury and the Attorney General.

(e) As used in this section—

(1) the term "**computer**" means an electronic, magnetic, optical, electrochemical, or other high speed data processing device performing logical, arithmetic, or storage functions, and includes any data storage facility or communications facility directly related to or operating in conjunction with such device, but such term does not include an automated typewriter or typesetter, a portable hand held calculator, or other similar device;

(2) the term "**Federal interest computer**" means a computer—

(A) exclusively for the use of a financial institution or the United States Government, or, in the case of a computer not exclusively for such use, used by or for a financial institution or the United States Government and the conduct constituting the offense affects the use of the financial institution's operation or the Government's operation of such computer; or

(B) which is one of two or more computers used in committing the offense, not all of which are located in the same State;

(3) the term "**State**" includes the District of Columbia, the Commonwealth of Puerto Rico, and any other possession or territory of the United States;

(4) the term "**financial institution**" means—

(A) an institution with deposits insured by the Federal Deposit Insurance Corporation;

(B) the Federal Reserve or a member of the Federal Reserve including any Federal Reserve Bank;

(C) a credit union with accounts insured by the National Credit Union Administration;

(D) a member of the Federal home loan bank system and any home loan bank;

(E) any institution of the Farm Credit System under the Farm Credit Act of 1971;

(F) a broker-dealer registered with the Securities and Exchange Commission pursuant to section 15 of the Securities Exchange Act of 1934; and

(G) the Securities Investor Protection Corporation;

(5) the term "**financial record**" means information derived from any record held by a financial institution pertaining to a customer's relationship with the financial institution;

(6) the term "**exceeds authorized access**" means to access a computer with authorization and to use such access to obtain or alter information in the computer that the accesser is not entitled so to obtain or alter; and

(7) the term "**department of the United States**" means the legislative or judicial branch of the government or one of the executive departments enumerated in section 101 of title 5.

(f) This section does not prohibit any lawfully authorized investigative, protective, or intelligence activity of a law enforcement agency of the United States, a State, or a political subdivision of a State, or of an intelligence agency of the United States.

(g) Any person who suffers damage or loss by reason of a violation of this section may maintain a civil action against the violator to obtain compensatory damages and injunctive relief or other equitable relief. Damages for violations involving damage as defined in subsection (e)(8)(A) are limited to economic damages. No action may be brought under this subsection unless such action is begun within 2 years of the date of the act complained of or the date of the discovery of the damage.

(h) The Attorney General and the Secretary of the Treasury shall report to the Congress annually, during the first 3 years following the date of the enactment of this subsection, concerning investigations and prosecutions under subsection (a)(5).

The Sarbanes-Oxley Act of 2002
http://financialservices.house.gov/media/pdf/H3763CR_HSE.PDF

SEC. 802. CRIMINAL PENALTIES FOR ALTERING DOCUMENTS.
(a) IN GENERAL.—Chapter 73 of title 18, United States Code, is amended by adding at the end the following:

§ 1519. Destruction, alteration, or falsification of records in Federal investigations and bankruptcy

Whoever knowingly alters, destroys, mutilates, conceals, covers up, falsifies, or makes a false entry in any record, document, or tangible object with the intent to impede, obstruct, or influence the investigation or proper administration of any matter within the jurisdiction of any department or agency of the United States or any case filed under title 11, or in relation to or contemplation of any such matter or case, shall be fined under this title, imprisoned not more than 20 years, or both.

§ 1520. Destruction of corporate audit records

(a)(1) Any accountant who conducts an audit of an issuer of securities to which section 10A(a) of the Securities Exchange Act of 1934 (15 U.S.C. 78j–1(a)) applies, shall maintain all audit or review workpapers for a period of 5 years from the end of the fiscal period in which the audit or review 21 was concluded.

(2) The Securities and Exchange Commission shall promulgate, within 180 days, after adequate notice and an opportunity for comment, such rules and regulations, as are reasonably necessary, relating to the retention of relevant records such as workpapers, documents that form the basis of an audit or review, memoranda, correspondence, communications, other documents, and records (including electronic records) which are created, sent, or received in connection with an audit or review and contain conclusions, opinions, analyses, or financial data relating to such an audit or review, which is conducted by any accountant who conducts an audit of an issuer of securities to which section 10A(a) of the Securities Exchange Act of 1934 (15 U.S.C. 78j–1(a)) applies. The Commission may, from time to time, amend or supplement the rules and regulations that it is required to promulgate under this section, after adequate notice and an opportunity for comment, in order to ensure that such rules and regulations adequately comport with the purposes of this section.

(b) Whoever knowingly and willfully violates subsection (a)(1), or any rule or regulation promulgated by the Securities and Exchange Commission under subsection (a)(2), shall be fined under this title, imprisoned not more than 10 years, or both.

(c) Nothing in this section shall be deemed to diminish or relieve any person of any other duty or obligation imposed by Federal or State law or regulation to maintain, or refrain from destroying, any document.

SEC. 1102. TAMPERING WITH A RECORD OR OTHERWISE IMPEDING AN OFFICIAL PROCEEDING.

Section 1512 of title 18, United States Code, is amended—

(1) by redesignating subsections (c) through (i) as subsections (d) through (j), respectively; and

(2) by inserting after subsection (b) the following new subsection:

"(c) Whoever corruptly—

"(1) alters, destroys, mutilates, or conceals a record, document, or other object, or attempts to do so, with the intent to impair the object's integrity or availability for use in an official proceeding; or

"(2) otherwise obstructs, influences, or impedes any official proceeding, or attempts to do so, shall be fined under this title or imprisoned not more than 20 years, or both."

APPENDIX ❖ C1

Sample Preservation Letter— To Client

January 1, 2004

_____

_____

_____

_____

RE: [Case Name]—Data Preservation

Dear _____:

Please be advised that the Office of General Counsel requires your assistance with respect to preserving corporate information in the above-referenced matter.

Electronically stored data is an important and irreplaceable source of discovery and/or evidence in this matter.

The lawsuit requires preservation of all information from [Corporation's] computer systems, removable electronic media and other locations relating to [description of event, transaction, business unit, product, etc.]. This includes, but is not limited to, e-mail and other electronic communication, word processing documents, spreadsheets, databases, calendars, telephone logs, contact manager information, Internet usage files, and network access information.

Employees must take every reasonable step to preserve this information until further notice from the Office of General Counsel. *Failure to do so could result in extreme penalties against [Corporation].*

If this correspondence is in any respect unclear, please contact [designated coordinator] at [phone number].

Sincerely,

_____

APPENDIX ❖ C2

Sample Preservation Letter— To Opponent or 3rd Party

January 1, 2004

_____
_____
_____
_____

RE: [Case Name]—Data Preservation

Dear _____:

Please be advised that [Plaintiffs/Defendants/Third Party] believe electronically stored information to be an important and irreplaceable source of discovery and/or evidence in the above-referenced matter.

The discovery requests served in this matter seek information from [Plaintiffs'/Defendants'] computer systems, removable electronic media and other locations. This includes, but is not limited to, e-mail and other electronic communication, word processing documents, spreadsheets, databases, calendars, telephone logs, contact manager information, Internet usage files, and network access information.

The laws and rules prohibiting destruction of evidence apply to electronically stored information in the same manner that they apply to other evidence. Due to its format, electronic information is easily deleted, modified or corrupted. Accordingly, [Plaintiffs/Defendants/Third Party] must take every reasonable step to preserve this information until the final resolution of this matter. This includes, but is not limited to, an obligation to discontinue all data destruction and backup tape recycling policies.

If this correspondence is in any respect unclear, please do not hesitate to call me.

Sincerely,

_____

APPENDIX ❖ C3

Sample Fed. R. Civ. P. 30(b)(6) Deposition Notice

UNITED STATES DISTRICT COURT
DISTRICT OF [enter district here]

Court File No.:

_____,

Plaintiff,

v.

NOTICE OF TAKING DEPOSITION PURSUANT TO FED. R. CIV. P. 30(b)(6)

_____,

Defendant,

PLEASE TAKE NOTICE that, [Plaintiff/Defendant Corporation] take the deposition, before a qualified notary public by oral examination, of [Plaintiff/Defendant Corporation] on [date] commencing at [time], at [location]. The deposition will continue thereafter until adjournment.

Pursuant to Federal Rule of Civil Procedure 30(b)(6), [Plaintiff/Defendant] corporate designee(s) shall be prepared to testify regarding the following subjects, all with respect to [Plaintiff's/Defendant's] information technology systems:

1) Number, types, and locations of computers currently in use and no longer in use;
2) Past and present operating system and application software, including dates of use;
3) Name and version of network operating system currently in use and no longer in use but relevant to the subject matter of the action;
4) File-naming and location-saving conventions;
5) Disk or tape labeling conventions;
6) Backup and archival disk or tape inventories or schedules;
7) Most likely locations of electronic records relevant to the subject matter of the action;
8) Backup rotation schedules and archiving procedures, including any backup programs in use at any relevant time;
9) Electronic records management policies and procedures;
10) Corporate policies regarding employee use of company computers and data;
11) Identities of all current and former personnel who have or had access to network administration, backup, archiving, or other system operations during any relevant time period.

Dated:

ABC LAW FIRM

BY:

Attorneys for [Plaintiff/Defendant]

APPENDIX ❖ C4

Sample Proposed Request for Production of Documents and Things

UNITED STATES DISTRICT COURT
DISTRICT OF [jurisdiction]

Court File No.:

_____,

Plaintiff,

v.   **DOCUMENT REQUEST**

_____,

Defendant,

Plaintiff's Request for Production of Documents and Things

Pursuant to Rules 26 and 34 of the Federal Rules of Civil Procedure ("FRCP") Plaintiffs, by counsel, hereby request Defendants to produce the documents specified below, within thirty (30) days of service, to **[counsel name and address]**, or at such other time and place, or in such other manner, as may be mutually agreed upon by the parties.

Defendants' production of documents shall be in accordance with the Instructions and Definitions set forth below and Rule 34 of the FRCP.

Instructions and Definitions

(a) Whenever reference is made to a person, it includes any and all of such person's principals, employees, agents, attorneys, consultants and other representatives.

(b) When production of any document in Plaintiffs' possession is requested, such request includes documents subject to the Plaintiffs' possession, custody or control. In the event that Defendant is able to provide only part of the document(s) called for in any particular Request for Production, provide all document(s) that Defendants are able to provide and state the reason, if any, for the inability to provide the remainder.

(c) "Document(s)" means all materials within the full scope of Rule 34 of the FRCP including but not limited to: all writings and recordings, including the originals and all non-identical copies, whether different from the original by reason of any notation made on such copies or otherwise (including but without limitation to, email and attachments, correspondence, memoranda, notes, diaries, minutes, statistics, letters, telegrams, minutes, contracts, reports, studies, checks, statements, tags, labels, invoices, brochures, periodicals, telegrams, receipts, returns, summaries, pamphlets, books, interoffice and intraoffice communications, offers, notations of any sort of conversations, working papers, applications, permits, file wrappers, indices, telephone calls, meetings or printouts, teletypes, telefax, invoices, worksheets, and all drafts, alterations, modifications, changes and amendments of any of the foregoing), graphic or aural representations of any kind (including without limitation, photographs, charts, microfiche, microfilm, videotape, recordings, motion pictures, plans, drawings, surveys), and electronic, mechanical, magnetic, optical or electric records or representations of any kind (including without limitation, computer files and programs, tapes, cassettes, discs, recordings), including metadata.

(d) If any document is withheld from production under a claim of privilege or other exemption from discovery, state the title and nature of the document, and furnish a list signed by the attorney of record giving the following information with respect to each document withheld:

(i) the name and title of the author and/or sender and the name and title of the recipient;

(ii) the date of the document's origination;

(iii) the name of each person or persons (other than stenographic or clerical assistants) participating in the preparation of the document;

(iv) the name and position, if any, of each person to whom the contents of the documents have heretofore been communicated by copy, exhibition, reading or substantial summarization;

(v) a statement of the specific basis on which privilege is claimed and whether or not the subject matter or the contents of the document is limited to legal advice or information provided for the purpose of securing legal advice; and

(vi) the identity and position, if any, of the person or persons supplying the attorney signing the list with the information requested in subparagraphs above.

(e) "Relate(s) to," "related to" or "relating to" means to refer to, reflect, concern, pertain to or in any manner be connected with the matter discussed.

(f) Every Request for Production herein shall be deemed a continuing Request for Production and Defendant is to supplement its answers promptly if and when Defendant obtains responsive documents which add to or are in any way inconsistent with Defendant's initial production.

(g) These discovery requests are not intended to be duplicative. All requests should be responded to fully and to the extent not covered by other requests. If there are documents that are responsive to more than one request, then please so note and produce each such document first in response to the request that is more specifically directed to the subject matter of the particular document.

(h) Any word written in the singular herein shall be construed as plural or vice versa when necessary to facilitate the response to any request.

(i) "And" as well as "or" shall be construed disjunctively or conjunctively as necessary in order to bring within the scope of the request all responses which otherwise might be construed to be outside its scope.

Document Requests

1. All documents or communications with reference to or written policies, procedures and guidelines related to Defendant's computers,

computer systems, electronic data and electronic media including, but not limited to, the following:

a. Backup tape rotation schedules;

b. Electronic data retention, preservation and destruction schedules;

c. Employee use policies of company computers, data, and other technology;

d. File naming conventions and standards,

e. Password, encryption, and other security protocols;

f. Diskette, CD, DVD, and other removable media labeling standards;

g. Email storage conventions (e.g., limitations on mailbox sizes/storage locations; schedule and logs for storage);

h. Electronic media deployment, allocation, and maintenance procedures for new employees, current employees, or departed employees;

i. Software and hardware upgrades (including patches) **for [relevant time period]** (who and what organization conducted such upgrades); and

j. Personal or home computer usage for work-related activities.

2. Organization charts for all Information Technology or Information Services departments or divisions from [relevant time period].

3. Backup tapes containing email and other electronic data related to this action from **[relevant time period]**.

4. Exact copies (i.e., bit-by-bit copies) of all hard drives on the desktop computers, laptop computers, notebook computers, personal digital assistant computers, servers, and other electronic media related to this action from **[relevant time period]**.

5. Exact copies of all relevant disks, CDs, DVDs and other removable media related to this action from **[relevant time period]**.

6. For each interrogatory set forth in Plaintiffs' First Interrogatories, produce all documents which Defendant referred to, relied upon, consulted or used in any way in answering such interrogatory.

7. All documents that contain or otherwise relate to the facts or information that Defendants contend refute, in any way, the allegations contained in the Complaint in this action.

8. All reports, including drafts, submitted by any expert witness or potential expert witness retained or consulted by any Defendant with respect to the issues raised in this case.

Date: Respectfully submitted,

_____

APPENDIX ❖ C5

Sample Interrogatories

UNITED STATES DISTRICT COURT
DISTRICT OF [enter district here]

Court File No.:

_____,/

Plaintiff,

v.   **INTERROGATORIES TO [party name]**

_____,/

Defendant,

---

1. Identify all email systems in use, including but not limited to the following:

   (a) List ail email software and versions presently and previously used by you and the dates of use;

   (b) Identify all hardware that has been used or is currently in use as a server for the email system including its name;

   (c) Identify the specific type of hardware that was used as terminals into the email system (including home PCs, laptops, desktops, cell phones, personal digital assistants ["PDAs"], etc.) and its current location;

(d) State how many users there have been on each email system (delineate between past and current users);

(e) State whether the email is encrypted in any way and list passwords for all users;

(f) Identify all users known to you who have generated email related to the subject matter of this litigation;

(g) Identify all email known to you (including creation date, recipient(s) and sender) that relate to, reference or are relevant to the subject matter of this litigation.

2. Identify and describe each computer that has been, or is currently, in use by you or your employees (including desktop computers, PDAs, portable, laptop and notebook computers, cell phones, etc.), including but not limited to the following:

(a) Computer type, brand and model number;

(b) Computers that have been re-formatted, had the operating system reinstalled or been overwritten and identify the date of each event;

(c) The current location of each computer identified in your response to this interrogatory;

(d) The brand and version of all software, including operating system, private and custom-developed applications, commercial applications and shareware for each computer identified;

(e) The communications and connectivity for each computer, including but not limited to terminal-to-mainframe emulation, data download and/or upload capability to mainframe, and computer-to-computer connections via network, modem and/or direct connection;

(f) All computers that have been used to store, receive or generate data related to the subject matter of this litigation.

3. As to each computer network, identify the following:

(a) Brand and version number of the network operating system currently or previously in use (include dates of all upgrades);

(b) Quantity and configuration of all network servers and workstations;

(c) Person(s) (past and present including dates) responsible for the ongoing operations, maintenance, expansion, archiving and upkeep of the network;

(d) Brand name and version number of all applications and other software residing on each network in use, including but not limited to electronic mail and applications.

4. Describe in detail all inter-connectivity between the computer system at [opposing party] in [office location] and the computer system at [opposing party # 2] in [office location # 2] including a description of the following:

   (a) All possible ways in which electronic data is shared between locations;
   (b) The method of transmission;
   (c) The type(s) of data transferred;
   (d) The names of all individuals possessing the capability for such transfer, including list and names of authorized outside users of [opposing party's] electronic mail system.
   (e) The individual responsible for supervising inter-connectivity.

5. As to data backups performed on all computer systems currently or previously in use, identify the following:

   (a) All procedures and devices used to back up the software and the data, including but not limited to name(s) of backup software used, the frequency of the backup process, and type of tape backup drives, including name and version number, type of media (i.e. DLT, 4mm, 8mm, AIT). State the capacity (bytes) and total amount of information (gigabytes) stored on each tape;
   (b) Describe the tape or backup rotation and explain how backup data is maintained and state whether the backups are full or incremental (attach a copy of all rotation schedules);
   (c) State whether backup storage media is kept off-site or on-site. Include the location of such backup and a description of the process for archiving and retrieving on-site media;
   (d) The individual(s) who conducts the backup and the individual who supervises this process;
   (e) Provide a detailed list of all backup sets, regardless of the magnetic media on which they reside, showing current location, custodian, date of backup, a description of backup content and a full inventory of all archives.

6. Identify all extra-routine backups applicable for any servers identified in response to these interrogatories, such as quarterly archival backup, yearly backup, etc. and identify the current location of any such backups.

7. For any server, workstation, laptop, or home PC that has been "wiped clean," defragmented, or reformatted such that you claim

that the information on the hard drive is permanently destroyed, identify the following:

(a) The date on which each drive was wiped, reformatted, or defragmented;

(b) The method or program used (e.g., WipeDisk, WipeFile, Burnlt, Data Eraser, etc.).

8. Identify and attach any and all versions of document/data retention policies used by [opposing party] and identify documents or classes of documents that were subject to scheduled destruction. Attach copies of document destruction inventories/logs/schedules containing documents relevant to this action. Attach a copy of any disaster recovery plan. Also state:

(a) The date, if any, of the suspension of this policy *in toto* or any aspect of said policy in response to this litigation;

(b) A description by topic, creation date, user or bytes of any and all data that has been deleted or in any way destroyed after the commencement of this litigation. State whether the deletion or destruction of any data pursuant to said data retention policy occurred through automation or by user action;

(c) Whether any company-wide instruction regarding the suspension of said data retention/destruction policy occurred after or related to the commencement of this litigation and if so, identify the individual responsible for enforcing said suspension.

9. Identify any users who had backup systems in their PCs and describe the nature of the backup.

10. Identify the person(s) responsible for maintaining any schedule of redeployment or circulation of existing equipment and describe the system or process for redeployment.

11. Identify any data that has been deleted, physically destroyed, discarded, damaged (physically or logically), or overwritten, whether pursuant to a document retention policy or otherwise, since the commencement of this litigation. Specifically identify those documents that relate to or reference the subject matter of the above referenced litigation.

12. Identify any user who has downloaded any files in excess of ten (10) megabytes on any computer identified above since the commencement of this litigation.

13. Identify and describe all backup tapes in your possession including:

   (a) Types and number of tapes in your possession (such as DLT, AIT, Mammoth, 4mm, 8mm);

   (b) Capacity (bytes) and total amount of information (gigabytes) stored on each tape;

   (c) All tapes that have been re-initialized or overwritten since commencement of this litigation and state the date of said occurrence.

APPENDIX ❖ D

Noise Words

The following table shows noise words (i.e., common words) that experts should ignore when performing text searches. Ask whether your expert can filter for these types of words.

$	here	some
about	him	still
after	himself	such
all	his	take
also	how	than
an	I	that
and	if	the
another	in	their
any	into	them
are	is	then
as	it and its	there
at	just	these
be	like	they
because	make	this
been	many	those
before	me	through
being	might	to
between	more	too
both	most	under
but	much	up
by	must	use

came	my	very
can	never	want
come	now	was
could	of	way
did	on	we
do	only	well
does	or	were
each	other	what
else	our	when
for	out	where
from	over	which
get	re	while
got	said	who
has	same	will
had	see	with
he	should	would
have	since	you
her	so	your

APPENDIX ❖ E

Electronic Evidence: Secondary Research Resources

Two Views From the Data Mountain
36 Creighton L. Rev. 607 (2003).

The Sedona Conference Working Group on Electronic Document Retention and Production
4 Sedona Conf. J. 197 (2003).

Electronic Evidence Can Unearth a Treasure Trove of Information or Potential Landmines
75 N.Y. St. B.J. 32 (September 2003).

Digital Dangers: A Primer on Electronic Evidence in the Wake of Enron
74 Pa. B.A. Q. 1 (2003).

Discovery Unplugged: Should Internal E-Mails Be Privileged Confidential Communications?
70 Def. Couns. J. 36, 39 (2003).

E-Discovery: Preserving, Requesting & Producing Electronic Information
19 Santa Clara Computer & High Tech L.J. 131 (2002).

Discoverability of "Deleted" E-Mail: Time for a Closer Examination
25 Seattle U. L. Rev. 895 (2002).

Electronic Data Discovery: Litigation Gold Mine or Nightmare?
58 J. Mo. B. 18 (2002).

Challenges for Corporate Counsel in the Land of E-Discovery: Lessons Learned From a Case Study
16 Andrews Delaware Corporate Litigation Reporter 11 (2002).

What—if anything—is an E-Mail? Applying Alaska's Civil Discovery Rules to E-Mail Production
19 Alaska L. Rev. 119, 140 (2002).

Electronic Discovery and the Litigation Matrix
51 Duke L.J. (November 2001).

Allocating Discovery Costs in the Computer Age: Deciding Who Should Bear the Costs of Discovery of Electronically Stored Data
57 Wash. & Lee L. Rev. 257 (2000).

Electronic Media Discovery: The Economic Benefit of Pay-Per-View
21 Cardozo L. Rev. 1379 (2000).

Electronic Discovery in Federal Civil Litigation: Is Rule 34 up to the Task?
41 B.C. L. Rev 327 (2000).

Computer-Based Discovery in Federal Civil Litigation
2000 Fed. Cts. L. Rev. 2 (October 2000).

E-Discovery: Preparing Clients for (and Protecting them Against) Discovery in the Electronic Information Age
26 Wm. Mitchell L. Rev. 939 (2000).

Michael Overly, Overly on Discovery of Electronic Evidence in California.
Eagan, MN: West Group (1999).

The Electronic Paper Trail: Evidentiary Obstacles to Discovery and Admission of Electronic Evidence
4 B.U.J. Sci. & Tech. L. 5 (Spring 1998).

How Companies Can Reduce the Costs and Risks Associated with Electronic Discovery
15 *Computer L.* 8 (July 1998).

A Practitioner's Overview of Digital Discovery
33 Gonz. L.Rev. 347 (1998).

Electronic Evidence: Discovery in the Computer Age
58 *Ala. Lawyer* 176 (May 1997).

When the Postman Beeps Twice: The Admissibility of Electronic Mail Under the Business Records Exception of the Federal Rules of Evidence
64 Fordham L. Rev. 2285 (1996).

APPENDIX ❖ F

Glossary of Terms

Active Data: Active Data is information residing on the direct access storage media of computer systems, which is readily visible to the operating system and/or application software with which it was created and immediately accessible to users without undeletion, modification or reconstruction.

Application: Software programs, such as word processors and spreadsheets that most users use to do work on a computer.

Archival Data: Archival Data is information that is not directly accessible to the user of a computer system but that the organization maintains for long-term storage and record keeping purposes. Archival data may be written to removable media such as a CD, magneto-optical media, tape or other electronic storage device, or may be maintained on system hard drives in compressed formats.

ASCII (Acronym for American Standard Code): ASCII is a code that assigns a number to each key on the keyboard. ASCII text does not include special formatting features and therefore can be exchanged and read by most computer systems.

Backup: To create a copy of data as a precaution against the loss or damage of the original data. Most users backup some of their files, and many computer networks utilize automatic backup software to make regular copies of some or all of the data on the network. Some backup systems use digital audio tape (DAT) as a storage medium.

Backup Data: Backup Data is information that is not presently in use by an organization and is routinely stored separately upon portable media, to free up space and permit data recovery in the event of disaster.

Backup Tape: See Disaster Recovery Tape.

Backup Tape Recycling: Backup Tape Recycling describes the process whereby an organization's backup tapes are overwritten with new backup data, usually on a fixed schedule (e.g., the use of nightly backup tapes for each day of the week with the daily backup tape for a particular day being overwritten on the same day the following week; weekly and monthly backups being stored offsite for a specified period of time before being placed back in the rotation).

Bandwidth: The amount of information or data that can be sent over a network connection in a given period of time. Bandwidth is usually stated in bits per second (bps), kilobits per second (kbps), or megabits per second (mps).

Binary: Mathematical base 2, or numbers composed of a series of zeros and ones. Since zero's and one's can be easily represented by two voltage levels on an electronic device, the binary number system is widely used in digital computing.

Bit: A measurement of data. It is the smallest unit of data. A bit is either the "1" or "0" component of the binary code. A collection of bits is put together to form a byte.

Burn: Slang for making (burning) a CD-ROM copy of data, whether it is music, software, or other data.

Byte: Eight bits. The byte is the basis for measurement of most computer data as multiples of the byte value. A "megabyte" is one million bytes or eight million bits or a "gigabyte" is one billion bytes or eight billion bits.

    1 gigabyte = 1,000 megabytes
    1 terabyte = 1,000 gigabytes

Cache: A type a computer memory that temporarily stores frequently used information for quick access.

CD-ROM: Data storage medium that uses compact discs to store about 1,500 floppy discs worth of data.

Compression: A technology that reduces the size of a file. Compression programs are valuable to network users because they help save both time and bandwidth.

Computer Forensics: Computer Forensics is the use of specialized techniques for recovery, authentication, and analysis of electronic data when a case involves issues relating to reconstruction of computer usage, examination of residual data, authentication of data by technical analysis or explanation of technical features of data and computer usage. Computer forensics requires specialized expertise that goes beyond normal data collection and preservation techniques available to end-users or system support personnel.

Cookie: Small data files written to a user's hard drive by a web server. These files contain specific information that identifies users (e.g., passwords and lists of pages visited).

DAT: Digital Audio Tape. Used as a storage medium in some backup systems.

Data: Information stored on the computer system, used by applications to accomplish tasks.

De-Duplication: De-Duplication ("De-Duping") is the process of comparing electronic records based on their characteristics and removing duplicate records from the data set.

Deleted Data: Deleted Data is data that, in the past, existed on the computer as live data and which has been deleted by the computer system or end-user activity. Deleted data remains on storage media in whole or in part until it is overwritten by ongoing usage or "wiped" with a software program specifically designed to remove deleted data. Even after the data itself has been wiped, directory entries, pointers, or other metadata relating to the deleted data may remain on the computer.

Deleted file: A file with disk space that has been designated as available for reuse. The deleted file remains intact until it has been overwritten with a new file.

Deletion: Deletion is the process whereby data is removed from active files and other data storage structures on computers and rendered inaccessible except using special data recovery tools designed to recover deleted data. Deletion occurs in several levels on modern computer systems: (a) File level deletion: Deletion on the file level renders the file inaccessible to the operating system and normal application programs and marks the space occupied by the file's directory entry and contents as free space, available to reuse for data storage, (b) Record level deletion: Deletion on the record level occurs when a data structure, like a database table, contains multiple records; deletion at this level renders the record inaccessible to the database management system (DBMS) and usually marks the space occupied by the record as available for reuse by the DBMS, although in some cases the space is never reused until the database is compacted. Record level deletion is also characteristic of many e-mail systems, (c) Byte level deletion: Deletion at the byte level occurs when text or other information is deleted from the file content (such as the deletion of text from a word processing file); such deletion may render the deleted data inaccessible to the application intended to be used in processing the file, but may not actually remove the data from the file's content until a process such as compaction or rewriting of the file causes the deleted data to be overwritten.

Desktop: Usually refers to an individual PC—a user's desktop computer.

Digital: Storing information as a string of digits—namely "1"s and "0"s.

Disaster Recovery Tape: Disaster Recovery Tapes are portable media used to store data that is not presently in use by an organization to free up space but still allow for disaster recovery. May also be called "Backup Tapes."

Disc (disk): It may be a floppy disk, or it may be a hard disk. Either way, it is a magnetic storage medium on which data is digitally stored. May also refer to a CD-ROM.

Disc mirroring: A method of protecting data from a catastrophic hard disk failure. As each file is stored on the hard disk, a "mirror" copy is made on a second hard disk or on a different part of the same disk.

Distributed Data: Distributed Data is that information belonging to an organization which resides on portable media and nonlocal devices such as home computers, laptop computers, floppy disks, CD-ROMs, personal digital assistants ("PDAs"), wireless communication devices (e.g., Blackberry), zip drives, Internet repositories such as e-mail hosted by Internet service providers or portals, web pages, and the like. Distributed data also includes data held by third parties such as application service providers and business partners.

Electronic Mail: Electronic Mail, commonly referred to as e-mail, is an electronic means for communicating information under specified conditions, generally in the form of text messages, through systems that will send, store, process, and receive information and in which messages are held in storage until the addressee accesses them.

Encryption: A procedure that renders the contents of a message or file unintelligible to anyone not authorized to read it.

Ethernet: A common way of networking PCs to create a LAN.

Extranet: An Internet based access method to a corporate intranet site by limited or total access through a security firewall. This type of access is typically utilized in cases of joint venture and vendor client relationships.

File: A collection of data of information stored under a specified name on a disk.

File extension: A tag of three or four letters, preceded by a period, which identifies a data file's format or the application used to create the file. File extensions can streamline the process of locating data. For example, if one is looking for incriminating pictures stored on a computer, one might begin with the .gif and .jpg files.

File server: When several or many computers are networked together in a LAN situation, one computer may be utilized as a storage location for files for the group. File servers may be employed to store e-mail, financial data, word processing information or to back-up the network.

File sharing: One of the key benefits of a network is the ability to share files stored on the server among several users.

Firewall: A set of related programs that protect the resources of a private network from users from other networks.

Floppy: An increasingly rare storage medium consisting of a thin magnetic film disk housed in a protective sleeve.

Forensic Copy: A Forensic Copy is an exact bit-by-bit copy of the entire physical hard drive of a computer system, including slack and unallocated space.

Fragmented Data: Fragmented data is live data that has been broken up and stored in various locations on a single hard drive or disk.

FTP (File Transfer Protocol): An Internet protocol that enables you to transfer files between computers on the Internet.

GIF (Graphic interchange format): A computer compression format for pictures.

GUI (Graphical User Interface): A set of screen presentations and metaphors that utilize graphic elements such as icons in an attempt to make an operating system easier to use.

Hard disk: A peripheral data storage device that may be found inside a desktop or laptop as in a hard drive situation. The hard disk may also be a transportable version and attached to a desktop or laptop.

Hard drive: The primary storage unit on PCs, consisting of one or more magnetic media platters on which digital data can be written and erased magnetically.

HTML (Hypertext Markup Language): The tag-based ASCII language used to create pages on the web.

Image: In data recovery parlance, to image a hard drive is to make an identical copy of the hard drive, including empty sectors. Akin to cloning the data. Also known as creating a "mirror image" or "mirroring" the drive.

Instant Messaging ("IM"): Instant Messaging is a form of electronic communication which involves immediate correspondence between two or more users who are all online simultaneously.

Internet: The interconnecting global public network made by connecting smaller shared public networks. The most well known Internet is the Internet, the worldwide network of networks which use the TCP/IP protocol to facilitate information exchange.

Intranet: A network of interconnecting smaller private networks that are isolated from the public Internet.

IP address: A string of four numbers separated by periods used to represent a computer on the Internet.

IS/IT Information Systems or Information Technology: Usually refers to the people who make computers and computer systems run.

ISP (Internet Service Provider): A business that delivers access to the Internet.

JPEG (Joint Photographic Experts Group): An image compression standard for photographs.

Keyword search: A search for documents containing one or more words that are specified by a user.

Kilobyte (K): One thousand bytes of data is 1K of data.

LAN (Local area network): Usually refers to a network of computers in a single building or other discrete location.

Legacy Data: Legacy Data is information in the development of which an organization may have invested significant resources and which has retained its importance, but which has been created or stored by the use of software and/or hardware that has been rendered outmoded or obsolete.

Megabyte (Meg): A million bytes of data is a megabyte, or simply a meg.

Metadata: Metadata is information about a particular data set which may describe, for example, how, when, and by whom it was received, created, accessed, and/or modified and how it is formatted. Some metadata, such as file dates and sizes, can easily be seen by users; other metadata can be hidden or embedded and unavailable to computer users who are not technically adept. Metadata is generally not reproduced in full form when a document is printed. (Typically referred to by the less informative shorthand phrase "data about data," it describes the content, quality, condition, history, and other characteristics of the data.)

Migrated Data: Migrated Data is information that has been moved from one database or format to another, usually as a result of a change from one hardware or software technology to another.

Mirroring: The duplication of data for purposes of backup or to distribute network traffic among several computers with identical data.

MIS: Management information systems.

Modem: A piece of hardware that lets a computer talk to another computer over a phone line.

Network: A group of computers or devices that is connected together for the exchange of data and sharing of resources.

Node: Any device connected to network. PCs, servers, and printers are all nodes on the network.

OCR: Optical character recognition is a technology which takes data from a paper document and turns it editable text data. The document is first scanned. Then OCR software searches the document for letters, numbers, and other characters.

Offline: Not connected (to a network).

Online: Connected (to a network).

Operating system (OS): The software that the rest of the software depends on to make the computer functional. On most PCs this is Windows or the Macintosh OS. Unix and Linux are other operating systems often found in scientific and technical environments.

PC: Personal computer.

PDA (Personal Digital Assistant): Handheld digital organizers.

PDF (Portable Document Format): An Adobe technology for formatting documents so that they can be viewed and printed using the Adobe Acrobat reader.

Plaintext: The least formatted and therefore most portable form of text for computerized documents.

Pointer: A pointer is an index entry in the directory of a disk (or other storage medium) that identifies the space on the disc in which an electronic document or piece of electronic data resides, thereby preventing that space from being overwritten by other data. In most cases, when an electronic document is "deleted," the pointer is deleted, which allows the document to be overwritten, but the document is not actually erased.

Private Network: A network that is connected to the Internet but is isolated from the Internet.

PST (Personal Folder File): The place where Outlook stores its data (when Outlook is used without Microsoft® Exchange Server). A PST file is created when a mail account is set up. Additional PST files can be created for backing up and archiving Outlook folders, messages, forms and files. The file extension given to PST files is .pst.

Public Network: A network that is part of the public Internet.

RAM (Random Access Memory): The working memory of the computer into which application programs can be loaded and executed.

Residual Data: Residual Data (sometimes referred to as "Ambient Data") refers to data that is not active on a computer system. Residual data includes (1) data found on media free space; (2) data found in file slack space; and (3) data within files that has functionally been deleted in that it is not visible using the application with which the file was created, without use of undelete or special data recovery techniques.

Router: A piece of hardware that routes data from a local area network (LAN) to a phone line.

Sampling: Sampling usually (but not always) refers to the process of statistically testing a data set for the likelihood of relevant information. It can be a useful technique in addressing a number of issues relating to litigation, including decisions as to which repositories of data should be preserved and reviewed in a particular litigation, and determinations of the validity and effectiveness of searches or other data extraction procedures. Sampling can be useful in providing information to the court about the relative cost burden versus benefit of requiring a party to review certain electronic records.

Sandbox: A network or series of networks that are not connected to other networks.

Server: Any computer on a network that contains data or applications shared by users of the network on their client PCs.

Software: Coded instructions (programs) that make a computer do useful work.

Stand alone computer: A personal computer that is not connected to any other computer or network, except possibly through a modem.

System administrator: (sysadmin, sysop) The person in charge of keeping a network working.

TIFF (Tagged Image File Format): One of the most widely supported file formats for storing bit-mapped images. Files in TIFF format often end with a .tiff extension.

Transmission Control Protocol/Internet Protocol (TCP/IP): A collection of protocols that define the basic workings of the features of the Internet.

VPN (Virtual Private Network): A virtually private network that is constructed by using public wires to connect nodes.

World Wide Web: The WWW is made up of all of the computers on the Internet which use HTML-capable software (Netscape, Explorer, etc.) to exchange data. Data exchange on the WWW is characterized by easy-to-use graphical interfaces, hypertext links, images, and sound. Today the WWW has become synonymous with the Internet, although technically it is really just one component.

ZIP: An open standard for compression and decompression used widely for PC download archives. ZIP is used on Windows-based programs such as WinZip and Drag and Zip. The file extension given to ZIP files is .zip.

INDEX